W9-CHI-120

Ann-ping Chin

CHILDREN OF CHINA

VOICES FROM RECENT YEARS

Cornell University Press

Ithaca, New York

Published by arrangement with Alfred A. Knopf, Inc.

Grateful acknowledgment is made to Random House, Inc., for permission to reprint excerpts from *The Selected Poetry of Rainer Maria Rilke*. Edited and translated by Stephen Mitchell. Copyright © 1980, 1981, 1982 by Stephen Mitchell. Reprinted by permission of Random House, Inc.

First published Cornell Paperbacks 1989 by Cornell University Press.

Printed in the United States of America

Library of Congress Cataloging-in-Publication Data

Chin, Ann-ping, 1948–
Children of China : voices from recent years / Ann-ping Chin. — Cornell paperbacks ed.
p. cm.
Bibliography: p.
Includes index.
ISBN 0-8014-9683-7 (alk. paper)
1. Children—China—Social conditions. 2. Family—China. 3. Children—China—Interviews. 4. China—Social conditions—1976– I. Title.
[HQ792.C5C46 1989] 305.23'0951—dc20 89–42933

⊗ The paper used in this publication meets the minimum requirements of the American National Standard for Permanence of Paper for Printed Library Materials Z39.48–1984.

To the memory of June Freier Esserman,
without whose initial collaboration
this book would not have been possible,
and to the memory of my father, Chin Chang-ming

But later, among the stars,
what good is it—*they* are *better* as they are, unsayable.
For when the traveler returns from the mountain slopes into the valley,
he brings, not a handful of earth unsayable to others, but instead
some word he has gained, some pure word, the yellow and blue gentian.

—*Rainer Maria Rilke,*
Duino Elegies

Contents

Acknowledgments

My very special thanks go to Paul Esserman for his belief in my work and in me. I am also grateful to Gerard and Eleanor Piel, my ebullient traveling companions, who helped me to establish many important contacts in the PRC, and to Lauren Esserman, who was a luminous presence throughout this endeavor.

While working on this book, I have benefited greatly from the helpful suggestions of William Decker and Robert Chessin. My gratitude goes to the June Esserman Fund for its grant, which made it possible for me to continue working on this book. I would like to acknowledge Chu Ron-guey, who did the initial transcription of a large portion of my tapes. Jonathan Spence and William Kessen read the first draft of this book. Their continuing encouragement kept me going, and they have my sincerest thanks. I am also deeply grateful to Elisabeth Sifton, for no author could wish for a more understanding, scrupulous, or caring editor-critic.

Finally, my warmest thanks to the Chin family—my mother, sisters, and brother—who helped me make sense of everything, and to my husband, Li-ping Woo, who strengthens me by simply being the vivacious, audacious person that he is.

Preface to the Paperback Edition

On June 3, 1989, nearly a decade after my first visit to China, tanks and armored personnel carriers of the People's Liberation Army advanced toward the Gate of Heavenly Peace, carrying troops frenzied in their determination to impose an inhuman order. Within minutes soldiers opened fire on thousands of unarmed student demonstrators who had been occupying the square in Beijing. The sight and sound of terror fed their madness, and by daybreak the Gate of Heavenly Peace had become a mockery of Heaven and of peace.

The hope and resolve of the young had been bulldozed by military equipment. There was no real test in this contest, just heavy metal against the human spirit, and the confrontation was brought to a swift conclusion. A defeat for the human spirit, these actions proclaimed, and the world is beginning to believe it as the dead burn in the incinerators and the living flee to the countryside.

In the aftermath of this obscene act of violence, I have been thinking intensely about the young Chinese men and women caught up in this tragedy. I knew some of them when they were children, when their world still included stray cats and the bogeyman and was not complicated by beliefs. They realized that I was studying them, but I was also a friend or an aunt without any ties to the family. So they were unabashed in talking about themselves.

Many in this generation still love the Communist Party as their parent, but, because they have taught themselves to observe and to listen, to read and to think critically, they are more inclined than their own fathers and mothers to see dogmas as dogmas and not as a set of truths. They also find humor in all that is staid and holy, and hilarity in the rituals of the elders. As events unfolded in April, May, and June of 1989, it appears that their irreverence and skepticism, and their audacity in addressing their political elders publicly, speaking as if they were charged with a moral responsibility to dissuade them from doing wrong, provoked a fury. The one whom they call Mom and Dad in the end betrayed their trust and beat them to death, making them the victims of the worst kind of child abuse.

On the streets of Homeric Argos, a boy "performed the ancient music of yearning"; as his first notes pierced through the muted void, he began singing the lament to Linus. Linus, himself a youth, was "as lovely as a god"; his voice was that of an angel, but he died young, killed, according to one myth, by his father, Apollo, in a jealous rage. The Argive children, moved by the singing that recalled Linus, danced a crazed dance, their bodies swaying to the powerful rhythm, their feet pounding the earth in unison, leaping and shouting for joy.[1]

On the streets of Beijing these days, there is no way of telling Linus apart from his muses. They are all dead, burned together on the funeral pyre. Perhaps they were indistinguishable to begin with, and the song they sang was not a lamentation but an encomium, a joyous celebration of their youthful spirit. "Those who were carried off early," Rilke wrote toward the end of his First Duino Elegy, "no longer need us: they are weaned from earth's sorrows and joys, as gently as children outgrow the soft breasts of their mothers." And he continued, "But we, who need such great mysteries, we for whom grief is so often the source of our spirit's growth—: could we exist without *them*?"

A.P.C.

Wesleyan University
June 12, 1989

[1]Adapted from the *Iliad*, xviii.563–575. The image of maidens and young men dancing to the lament of Linus of Argos was carved on the shield the smith-god Hephaestus fashioned for Achilles. The scene was in a vineyard.

Preface

Most serious undertakings begin with farfetched ideas. This is certainly true in the case of my book. In 1979, I was a graduate student at Columbia University, working on a doctoral thesis in Chinese thought. Although at the time my family and I had already moved to Connecticut, every other weekend I would commute to New York to give Chinese lessons to June Esserman and her daughter Lauren. I was their tutor, but my relationship with them was more complex. Since I was not a strict teacher and they were lax students, our Chinese lessons became tea parties, and our fondness for each other grew over the years.

When I first met June, she was the director of a company that did child research. A child psychologist trained in New York University, she consulted for private firms and government agencies and had done in-depth studies of the effects of television advertising on children. In the spring of 1979, she and her family were preparing for a summer trip to the People's Republic of China. It would be their third visit to China, and June wanted to spend some time understanding Chinese children. During her past trips she had visited schools but had learned very little about the children themselves. This time she planned to interview them, a technique she had used widely in her studies of American children.

When June first sounded me out with her plan, I was skeptical. In post-Liberation China, up to that time, no one had attempted any field research based on interviews. Moreover, in the period immediately following the Cultural Revolution, it was extremely difficult to predict what official reactions might be to such a proposal. Finally there was the unsettling question of whether it was possible to relate to children through an interpreter. But June did not believe in the improbable. She proposed that I join them. Because I was a native speaker with native instincts and was versed in the Chinese cultural tradition, I would be able to talk to Chinese children directly. I was elated with her proposal, and within weeks the preparations for my exit and return were completed.

The group, in this first trip, comprised the Esserman family, the Piel family, and myself. Paul Esserman and the publisher Gerard Piel went with clearly defined goals—one was to propose scholarly exchange programs with several major universities in China, and the other was to authorize the publication of *Scientific American* in Chinese. June and I had our proposal vaguely sketched, and that was all.

From the beginning the transformation from farfetched idea to reality depended on trust. Paul had been the physician to the Chinese delegation at the United Nations. His humanity as a doctor and a person was deeply appreciated by the Chinese who were under his care and it was generously returned at the right time and place. It was Paul's former patients at the Chinese Foreign Office who led us to the right vice premier, who in turn gave oral consent to June's and my proposal. Even though we had to depend on ourselves to carry out our intent, the few words of approval came in handy when circumstances called for them. And shamelessly we used them to our advantage.

June passed away three years after that trip to China in 1979. Her untimely death had a profound effect upon me. It was my first experience of losing someone so close. My youthful belief that life will go on forever came to an end at that moment. The painful realization quickened my own growth as a person.

By then I had developed ambivalent feelings about our project. Up to that point our work had not gained the kind of momentum that would carry it into print: June had been preoccupied with various professional responsibilities and I with my studies. But I had finished transcribing our taped interviews with the Chinese children, and we had often discussed approach, methodology, even the outline of specific chapters. June had also been talking to other child psychologists and educators about our project. Their response had been one of enthusiasm and delight, but the general consensus was that a follow-up trip was necessary. In our last conversations, we had made tentative plans for a return trip to China in the spring of 1983.

Why then was I hesitant about continuing the work alone? Without June, I thought, our study lost not just the perspective of a child psychologist but its overall perspective. For it had been decided that the book was to be written from a psychologist's point of view. In our division of labor, June was to begin with a discussion of those traits and behaviors she observed to be common to all children—Western or Chinese or those of any other culture. I was to put our findings in the

Chinese cultural context. Our intent, therefore, was to understand Chinese children first as *children* and then as *Chinese children*. Conceptually it meant adopting "the universal to the particular" approach. When June died, I realized that in matters regarding children I had neither the knowledge nor the experience to speak of shared traits or the natural order in human behavior.

In the years since, my own concerns with cultural interpretation have led me to explore other horizons. In the process of reconsidering and revising my own ideas, I have found the anthropologist's reverse argument—that understanding must begin with a context—to be particularly compelling and convincing. (I am not, however, ruling out the possibility that my own inability to deal with issues from a psychologist's point of view has pushed me in that direction.) So I have chosen to approach the problem of understanding these children from the opposite end—beginning with *them*.

I have tried in my book to follow this general approach regarding the translation of cultures. First I present the context—a context within which modes of thinking and action can be "thickly described," to use the famous phrase. And then we encounter the children in a dialogue. My aim has been what Clifford Geertz has called the aim of cultural anthropology, "the enlargement of the universe of human discourse." And what of the universals? To this, I answer: when children themselves through their discourse express their minds and spirits clearly and effortlessly, must we talk of universals?

In the summer of 1984, I journeyed back to China with my husband and two children. This was the follow-up trip that June and I had wanted to take together. This time, watching my two playing with the native children as June's daughter had done five years before, I felt more a part of the landscape, though there was never a full sense of belonging. My relation with the Chinese children was one of greater ease; I conversed *with* them and understood them more intimately.

In preparing this book, I tried to reconstruct in my mind the many conversations June and I had over the years. The urge to debate again with her the issues that seem to divide us now was always present. For I was certain that a clash of the creative kind could only broaden the scope of this study.

Author's Note

PRONUNCIATION OF CHINESE NAMES AND WORDS

I have used the Pinyin system of romanization. Most letters in Pinyin are pronounced roughly as written, with these exceptions:

Pinyin		*English sound*
Q	=	ch
C	=	ts
X	=	hs

CURRENCY

A fen is a Chinese cent. Ten fen equal one jiao. Ten jiao equal one yuan.

Frequently Used Chinese Terms for Family Relationships

yeye or gonggong = paternal grandfather
nainai or popo = paternal grandmother
laoye or waigong = maternal grandfather
laolao or waipo = maternal grandmother
baba = dad
mama = mom
gege = older brother
jiejie = older sister
didi = younger brother
meimei = younger sister

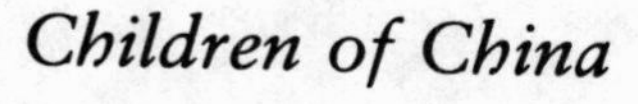

Children of China

Introduction

The study of Chinese children poses many challenges, the most important of which has to do with the question of understanding. How do we understand children, their minds, hearts, and spirits? How do we understand *Chinese* children, who partake in a cultural tradition decidedly different from our own.

Understanding begins with listening. Zhuang Zi, a Taoist thinker of the fourth century B.C., said this about listening: "Don't listen with your ears, listen with your mind. No, don't listen with your mind but listen with your spirit. Listening stops with the ears, the mind stops with recognition, but the spirit is open and receptive and waits on all things."[1]

How do we listen with our spirit? When deliberation gives way to spontaneity, mind yields to spirit. Why must we listen with our spirit? A high school student from Chongqing (Sichuan) told me of a wish: "I want to be even younger because I remember seeing things even more clearly then, and the world was full of wonder." Listening to children with our spirit allows us to participate in their sense of wonder.

Throughout my endeavor I was aware of its inherent paradox: my intent was to understand Chinese children, but all understanding is anticipatory. In trying to understand others, we do more than share in their experience; we expect them to inform us of something. Understanding is, therefore, listening with a deliberate mind.

At some point of this project, I wanted to abandon altogether my attempt to understand. I was hesitant about finding truths and meaning in the data I had gathered. A book, I thought, could serve to provide source materials for others, becoming useful in that way. During my two trips to the People's Republic of China, I had gained the trust of the children I talked to, and they allowed me, a stranger, to share in their experiences and dreams and to capture their thoughts and feelings on tape. For me, their voices are what mattered; they ought not serve an ulterior motive. Let others make of their voices what they will.

An adolescent from a farming village in Zhejiang Province insisted that boys, like girls, are sensitive to a mother's tears: "When she starts to cry, I soften my stand. I give in. The other day I had an argument with her. At first she tried to convince me, but I didn't listen. Then she became *that way*—she seemed to be very unhappy—and I backed down; I didn't insist on my point." What matters here is not that the mother-son relationship conforms to a pattern, that it proves a particular social theory. What is memorable is the relationship itself. And we learn more:

> There is work in the fields and at home. We have to do everything. I do some work, but my mama doesn't let me do too much. She wants me to study. My mama is always so tired. She is tired because she wants to put us through school. She doesn't want us to do any work, but we can't just sit around and watch her work so hard, so we do what we can to help. We plant rice and wheat, but we also have to have another business on the side. So we grow mushrooms, lots of mushrooms. Growing mushrooms is also hard work. You have to pick them at the right time . . . to make sure they don't pop. . . . A lot of the time my mother plants rice during the day and watches the mushrooms at night. She hardly gets any sleep. But if my parents didn't grow mushrooms, we couldn't afford to go to school. So it's very hard on them.

What emerged from our conversations with the Chinese children were persons, not statistics, and if we open ourselves to these persons, they speak to us directly. In a way this is what Zhuang Zi meant by listening "with the spirit." But listening with the spirit, pushed to its logical conclusion, suggests that we might subsume ourselves within someone else's experience. Yet is this actually possible? Listening to others, are we able to escape from our own standpoint—to forget our prejudices and prejudgments—and to leap into someone else's situation? It is not possible to listen to others with *total* detachment. But then, is it necessary or even desirable to try to get under someone else's skin? Prejudices and prejudgments are handed down to us through the tradition that shapes us. They are constitutive of what we are, and they condition the way we read a text and the way we listen in a conversation.

Recognizing that to listen is to understand and that no understanding is freed from the bias of the listener takes us back where we started. But now we can make a clear distinction between two kinds of understanding: understanding in order to confirm a hypothesis or preconceived notion, and understanding in order to enlarge our views and to transform ourselves. The former risks enclosing us within the walls of our prejudices, while the latter points to risking and testing our prejudices, to the openness of experience.

The German philosopher Hans-Georg Gadamer, who made the controversial claim that prejudices constitute our being and condition our understanding, illustrates the "human situation" with the idea of a horizon: "Every finite present has its limitations. We define the concept of 'situation' by saying that it represents a standpoint that limits the possibility of vision. Hence an essential part of the concept of situation is the concept of 'horizon.' The horizon is the range of vision that includes everything that can be seen from a particular vantage point." A horizon is limited but remains open; it is finite but changing. We speak of its "narrowness" but also of its "possible expansion": "The closed horizon that is supposed to enclose a culture is an abstraction. The historical movement of life consists in the fact that it is never utterly bound to any one standpoint, and hence can never have a truly closed horizon. The horizon is, rather, something into which we move and that moves with us. Horizons change for a person who is moving."[2]

The fact that we are always surrounded by a horizon rules out the possibility of leaping into someone else's situation through a pure act of empathy. How then do we understand a world with a horizon other than our own? Here Gadamer employs the metaphor of the "fusion of horizons." During a fusion of horizons, there is an encounter of one's own with others. The range of one's vision is extended, for through a knowledge of others one arrives at a deeper and more expansive understanding of oneself.

The fusion of horizons happens during an encounter: understanding begins with a dialogue. Gadamer distinguishes between a dialogue with a text or tradition and a dialogue with other persons. In a live conversation, whose participants have respect for one another and a sincere desire to grasp what the other is saying, mutuality is present. Our talks with the Chinese children did not quite tally with Gadamer's notion of an ideal conversation, for this mutuality was absent. The kids did not come to see us with an intent; they did not seek to understand us or themselves, to explore the possibility of widening their horizons; from their standpoint, there were no prejudices to transform. Their openness came from within, effortlessly and without expectation. In these unconstrained dialogues, we were the beneficiaries. We alone gained a genuine knowledge of them and of ourselves.

From these children we took much and gave little, then. But despite this imbalance, they remained patient and responsive. Many went home after our talks and then came back with favorite toys and photos—trinkets for remembrance. They were eager to strengthen the bonds between us.

In a live conversation, we can sense intuitively how things are going between us—whether there is a rapport. When we both feel at ease and the conversation offers mutual pleasure, there is no need to reflect consciously whether we understand each other. We share in what each says, and through this common experience we forget the differences between us. In my talks with Chinese children, this often happened. Minimum effort was needed to move from strangeness to familiarity. Speaking the same language greatly facilitated the understanding, of course. If a dialogue is "a process of two people understanding each other," language is the medium. In the fusion of two different cultures, a common language does more: it invites the participants to be spontaneous, since if I know that you will immediately comprehend what I say, I will feel relaxed and at ease. There is less chance of misunderstanding.

In my talks with Chinese children, the swift transition from stranger to friend can be further explained by the fact that the children and I are shaped by the same tradition. I am an American and live in America, but I was raised as a Chinese—once I, too, was a Chinese child—so we shared the same myths and stories and were grounded in the same cultural horizon; the range of our vision was often set from the same vantage point.

Still, the common language and the shared cultural tradition do not quite explain the affection that so often sprang up between us, the desire to stay and talk a few minutes longer. At a model grammar school in Beijing, I met a thin, bright-eyed girl of about twelve. She told me about her pet rabbits:

> Someone was selling rabbits on the street. [My mama] took me out to see the rabbits. Once I saw them, I refused to leave. I kept pestering my mother to buy me some. She said, No. She thinks rabbits smell awful. She doesn't like small animals. Later I took some money and bought two rabbits behind her back. I put them in a grocery basket. I lined the basket with newspapers in case they peed. I also went to the kitchen and quietly took some vegetables for my rabbits.

When her mother later discovered her rabbits, she was furious and warned her daughter of more serious consequences if her father were told about her mischief. In the end, the girl had to give up her rabbits. She entrusted them to her aunt, but they died soon after, she told me. And in turn I told her Beatrix Potter's story about Peter Rabbit.

Our morning session that day lasted longer than usual. At the end I didn't have a chance to talk to the two boys who were waiting patiently for their turn. In the afternoon, when the boys came to my hotel room to talk, the girl who loved rabbits tagged along, bringing a little photo album with her. At one time she had been trained as a gymnast, and the photos showed her on the balance beam and the parallel bars. These were her prized possessions, and there were only a few in her album. She let me choose—"Any two you like," she said. When it was time to go, she told me, "A-yi [Auntie], you must come back very soon." The parting was difficult.

Our natural affinities and linguistic and cultural linkages enabled something magical to happen. The children opened themselves to this inquisitor-stranger-friend-auntie. Comfortable and spontaneous, they talked about themselves—their dreams and grievances, joys and hurts. These were private conveyances. They were letting go buried thoughts and feelings. And as they were reflecting and expressing, some were a little surprised about what they had said: "I have never thought of this question before, but I guess this is how I feel."

In transcribing these conversations into English and putting them in this book, my aim is to let the children's voices speak to us directly, and here the reader is immediately involved and must temper his understanding to the messages themselves. (This is listening with the spirit.) But since the dialogue is with representatives of a foreign tradition, a receptive attitude alone cannot beget understanding; a reader must have a basic knowledge of the other tradition—its underlying assumptions and the prejudgments derived from them. This explains in part my intent in Chapter One, where I have tried to describe in broad terms the

Chinese perception of reality and to locate the source of Chinese traditional values. I have focused on the concept of the self, for it bears a direct relationship to the experience of growing up. After all, growing up is the process whereby a person gains a sense of the emerging self; he realizes his possibilities and learns to come to terms with his limitations.

The Chinese have traditionally conceived of the self as a relational self. From this basic premise, the early Confucians put forth their own assumptions regarding the nature of mankind. For them everyone was equally endowed with the innate ability to know right and wrong and to act morally. Thinkers from this tradition tried to come to grips with the question of how to extend this goodness to others. At about the same time (fifth to third century B.C.) the Taoists advanced their own theories, asking us to look beyond human relationships, since they saw man's relation to man as part of his relation to the total reality. In their view an understanding of the Way of Heaven and Earth (or Nature) broadens and deepens our understanding of the way of mankind.

These Confucian and Taoist concerns are reflected in the questions we asked the children. How did they relate to others—their families, friends, neighbors, teachers—to society as a whole, to nature, and to their history and tradition? How did their relationships change with the vicissitudes of time and social and political circumstances? How did the children themselves perceive the transformations, within themselves and in relation to others? Here the reflections of the older children (in particular two girls and three boys whom I interviewed on both trips) are especially illuminating; indeed my encounters with them were emotional and at times disturbing.

The structure of the rest of the book is fairly simple. Chapters Two and Three focus on individual children, half of whose comments I extracted from what were originally group discussions. In doing so, I sacrificed the special tone of a child's response in a group situation in the interests of a more coherent presentation of the individual. The interviews in these two chapters are divided according to age—grammar school and junior high school students in Chapter Two, and high school students in Chapter Three—and further arranged according to geographical location.

Here a word must be said about the school system in present-day China, which actually resembles the system found in the United States in its temporal division. The initial six-year period and then two three-year periods mark the three stages of formal education prior to college: what Americans would call primary school, junior high, and high school. (This twelve-year course was shortened to ten—five years of primary and five years of middle school—during the Cultural Revolution in 1966–76 and immediately after it. In 1979, when I made my first trip, it was a time of transition. The schools were waiting for directives about reviving the former twelve-year system.)

In Chapter Four children aged between seven and fifteen from five major cities are represented in group discussions. Here the underlying theme is still "children as individuals," only the method has changed. In these interviews each child comes through in his interaction with others. In selecting the interviews to be included in this chapter, I again took into consideration the age and the geographic location.

Chapter Five is one big interview with a group of high school students who were attending a computer camp in Hangzhou's Zhejiang University. These students were from the Huadong (Eastern) region, which includes six provinces: Fujian, Zhejiang, Jiangsu, Jiangxi, Anhui, and Shandong. Our conversation began on the Zhejiang University campus one early afternoon and finished late that night in my hotel room, after a pleasant dinner.

All the transcribed interviews are the result of careful editing and conscious selection. Although this is *my* version of what I think I heard these children say, it is *their* stories I have sought to deliver; their voices are doing the telling.

I have also tried to recapture the spirit of each encounter, and those body idioms—gestures and movements—characteristic of each storyteller. Each interview begins with a description of the circumstances of the conversation. Whenever a child's voice is introduced for the first time, her presence is acknowledged with a brief note on her background. In all cases, my questions, observations, and comments, integrated and yet kept separate from the children's narration, are found in italics.

Finally, to protect the privacy of the children, I have changed a number of their names, but I have done this with great reluctance. In China, names give meaning to a person. He is not just an Andrew or a Samuel. He is "tranquil" (*jing*) or "resolute" (*jin*); he is "a cloud followed by a dragon" (*yun*) or one who "holds on to his humanity" (*shou-ren*). A person's name is what his parents and grandparents expect of him, and, later on, perhaps, what he expects of himself. Thus to give him a new one arbitrarily, as I have done, is, in a way, to take away his essence.

During the first trip, in the summer of 1979, June Esserman and I interviewed thirty children between the ages of six and thirteen, and most of them lived in coastal cities—Beijing, Tianjin, Shanghai, and

Guangzhou. When we saw them, the schools were coming to the end of the spring semester. The children were getting ready to take their final examinations, and some of them were preparing for middle school entrance exams. In most cases our meetings were arranged by school administrators and were held primarily in school environments—with two exceptions, once in the home of a model commune and another time in a park.

Many of the children from the coastal cities grew up in the country with their grandparents, for with both parents holding jobs, there was usually no one at home to take care of them when they were very young. They returned to their parents around the age of six or seven. Most could recall in detail their earlier childhood experiences. The children all carried distinct regional traits. In their speech I detected heavy dialect tones and a liberal use of local slangs. (This was very different from my experience in 1984, when most of the grammar school children whom I talked to spoke perfect *pu-tong-hua,* the standard Chinese based on the Beijing dialect.)

Western sociologists and psychologists have noted the many difficulties in attempting psychological research in China. Of course, for years post-Liberation China was largely closed to direct observation by foreigners. Some researchers tested their hypotheses through interviews with Chinese emigrés in Hong Kong and Taiwan. In 1979, the only book available in English that dealt extensively with children growing up in the People's Republic of China was *Childhood in China,* a work based on observations made by a group of distinguished American child psychologists and sociologists, which included William Kessen, Jerome Kagan, Urie Bronfenbrenner, Martin Whyte, and others. Though a highly informative book, *Childhood in China* allows us only the kind of knowledge acquired largely through "impressions," and, in several instances, its authors express frustration at not being able to "register and understand variations in personality among Chinese children" and "to penetrate [China's] underlying social reality."

During our first trip, with virtually no past experiences to guide us in our field investigations, June and I knew only that we had to be extremely flexible and adaptable. It was difficult to structure an approach ahead of time, but we did decide not to carry any standardized questionnaires or psychologically projective tests. These tools, used to analyze and predict the attitudes and concerns of American children, do not necessarily work cross-culturally, and we ran the risk of grasping inaccurately and insufficiently the social and psychological make-up of children growing up in a decidedly different cultural context. Again I was reminded of Gadamer's claim that no methods are truly objective. Aside from these considerations, we also guessed that since Chinese children were not familiar with questionnaires and psychological tests, they would probably associate them with regular academic examinations, which might make them anxious and uneasy. In fact, many children at the beginning of our conversations wanted to know what our questions would be like: "Is it like a test?" "Do we have to give the correct answers?" And at the end of our sessions, a few said, "This is it? That's all you want to know? It sure was easy!"

Because circumstances did not allow us to be "well prepared," it is more accurate to describe our undertaking as an adventure rather than a field study. We went as explorers rather than investigators. Ironically, this was to our advantage. With children as our guides, we discovered more unknown lands and had more fun along the way.

Since during our first trip most of our conversations were carried out in school environments, a typical visit began with a brief introduction by the school principal, who would ask us if we'd like to tour the school and observe classrooms. We politely declined and explained our wish to talk to some children instead. The immediate response was one of surprise. "We have never been approached this way," one principal told us. They wanted to know the purpose of our interviews, and, in some instances, to hear a few sample questions. But generally they were receptive to our unusual request, and we met little resistance—up to the point when we asked to be left alone with the children. Yet this last part of our request was essential. For the children to feel comfortable and unconstrained while they talked, they had to be left alone with us, away from the attentive ears and the watchful eyes of parents, teachers, school administrators, and even interpreters. The school officials were always tactful but persistent: "We are interested in your studies. Listening to your exchange with our children would be a learning experience for us." But we, too, were persistent, and at the end our request was granted, primarily because of the trust we had established with our hosts. So in all the schools we visited, we were allowed to talk to the children alone. When we finished, we offered to let the principals and teachers listen to our tapes. "There is no need," they assured us.

The primary schools we saw had all been built in the 1950s or early 1960s, after the Liberation and before the Cultural Revolution. The buildings were two- or three-story brick or concrete structures, and the colors were uniform shades of gray. The playgrounds were usually paved. All had only minimal stationary equipment: swing sets, slides, monkey bars, and basketball hoops. For most children, the playground was primarily a gathering area during recess, where they could chat or skip rope with friends.

Before sitting down to converse, we played with the children in the schoolyards. There would usually be twenty or thirty of them in the playground, some because it was their recess, others brought out to us by the teachers. We brought along Frisbees, balls, jacks, and other games that American children play. Very soon they all joined in, and in return they showed us their games. When the children were relaxed and felt at ease with us, then we began to talk in a more direct way with them; we either asked for volunteers or picked children ourselves. Given our limited time, we made obvious choices of children who seemed likely to be responsive, who appeared to be lively and spontaneous. We realized that our methods of choice were far from perfect or objective.

We interviewed the children two or three at a time, with boys and girls in separate groups. Each session lasted from sixty to ninety minutes.

When I returned to China in 1984, the circumstances of my encounters with the children depended more on chance and improvisation. It was the middle of summer vacation, and many were with their grandparents in the country. Though they returned to their schools once a month to hand in summer homework, the schools were in recess and administrators and teachers were nowhere to be found. It was therefore impossible to solicit their help.

Yet from the beginning luck was on our side. In Shanghai my husband Li-ping's contact at the local Science and Technology Exchange Center telephoned the school June Esserman and I had visited in 1979. The teacher who happened to be there to pick up his bimonthly paycheck remembered me: he was the English teacher who had received us five years before and was eager to help me again. The next day he gathered a group of children from the neighborhood, all pupils from his school, and among them was one of two sisters I had interviewed on my first trip. That afternoon she brought over her older sister. Five years ago we had spent half an afternoon together, but many changes had taken place since then, and they were eager to talk. When we finished, the sisters brought us (Li-ping, my two children, and me) home to meet their parents. It felt like a reunion, even though we had never met before. The parents talked about themselves, their children, and the transformations over the years. They were affectionate to my daughter and son. The father even suggested that we exchange children for a year.

The same English teacher in Shanghai also tracked down for me three boys whom I had interviewed in 1979. Then, in Hangzhou, there was a boy named Zheng Gao-xing. He was from Haiyen, a small town in

Zhejiang Province, and he had come to visit Hangzhou that day with a friend. We were sitting by the West Lake when he passed by, and he stopped to listen to our children because they were speaking to each other in English. Before long, he was sitting next to me on the bench. I turned on my tape recorder, and we talked for an hour.

Throughout this trip I was dependent on the kindness of others: relatives, friends, friends of friends, strangers-becoming-friends. They guided me to children. Our contacts at the Institute of Scientific and Technical Information in Chongqing and Beijing, and at the Science and Technology Exchange Centers in Shanghai and Hangzhou, also played a direct role in helping me to find children. Many were parents themselves and, taking a genuine interest in my effort, went out of their way and used unconventional means to assist me. I think they were interested in what the children had revealed to me because they wanted to understand their own children.

The circumstances under which I talked to children in 1984 varied as much as the circumstances that led me to them. Because it was summer vacation, the children and I could spend more time together. We went on outings together, had lunch and dinner together; I went to their homes, their friends' and neighbors' homes, their parents' work units, to restaurants, hotel rooms, schools, and parks. I was still pressed for time, but my schedule was not dictated by factors completely beyond my control. We did not have to cut short a conversation because the children had to go home for lunch, as had often happened in 1979. The children could have lunch with me, and we could continue to talk. And of course, since we had more time together and the freedom to choose where to go, we had greater pleasure in relating to one another.

Our conversations differed from conventional interviews. In 1979, June and I had tried to use the question-and-answer format only sparingly, for, as Studs Terkel has put it, it "may be of some value in determining favored detergents, toothpaste and deodorants, but not in the discovery of men and women." Since these were children between the ages of six and thirteen, their responses to any given question tended to be brief and to the point, and we had to work hard to tease out the specifics; as a result the interviews often did fall into the question-and-answer pattern, even when we had planned it otherwise. But my experience the second time was different. The children had more time to ease into a conversation; most of them were teenagers who were able to sustain and often expand a discussion. The talks we had were for them like those they might have with an older friend or an aunt or uncle, only less restrained. We shared experiences and disagreed on issues. We traded stories and even gossip. A teenager from Jiangsu, for instance, told me about his former neighbors: "The mother was sick in bed. The daughter-in-law never looked after her. But whenever the mother got a little better, the daughter-in-law would ask her to do the wash. She'd go to the movies while her mother-in-law was home doing the wash."

On this second trip to the PRC, I talked to more than a hundred children between the ages of six and nineteen. They were primarily from five cities I visited: Shanghai, Hangzhou, Beijing, Xian, and Chongqing. In addition, I had the rare opportunity of holding an informal round-table discussion with a group of high school seniors from the Huadong region.

Only on a few occasions did I get to know children who were from a genuine peasant background. Many children had lived in the countryside before starting first grade, but their parents were either intellectuals or factory workers. We know that 80 percent of the Chinese population are peasants, and yet less than 10 percent of the children in this volume represent this enormous mass of people. Statistically, therefore, I cannot say that I have any claim to understanding how *most* Chinese children think and feel, and this is a major shortcoming of my study. Still, given the special nature of the Chinese experience and, in particular, of the experience of Chinese children, the shortcoming is not so severe as it might be in other countries. Children reared in a long and stable social tradition like China's share the same cultural values regardless of their economic class or their parents' educational background; and, being children, they are less conscious of status, less deliberate in their thought and action. They may have more affection for the land if they are from the country, and a more heightened awareness of their parents' labor if they observe daily agricultural work, but in the end they feel the same pains and dream the same dreams. The daughter of a tea farmer from Longjing, a tall soft-spoken girl who had just finished junior high, told me that her mother had picked tea leaves since she was a girl, but she wanted to become an athlete—a runner—or a doctor.

1

A Backdrop for . . .

Clifford Geertz tells us that "as culture shapes us as a single species—and is no doubt still shaping us—so too it shapes us as separate individuals."[1] A person begins his life in a cultural framework that confines him and continues to define him. But being the questioning, pondering, morally and aesthetically sensitive animal that he is, he does not merely receive what is given. He is an actor, a player. He responds to his circumstances and often redefines the rules that govern his reality. In the course of becoming, he emerges as an individual and as a maker of his culture.

Listening to children allows us, I believe, a glimpse of how the process works—how we become a part of the whole, while growing more distinct as a part. Childhood is a unique period in our lives when, without being deliberately reflective, we feel the anguish and the joy of coming into being; when we are experiencing and not analyzing; when we still have the power to be honest about our thoughts and feelings. Childhood is also a period when we become increasingly aware of the polarities between the whole and the individual, and of the necessity to choose or, rather, to come to terms with the conditions of being human.

Exactly what is the cultural framework into which a Chinese is born, and what do its underlying assumptions tell him regarding what a person is? The children's responses recorded in this book should be set in the frame of what the Chinese perceive as normal and be understood in terms of that vision. A description of the extrinsic forces of their culture renders the Chinese children more accessible and provides a backdrop against which their thoughts and actions can be better understood. But ultimately it is the children themselves, and their interaction with their preexisting circumstances, that matter. The tales they tell are revelations of that mysterious and magical process that is becoming human. Although the voices we hear are distinctly those of Chinese children, in the end they involve us in a kind of universal human discourse. In understanding what they are, we catch a glimpse of what we are.

EARLY RELIGIOUS ORIENTATIONS

Archeological expeditions of this century have led to the uncovering of a remote past that continues to throw light on the immediate present. In China, material artifacts and archeological data have greatly enriched our knowledge of the period between the second and first millennia B.C. More important, we have moved steps closer toward answering the question, what is Chinese? What defines the Chinese perception of the world and how? What makes them respond to their world in their unique ways?

A principal source of our information regarding this period is the oracle bone inscriptions. The oracle bone inscriptions are evidence of the practice of divination: large animal bones and tortoise shells were heated until they cracked, and the patterns of the cracks thus formed were then interpreted by diviners; the questions the diviners posed to the ancestral spirits and their explanations of the patterns were then inscribed on the bones and shells. These inscriptions reveal the pervasiveness of ancestor worship in China's early religious orientations. Although the material artifacts and data come from the imperial archives, scholars are reasonably certain that they reflect widely shared orientations, that people on all levels of Chinese society participated in the ancestor cult.

The ancestor cult as practiced by the nobility of the Shang dynasty (1766?–1122? B.C.) involved making human and animal sacrifices to the ancestral spirits to obtain their approval and blessing. At fixed dates the ruler, assisted by priests and ministers, attempted to communicate with the spirits of the noumenal world by performing certain religious rites; he and his assistants prayed to the spirits of deceased rulers and ministers and to the Lord-on-High (*shang-di*). The Lord-on-High, conceived either as the first of the Chinese progenitors or as a purely numinous being (scholars disagree on this question), was not an anthropomorphic representation of an absolute ideal. The question whether he was perfect or not was not a concern for the Chinese. What was important was that he was either the first in an ancestral line or a spiritual being to whom the ancestral spirits had direct access. He was regarded with awe because of the ancestral connection and the numinous aura surrounding him. He could confer benefit or misfortune; therefore men had to decipher his wishes and seek his blessings.

It is also significant that the Lord-on-High was not conceived as the creator of humankind. In fact, during this early period in their history the Chinese did not have a creation myth. Questions regarding the origin of the universe and the beginning of humankind were simply not asked. The Chinese people were not interested in speculating on how and why life began. Life was "as it is," given to humankind through the natural process of procreation. It was linked with the biological notion of production and reproduction (*sheng-sheng*), not with the idea of creation. Life began with spontaneous self-generation—a view articulated by the Neo-Taoists of the third and fourth centuries—and continued through the process of begetting. It was not something fashioned from nothing, and there was no eternal entity, such as the soul, attached to the temporal body. For the Chinese, there was nothing beyond the biological continuity of life, perpetuated through the family line.

It was only natural, therefore, that by the next dynasty, the Zhou (1122?–256 B.C.), the notion of the Lord-on-High was gradually replaced by the concept of Heaven (*tian*), a term closely associated with Nature (*zi-ran*). In Shang ancestor worship, the division of the human world and the noumenal world was unclear on account of the biological link between them through the ancestors. Even in the case of the highest deity, there was a natural bond between him and human beings.

In the early Zhou, the notion of an anthropomorphic deity receded to the background, and the two worlds—human and noumenal—became closely identified. That which was conceived of as greater than human beings was no longer a divine entity wrapped in a numinous aura, but the cosmic force that gives us life and continues to transform us: Heaven is here and now; it is one with this world.

The concept of Heaven brought together the two dominant metaphors in Chinese thought: of birth and spontaneous growth, and of a preestablished holistic order. Heaven is a dynamic whole, and everything is an inseparable part of it; everything belongs to it and nothing lies outside it. The whole—understood here as a kind of *élan vital*—nourishes all things and advances them. However, it does not proceed haphazardly; it follows a definite order and set patterns. The individual components, for their part, "cooperate" and "harmonize their wills" to preserve the whole.[2] The cooperation and harmonization of wills suggest a hierarchic relationship, which in Chinese culture has its beginning in the family. And because the notions of authority and hierarchy are first learned in the home, where "Father" is not only a power figure but one who has produced me and who nurtures me, it is easier for me to accept them. This does not mean that the families actually constitute harmonious wholes, however. "They ought to [but] do not necessarily do so," as Benjamin Schwartz has observed.[3] And it is in the abyss between what is ideal and what is real that we find the Chinese individual.

THE SELF AND THE FAMILY

In the Chinese perception, a person is born a son or a daughter, a brother or a sister; in time, he or she will become a father or a mother and a friend to others. A person is born into a web of human relatedness; he is a link in the human nexus, his identity predetermined by his relations to others. ("I am the third son of the Guo family" is how a man might refer to himself.) Who he is becomes clearer as he fulfills his social responsibilities. ("He is the third son of the Guo family, the one who sided with his wife, instead of his mother, the last time the two quarreled," a neighbor might say.) In the Confucian framework, a normative sociopolitical order becomes possible where social roles are realized according to proper steps. When asked about government, Confucius replied, "Let the ruler be a ruler, the subject be a subject, the father be a father, and the son be a son."[4]

Does a person lose himself in the process of fulfilling these roles? No, not when the self is itself defined in relational terms. The roles he assumes are not external to his personhood but, in fact, constitute his identity. Realization of one's social responsibilities is the realization of oneself.

In the West we have a decidedly different notion of the self. Shortly before Mencius (371?–289? B.C.), the most important interpreter of Confucius' teachings, drew analogies between the four moral principles—humaneness (*ren*), righteousness (*yi*), propriety (*li*), and wisdom (*zhi*)—

and the four limbs of the body, Plato was propounding his theory of the self as consisting of two separate entities, a temporal body and an eternal soul. The soul is entrapped in the body, but the body is the servant of the soul, a relationship corollary to Plato's theorem that "the universal finds its expression in the particular." Later, in the Christian tradition, the soul becomes the person's emotional seat and moral source, created for us by God so that we may experience the lyrical and tell right from wrong. The path the soul traverses in this life determines its career in the other life, when it stands before God on Judgment Day. Whether a person will be judged to receive eternal bliss or damnation depends on the choices his willful soul has made in the temporal life. St. Augustine in his *Confessions* asked: "For I wondered how it was that I could appreciate beauty in material things on earth or in the heavens, and what it was that enabled me to make correct decisions about things that are subject to change and to rule that one thing ought to be like this, another like that." "So step by step," he continued, "my thoughts moved on from the considerations of material things to the soul" and to "the soul that wills." And we read further:

> When I was trying to reach a decision about serving the Lord my God, as I had long intended to do, it was I who willed to take this course and again it was I who willed not to take it. It was I and I alone. But I neither willed to do it nor refused to do it with my full will. So I was at odds with myself. I was throwing myself into confusion. All this happened to me although I did not want it, but it did not prove that there was some second mind in me besides my own.

Augustine placed the burden upon the "I": "I had the *free will* to choose and I did not. I wavered in my decision and was torn between both inclinations because I did not will it in a 'wholehearted' and 'resolute' way."[5]

In the West, ever since the appearance of the *Confessions,* the Augustinian notion of free will has continuously transformed our perception of what a person—an individual—is. Sixteenth- and seventeenth-century European philosophers understood the weighty responsibility of "It was I who willed to take this course and again it was I who willed not to take it"; they took it to mean, I have the *natural right* to the privacy of my thought and beliefs, and I have the freedom to make autonomous decisions concerning them. Now we say that each individual has a unique identity, for the sake of which we embark on a private and often painful journey "to find ourselves," beginning (so psychologists tell us) around the age of twelve or thirteen. Whether or not we actually find ourselves is not the most important question. What is critical is that we commit ourselves to this task. Otherwise we "lose ourselves." Thus, like Oedipus, who was sent packing as an infant, we learn to hold a spoon before our first birthday. Teaching children to be independent is one of the first principles in child rearing. When we are young, others applaud our individual expressions, and we are fulfilled. When we grow older, the individuality of our expressions translates into privacy and autonomy that form a separate domain of the self, jealously guarded from the encroachment of others.

In the Chinese conception of the self, there is no clear division between the private and the public self. In Confucian teaching, moral responsibilities are construed in terms of relationships. They are not grounded on the "I and I alone." Since there is no willful soul to speak of, not being responsible does not mean that one did not exercise one's will either to act or not to act, that "I was at odds with myself, throwing myself into confusion." For the Chinese, responsibilities are social and are thought of in terms of relationships. Being responsible means realizing one's roles or "exerting one's mind to the utmost" in relation to others.[6]

Why did the Confucians conceive responsibilities in this way? Confucius' answer is preserved in the *Analects*. He believed there was a high degree of stability attached to relationships and to the identities derived from them. When moral responsibilities were defined in terms of these relationships, their fulfillment would ensure a normative sociopolitical order.

Is there a person at all at the center of the web? Is there an inner dimension to that person? Or do his relations to others represent the totality of his being? At one point in the *Analects,* Confucius turned to one of his disciples, Zeng Shen, and said, "Shen, there is one thread running through my teachings [*tao*]." Shen replied, "Yes." When he heard that, the Master left the room. The other disciples asked Zeng Shen, "What did he mean?" Zeng Shen responded, "The way of our master is to be truthful to our heart-and-mind [*xin*] and to extend sincerely this heart-and-mind to others."[7]

Truthfulness and reciprocity point to the underlying significance of the Confucian teaching of rites or propriety (*li*). In performing social rites, one gives proper expression to one's concerns and regard for others. The ceremonial act is an embodiment of one's inner reverential attitude. Confucius said, "Courtesy without [the reverential spirit of] *li* becomes laborious bustle. Cautiousness without *li* becomes timidity.

Boldness without *li* becomes insubordination. Straightforwardness without *li* becomes rudeness." Similarly, rituals performed without sincere intent are merely perfunctory acts. Again, Confucius said, "If a man is not humane, what has he to do with ceremonies? If he is not humane, what has he to do with music?"[8]

With truthfulness and reciprocity as its basis, filial piety is no longer simply a fulfillment of duty to one's parents; it is a moral act. To serve one's parents is an outward expression of a child's deep love and respect. Confucius said, "A filial son is not just a man who keeps his parents fed. Dogs and horses can do that. If there is no feeling of reverence, wherein lies the difference?"[9]

The "one thread," as Zeng Shen understood it, concerns the realization of an inner moral life through the fulfillment of relational responsibilities. Confucius described the ideal man as one who "cultivates himself [seriously] so as to give common people security and peace."[10] A person's inner and outer dimensions are not and ought not to be disjoined. There is only one way of being a person: outward expressions acquire depth through a sincere mind; inner intent finds actualization through concrete actions. The discourse in the *Analects* seems to suggest that there *ought* not to be any tension between the two. But then we encounter a passage such as this one: "In serving his parents, a son may remonstrate with them, but gently; when he sees that they do not incline to follow his advice, he shows an increased degree of reverence, but does not abandon his purpose; and should they punish him, he does not allow himself to murmur."[11] Here we must read beyond the apparent—the authority endowed in the parents and the constraints placed on the son. This passage does not simply tell us the "do's" and "don'ts" in a parent-child relationship. It introduces questions and poses problems. Confucius said that he who cultivates himself is one who can develop others. The son's failure in this case, despite repeated effort and extreme sensitivity in approaching his parents, points to the gap between what ought to be and what is. Confucius' words seem like moral prescriptions, but are they? In this example he has employed his favorite teaching method: holding up one corner of a square and asking us to find the remaining three for ourselves;[12] he is telling us what ought to be but has left the rest for self-discovery and self-realization.

Passages like this one allow us a glimpse of what happens in actual relationships, so far removed from what ought to happen. The abyss between the two is open, and an individual is often frustrated by what the space implies—that the ideal and the actual do not come together. Yet the space also allows him to make sense of his own existence, inviting him to reflect and explore further, suggesting potentialities that await realization. The potentialities are the three remaining corners, and the process of seeking the three corners is the self becoming.

The son who resists abandoning his purpose is an individual emerging. His own moral inclination gives him a locus, an anchor point. Being Chinese, he perceives his purpose in terms of his role—in this case his role as a son. His purpose is to persuade his parents not to stray from what he sees as the correct path. His moral inclination is extended in the process of relating to others. It is not cultivated in isolation, as the mind becomes more resolute in exercising free will to choose between this or that. For a Chinese, it is a test of the individual's moral strength to be able to remain true to his endowed humanity as he tries to fulfill his relational responsibilities.

The Chinese person is confronted with another challenge: how is he to fulfill his responsibility to himself and to others without putting any strain on relationships? In Confucian teaching, individuals must try to avoid conflicts when associating with others, since relationships are the stabilizing force in the society. The son, who remonstrates with his parents, "but gently," is cautiously balancing himself within an established order. And as he positions himself in the web of relations, he feels pulls from various directions; but he must not lose his balance. As the lines tighten, he must maintain equilibrium. The web must not break, or he will fall.

The perception of the self as a relational self born with social responsibilities is not confined to the Confucians. Even a Taoist thinker such as Zhuang Zi, who created many delightful parodies of the purposeful Confucians weighed down by their determination to save the world, shared such a vision. In Chapter Four of the *Zhuang Zi,* he speaks of serving one's parents and ruler as something one "cannot avoid." His advice to Yen Ho, who had to tutor a prince who lacked virtue, is this:

> In your action it is best to follow along, and in your mind it is best to harmonize with him. However, these courses involve certain dangers. Though you follow along, you don't want to be pulled into his doings, and though you harmonize, you don't want to be drawn out too far. . . . If he wants to be a child, be a child with him. If he wants to be reckless, be reckless with him. Understand him thoroughly, and lead him to the point where he is without fault.[13]

Both Confucians and Taoists suggest the approach of following along and harmonizing with the other. (Here, "the other" refers to an authority figure, a father or ruler.) But there are subtle differences, and in them one sees clear distinctions. In an earlier passage of *Zhuang Zi*, one finds Confucius giving advice, in the manner of a Taoist sage, to his favorite disciple, Yen Hui, who wants to do a very Confucian thing—"to restore a chaotic state to health":

> Though your virtue may be great and your good faith unassailable, if you do not understand men's spirit, though your fame may be wide and you do not strive with others, if you do not understand men's minds, but instead appear before a tyrant and force him to listen to sermons on benevolence and righteousness, measures and standards—this is simply using other men's bad points to parade your own excellence.[14]

Taoists fault Confucians for "forcing" others "to listen to sermons," which, according to them, is "simply using other men's bad points to parade your excellence." Numerous passages in the *Analects* lend support to the Taoists' claim that the Confucians relate to others self-righteously. When the head of the powerful Ji family from Confucius' native state of Lu asks the Master about government, he answers, "To govern means to rectify. If you lead on the people with correctness, who will dare not to be correct?" When questioned further about "how to do away with thieves," Confucius replies, "If you, sir, were not covetous, although you should reward them to do it, they would not steal."[15] In these responses Confucius is making clear who is to be blamed for the state of affairs: the ruler lacked virtue, and therefore the people lacked virtue.

Throughout Chinese history scholar-officials whose "virtue may be great" and "good faith unassailable" have put into practice the Confucian principle that "to govern means to rectify." In their memorials to the throne, they point out what is correct and then they remind their rulers, "If you lead on the people with correctness, who will dare not to be correct?" Rarely did the rulers heed such advice. Most either ignored what they felt as "tiresome sermons on benevolence and righteousness" or imposed their own views on their subordinates. Their reactions merely confirm what Zhuang Zi forewarned: "Kings and dukes always lord it over others and fight to win the argument." For him, the self-righteous Confucian is like "the praying mantis that waved its arms angrily in front of an approaching carriage . . . such was the high opinion it had of its talents."[16]

What is the Taoist way of following along and harmonizing with the one who has power and authority? "If he wants to be a child, be a child with him. If he wants to be reckless, be reckless with him. Understand him thoroughly and lead him to the point where he is without fault." One essential difference between this and Confucius' recommendation to the head of the Ji clan and his advice to the son rests on the question of understanding. "Understand him thoroughly," his "spirit and mind," Zhuang Zi tells us, and then "lead him." In his view, the strain in any relationship initiates with the recognition of right and wrong. In a ruler-subject relationship, the situation is usually brought to a head with the obstinate one getting himself executed and the compromising one prostrating himself before the dragon throne, "with eyes growing dazed, color changing, and mouth inventing excuses."[17] They may both be virtuous, but neither has succeeded in persuading his ruler to change his ways.

In a parent-child relationship, natural affection, being an inseparable part of this bond, softens the obstinate mind. A child who believes he is right is less self-righteous; he is more yielding and, therefore, gentler. He hopes to exert influence through his reverential attitude, but in the end, should he fail, should his parents punish him, "he does not allow himself to murmur"—this was Confucius' counsel; the thread must not be severed—this was Confucius' warning. As for the father, he loves his child but also takes his endowed authority seriously. From the Taoist point of view, he nurtures his child while taking possession of him. "The best person," Lao Zi said, "is like water," benefitting all things without contending with them or taking possession of them. "The best of all rulers," he continued in another chapter, "is but a shadowy presence to his subjects. . . . When his task is accomplished and his work done / The people all say, 'It happened to us naturally.' "[18] Zhuang Zi echoed these same words with greater resonance: "Therefore the Great Man in his actions will not harm others, but he makes no show of benevolence or charity. He will not move for the sake of profit, but he does not despise the porter at the gate."[19]

When we listen to the voices of Chinese children today, we wonder whether they, too, however unconsciously, are drawn to the Confucian-Taoist debate that began more than two thousand years ago. A girl of thirteen from the city of Chongqing told me about her dreams and her parents' expectations:

> Sometimes I'd like to be a zoologist. Sometimes I'd like to be a writer because I like literature very much. But my mother wants me to become an engineer or some kind of a specialist. And so I don't tell them what I want to be. I like to collect butterflies, to press them

> in my books. I like to take their scales off and see what they look like under the scales. But if my parents see me doing this, they say I'm not doing "proper work."

The child paused to listen to her classmates' comments, and then reflected further:

> My father is very good to me. He thinks I should choose the path I walk on for myself. But my mother is not like that. I like to read literature, but she says: "This is not going to be on your exams. Study something more useful!" If my father catches me reading, he just sighs, not saying a word. Still it makes me feel bad, and so I try not to read in front of them. At home, I don't openly do the things that I like to do. I don't want to hurt their feelings.

The central issue here is understanding, which for the Chinese always involves the other, since it acquires meaning only when there is a relation (this is true even with self-understanding). Zhuang Zi tried to tell the Confucians two thousand years ago that they talked too much about what relationships ought to be like and not enough about what they are like; given what they *are* like, they require understanding of the most expansive kind—they require "listening with the spirit."

Zhuang Zi's words have far-reaching resonances even today in China, and perhaps for all of us. They vibrate in the reflections of the thirteen-year-old girl from Chongqing even though she is unaware of the source. The child's mother, who no doubt loves her and wants to see her succeed, has decided for her what is useful and what is not. Her high-handedness has produced tension between her and her daughter. The girl's father appears to be more empathetic. He has his own opinions but only sighs and says nothing. The girl is sensitive to this, and does not want to hurt his feelings. In not challenging her parents openly, not even telling them what she wants to be, she is following Confucius' guideline for the parent-child relationship. At the same time, she tells us of her desire that her parents listen to her with an open spirit and try to understand her likes and dislikes. While reluctant to let her parents know her wishes, she longs to be understood; avoiding direct confrontation with them and genuinely concerned about their feelings, she resents their domineering ways. Here we can catch a glimpse of how the forces of tradition are worked into the complex texture of a child's moral life, creating deep inner conflicts. The child, intense and somewhat bitter (one detects this in her unusual candor about her mother), is trying to understand—herself, her parents, and her reality. Soon enough she will recognize how troubled and difficult is the tension between reality and ideals. A college student from the same city had this to say about himself and his younger brother, a high school junior:

> I'm not really interested in what I'm doing, except maybe the computer science courses I've taken. . . . Even with computer science, our school is short of good teachers and facilities. We don't have the same learning conditions as the students at Qinghua University. Then after college we're assigned to work units according to "need." There's no choice involved. . . . In this society, it's difficult to make changes. You just have to adjust to your environment. My brother and the kids from his generation are too idealistic. Life out there is not the way they perceive it.

When the girl's mother tells her that something that is not going to be on the exams will not be useful, is she making her aware of "life out there"? Is she saying that if you do not do well on your exams, you will not get into a good university and you will end up like that discontented college student? Adopting the mother's position, one might ask whether understanding a child's likes and dislikes is going to help her deal with "life out there." Again we return to a central question in the Confucian-Taoist debate: does the recognition that there is a "this" and a "that"—a "right" and a "wrong"—in every position help to solve real problems? The mother decides what is right and wrong for her child, and the child is unhappy. In the words of Lao Zi, she nurtures her child but at the same time takes possession of her. But if she does not do that, if she sees the "right" in her child's position, will her child be prepared for the requirements of the larger reality—requirements that, as the college student says, are hard to change?

One of the conditions that Chinese children today still must come to terms with is the intimate connection between their aspirations and exams. The examinations limit immediate choices but, if dealt with successfully, open up more and better opportunities in the future. The examination system, first introduced during the reign of Han Wu-di (141–87 B.C.) as a means of civil service recruitment, has for millennia shaped the Chinese attitude toward learning and education—and indeed, toward the future. This attitude, as we have already observed, touches the lives of the college student and the thirteen-year-old girl in a most profound way. For this reason, traditional Chinese views on education and their relationship to the examination system merit some attention. The evolution of this traditional attitude through time and historical circumstances affirms what Benjamin Schwartz said about individuals and their relationship to their pregiven culture: they "do not merely expound the rules. . . . They reflect on and wrestle with the meanings of the older cultural orientations even when they remain within the boundaries of these orientations."[20]

LEARNING AND EDUCATION

The *Analects* opens with the Master putting forth the following rhetorical questions: "Is it not a pleasure to learn and to repeat or to practice from time to time what has been learned? Is it not delightful to have friends coming from afar?!" Here the descriptive words *yueh* (pleasant) and *le* (delightful) and the particle *hu* (?!) betray the speaker's emotion. Confucius found joy in learning and association with others. Elsewhere he said: "Those who know the truth are not up to those who love it; those who love the truth are not up to those who delight in it," and "In a hamlet of ten families, there may be some as faithful and as truthful as I but no one who so loves learning."[21] Where does this singular love-delight come from? Perhaps it can be understood from Confucius' fervent commitment to the project of culture and civilization, from learning about "the resplendent Chou culture" and relating to others through the Chou rituals. When speaking of the ideal man (the noble man, *jun-zi*), Confucius said that he "extensively studies culture and restrains himself with the rules of propriety."[22] By culture he referred to the early Chou rituals and ceremonial prescriptions and Chou history, documents, poetry, and music. Is Confucius telling us that being civilized alone does not make us whole persons; that we must complete ourselves through "highly particular forms of culture"? Is his joy related to the realization that, as Geertz says, we are "unfinished animals" who must "finish ourselves" through the learning of culture? Here one is reminded of what Geertz understood when he heard the Javanese people say: "To be human is to be Javanese," that "to be human here is thus not to be Everyman; it is to be a particular kind of man."[23] Confucius would probably say, "To be human is to be a man of Chou," though he does not share Geertz's cultural relativism.

Beyond the pleasure he derived from learning, Confucius earnestly believed that through the pursuit of knowledge—specifically, the empirical knowledge of the past—one could arrive at a "synoptic vision" of reality. This vision of the whole, which Confucius called "an all-pervading unity" or "thread that runs through my teachings," when applied in everyday life, will effect exemplary conduct.[24]

Confucius' love and delight in learning explain the most important role he played: He was a teacher and perhaps the first in Chinese history who made a career out of teaching.[25] He wanted to transmit his faith in learning to those who were young, hoping they would "catch it" and share in his love and delight. His brimming enthusiasm made him popular as a teacher. (His disciples were said to have numbered three thousand.)[26] He accepted anyone who was willing to learn: "From the man bringing his bundle of dried flesh [the smallest offering to a teacher] for my teaching upwards, I have never refused instruction to anyone." "In education," he believed, "there are no class distinctions." A noble man (*jun-zi*), according to Confucius, is one who is noble not by birth but by his moral integrity.[27]

Confucius himself never made clear the reasons for his conviction that all persons could be educated. Two statements in the *Analects*—"Man is born with uprightness" and "By nature men are alike. Through practice they have become far apart"[28]—only hint at a possible explanation. Not until some centuries later, in the teachings of Mencius, do we find a definitive Chinese explanation of why learning should be accessible to everyone.

In a central debate he carried on with a leading thinker of his time, Kao Tzu (of whom we know very little), Mencius argued that humans' desire for morality can be seen in the same terms as their desire for food. He said, "Moral principles please our minds as beef and mutton and pork please our mouths."[29] The *desire* for morality suggests an inborn impulse to do good. For Mencius, this inborn impulse, common to all humans, is what distinguishes them from beasts. He wrote:

> Suppose a man were, all of a sudden, to see a young child on the verge of falling into a well. He would certainly be moved to compassion, not because he wanted to get in the good graces of the parents, nor because he wished to win the praise of his fellow villagers or friends, nor yet because he disliked the cry of the child. From this it can be seen that whoever is devoid of the heart of compassion is not human.[30]

The heart of compassion is the beginning of humaneness, which together with the beginnings of righteousness, propriety, and wisdom makes up the moral "stuff" of the self. And a person "has these four beginnings just as he has four limbs." Mencius went on to say: "For a man possessing these four beginnings to deny his potentialities is for him to cripple himself." To have moral goodness and not to develop it is to inflict injury on the self. If the moral deprivation continues, it would be like the Ox Mountain, once covered with luxuriant trees, but because of cattle and sheep grazing on it, no longer forested.[31] Similarly, a person's native endowment can be lost if no effort is made to preserve and nourish it.

In these passages Mencius made two basic points: that "no person is devoid of a heart sensitive to the suffering of others," and that "to finish ourselves" as humans, we must "exert our nature to the utmost."[32] Although Mencius was speaking exclusively of moral nature and its extension, his ideas have helped to define an attitude that is central to the Chinese sense and sensibility.

A high school senior from Shanghai told me: "Of course everyone needs some inborn ability to succeed, but we believe that even geniuses have to be industrious. They have to apply a lot of effort in order to succeed." Many of the Chinese children I spoke to shared this view, but they also asked questions about "how much is enough" and whether the kind of effort stressed in their education indeed helped them to develop their potential. A college student made this observation about their way of learning mathematics:

> It's the notion of "practice makes you more proficient." The whole idea is to keep on doing as many of these problems as you can. Those kids who do fewer problems and prefer to do other things are more likely to make mistakes. There are pages and pages of work, huge quantities. . . . Kids are given more and more tests all the time, and on tests they don't use what they've learned to find the answer. So the kind of life they live is quite rigid. They face entrance exams for junior high and high schools, and they are pressured to get into a "key school." On every level there is an elevator, and you have to get on. It's very hard on them.

The central issues here are *the reason for* and *the way of* learning. Is the learner motivated by the desire to ride the "elevator" up or by his love of learning? Does he merely accumulate knowledge or does he steep himself in the learning? This college student seemed to suggest that for most Chinese people the image of ascension provides the impetus, and that in their view learning by rote is the safest way of rising to the top. She does not like it, even though she has prepared herself well for the ride. But now that she is looking down, she feels uneasy about what she sees. The Confucian scholars of the Song (960–1279) and Ming dynasties (1368–1644) shared much the same concern.

Around the year 136 B.C., the powerful Confucian minister Dong Zhong-shu (179?–104? B.C.) made the following recommendation to the Emperor Wu-di of Han: "Among the things paramount for the upbringing of scholars, none is more important than a university. A university is intimately related to the fostering of virtuous scholars, and is the foundation of education. . . . Your servant desires Your Majesty to erect a university and appoint illustrious teachers for it, for the upbringing of the empire's scholars." When he presented his memorial, Dong had an ulterior motive: to educate the young scholars in the Confucian classics and the Confucian classics alone. This was part of a design "to put an end" to "the evil and licentious talk" or the teachings outside of "the arts of Confucius."[33] Dong succeeded. Emperor Wu-di adopted Confucianism as the official state ideology during the Former Han (202 B.C.–A.D. 9). A national university was established to educate promising scholars in the Confucian way. Its graduates provided the principal resource from which local authorities—princes, marquises, and governors—made their recommendations for appointments. The Emperor Wu-di, in addition, introduced a separate measure to verify the candidates' abilities: he gave written examinations. These were the world's earliest known civil service examinations.

During the next phase of a unified China, the Sui (581–618) and Tang dynasties (618–907), the examination system was firmly established as the most important channel for personnel recruitment, and it remained so until its abolition in 1905.* The existence of such an institution in the bureaucratic structure over thirteen hundred years had an enormous impact on China's notions of learning and education. In the *Analects* we have observed a love of and delight in learning and a faith that there is a direct correlation between learning and making correct judgments in action. Ideally, learning should be accessible to everyone, even though Confucius recognized that the peasants working in the fields had neither time nor energy to devote to such an enterprise. He himself never refused instruction to anyone, and as for his method of educating others, he stressed finding it for oneself. One *can* find it for oneself, he would insist; strength will not fail one who sets his mind to it: "I have not come across such a man whose strength proves insufficient for the task."[34] This effort was thoroughly explored and given particular emphasis in Men-

* During the Tang, most of the examination candidates were from the wealthy and prestigious families since only the upper class could give their children an education. But under the Tang system China also witnessed an expansion of the literate class. Education became more widespread; the government sponsored more schools at the prefectural level, and ironically, the Buddhist monasteries also played a major role in instructing the young in the Confucian classics. Thus, during the eighth and ninth centuries the chances for men of humble birth to participate in the civil service were better than during earlier periods.

cius' teaching. "Either you exert effort and extend your 'good' inclinations or you will lose them and become morally depraved"—this was Mencius' message.

The civil service examination, founded on Confucian ideals and theoretically open to all men, was intended to select only the most learned to govern, while emphasizing that effort was what allowed one to make a leap from lower to higher. Yet, when institutionalized, the system redefined the meaning of the Confucian ideal in a fundamental way. For Confucius and Mencius, effort can effect a moral transformation; the ordinary can become the noble. Under the examination system, success actually means an upgrading of one's social status, but whether the process of getting there actually brings about one's moral transformation is highly questionable. For the incentive to learn no longer originates in a desire to develop one's moral potentialities but rather in practical considerations and tangible goals: status and prestige, job security, and the fulfillment of one's parents' expectations.

This issue generated intense debate during the early Song dynasty. Many of the Song reformers—conservative, progressive, and all Confucians—thought that questions regarding the examination system should be addressed first. They were all deeply disturbed that the examinations tested the candidates' ability to memorize and recite the classics and the commentaries, but did not reflect their moral character or convictions, or their skills in applying learning to practical affairs. The controversy continued during the Ming dynasty, and serious-minded intellectuals engaged in inner debates; a number of them, while remaining true to the Confucian ideals, decided not to take the examinations, thus forgoing any chance of rendering public service.

Beginning in the seventeenth century, China witnessed a shift in intellectual and philosophical orientation. Partly as a response to the Ming debacle—the collapse of a Chinese dynasty and its fall to the Manchus—the Confucian scholars of the Qing dynasty (1644–1911) were no longer certain that moral cultivation alone could bring about political and cultural stability. As Confucians, they believed that an ideal order was possible. The founders of the Shang and Zhou dynasties had created and maintained order in the world when they were rulers. But for the Qing literati, these kingly rulers accomplished what they did, not because they were paragons of moral perfection but rather because they had mastered the techniques of world-ordering. Their charge, they felt, was to retrieve the ancient past and thereby to "locate a bedrock of timeless order."[35] Their efforts at reconstruction centered upon evidential research (*kao-zheng*)—the gathering and the analyzing of evidence found in ancient artifacts, historical documents and texts. For serious-minded scholars, the shift in concern and methodology altered the aim and content of learning but not their attitude toward the examination system. Many remained critical of the content of the examinations and the curriculum offered at the official academies.

The civil service examination was abolished in 1905, but the examination system has nonetheless continued in the twentieth century, with a ten-year lapse during the Cultural Revolution. Examinations are no longer offered at the county and prefectural level, nor at the capital. Now the ascension takes both boys and girls from primary school to junior high to senior high to college and finally to graduate school, if they manage to get onto the "elevator" on each floor. The basis of the examination since 1905 is no longer the Confucian classics. Students in China today are tested on language, mathematics, the sciences, English, history, geography, and politics. But the changes in rules, format, and content have not lessened the hold that examinations have on the Chinese people. They still determine the course of their lives. For most Chinese children, passing the examinations is the only way they can "realize some of their ideals."

Up to this point the ideas I have considered are wholly within the concerns of China's elite culture; they are articulated in texts, subjects for learned men. What relationship do they have, if any, with traditional assumptions translated into habits "without thought," which dominate the lives of ordinary people?

FROM TEXTS TO REALITY

Robert Coles, that fine listener to children and mothers, has caught for us the words of a Pueblo woman from New Mexico:

> I have to tell my children what to say, and what not to say, when they talk with Anglos. I think you learn to keep some thoughts—well, keep them out of your mind completely. If you don't, you're headed for trouble. The Anglos own this country, and the Indians are guests, even if we were here first—that's what I remind my oldest son, especially. He tells me about what he's read in school about "all men being created equal," and I tell him the words are great, but you should believe only what you see before your eyes if you want to survive in Albuquerque. When the government people

don't like what you say or do, the words from some history book won't help you much.[36]

In his most recent work, *The Moral Life of Children,* Coles remembers the remarks of Paul Tillich: "Morality for ordinary people is not the result of reading books and writing papers, as we're doing. Morality is not a subject; it is a life put to the test in dozens of moments. Morality and social class—that is a subject for us, an important one. For ordinary people, it is not a subject; it is affecting the views of people every day."[37]

Morality for a peasant tending his rice plants is not a subject. Each day he works long hours in the rice paddy to provide food and shelter for his family. He serves his parents dutifully. At times he finds himself mediating quarrels within his extended family. But he does not reflect consciously upon the meaning of his actions. He does not ask himself, for instance, whether when he feeds his feeble and bedridden mother every night he is actually reciprocating her love spoonful by spoonful. He performs this task without thinking. In fact a good part of his life is dominated by habits and based on implicit assumptions consisting of "ancient opinions and rules of life" or "untaught feelings."[38] Cultural assumptions "think themselves through him without his knowing them."

Morality for a Confucian scholar is a subject. He reads the *Analects:* "Filial piety and brotherly love, are they not the bases of humanity [*ren*]?," and he ponders questions regarding human nature. He thinks about the "stuff" that makes up what is human and formulates moral principles from our "untaught feelings" toward our relations. He reads further in the *Analects:* "A filial son is not just a man who keeps his parents fed. Dogs and horses can do that. If there is no feeling of reverence, wherein lies the difference?"; and the meaning of filial piety becomes clearer to him. It is not the ritual we perform that defines our humanity, rather it is the attitude we embrace that separates us from the birds and beasts. The peasant in the meantime continues to work in the field. He feeds his mother every night. He is not conscious of his attitude, but he knows that he is right and he is certain that he is human.

To say simply that the peasant, whose moral moments are in the everyday, and the scholar, who reduces human experiences to moral lessons and propounds them in texts, are on opposite sides of the social and cultural divide is to ignore the "complex and troubled and never totally resolved interaction between the two."[39] In his short story "The Diary of a Madman," Lu Xun, the most arresting Chinese writer of this century, brought out the relationship of texts to everyday morality through the perception of a "madman." The madman is convinced that all people around him—including his friends, neighbors and elder brother—are mad with the desire to eat him. Even children "eyed him strangely." "They must have learned this from their parents" is his conclusion. To understand this secret desire to eat people, he tries to look it up in the ancient texts: "but my history has no chronology and scrawled all over each page are the words 'Confucian Virtue and Morality.' Since I could not sleep anyway, I read intently half the night until I began to see words between the lines. The whole book was filled with two words—'Eat People.' "[40]

It is absurd to think that words have inherent authority. Words as a language denote a system of naming and evaluating. When we as children learn a language, we are taught to apply distinctions between this and that, good and bad, right and wrong, distinctions that in turn define our goals—what to avoid and what to pursue—and direct our actions. We can say, therefore, that our thought and action depend on the discourse particular to our group or our culture, that our language shapes our perspective of reality and directly controls our lives.

What Lu Xun seems to suggest in "The Diary of a Madman" is that Chinese texts are overladen with words that "eat people." For him, "Confucian Virtue and Morality," whose presence has been felt in every historical instance, are oppressive; they devour what is human. His painful conclusion that the Chinese had "four thousand years of man-eating history"[41] is a confession made public on behalf of the people and their tradition.

Lu Xun's voice is the voice of a generation that entered the twentieth century with an acute sense of urgency. This sense of urgency was first expressed in the famous incident of May 4, 1919, when some three thousand students from Beijing staged a demonstration protesting the way in which the Shandong question was being handled at the Versailles Peace Conference. The Allies' decision to transfer to Japan all Germany's interests in the Shandong peninsula, from the students' point of view, was a mockery of China's right to independence. The May Fourth incident was the beginning of a new epoch—"an epoch," as Jonathan Spence observed in *The Gate of Heavenly Peace,* "in which China's indigenous cultural yearnings were combined with a new international political awareness and a new and wider social consciousness."[42]

The May Fourth epoch was also a period of intense self-examination. Intellectuals like Lu Xun were frightened by the vision that the cannibals—tradition personified as people—might "finish off" all that was human if there was no mirror to reflect the harrowing ritual they were performing. Was there a basis for such a vision? Were these young iconoclasts capable of creating a mirrored image of their tradition and people? What they composed were powerful metaphors with the ability to pierce the mind and heart, but do they suggest things as they were? Some insisted that the question of spiritual awakening was inseparable from the more emotional issue of China's survival as a nation, that it was impossible under the circumstances to have a clarity of vision. Did they betray their tradition, as their critics claimed? And were they in turn betrayed by their own imagination? It is difficult to answer these questions, and all but impossible to know whether their judgment of their tradition was accurate.

At one point in the "Diary," Lu Xun compared the Confucian tradition to the beams and rafters in the madman's room: "The beams and rafters shook above my head. After shaking for a while they grew bigger and bigger. They piled on top of me. The weight was so great, I couldn't move. They meant that I should die. However, knowing that the weight was false, I struggled out dripping with sweat."[43] Lu Xun and the May Fourth intellectuals were not the only ones who struggled to get out from under the "beams and rafters." Many eminent Confucians of the Ming and Qing dynasties felt weighed down by the burden of their cultural inheritance,[44] and they too were "dripping with sweat." Nonetheless, there is a fundamental difference between them. In their effort to integrate China into the modern world, the twentieth-century Chinese intellectuals devoured Western knowledge with their eyes and minds and in the process gained a comparative perspective that made them even more aware of the weight "piled on top of them." Western ideas and methodology seemed to underscore the shortcomings of their native culture. But were they correct in thinking that the Confucian tradition was more burdensome than other cultural traditions? How does one measure the weight of a tradition anyway?

First of all, how did the May Fourth generation arrive at such a conclusion? Within the Confucian framework, moral responsibilities are construed in terms of relationships, the fulfillment of which ensures social stability; morality begins at the mind-and-heart; it is naturally endowed in us but is realized through the process of relating to others. In Mencian terms, if we do not fully exert ourselves in the extension of our moral beginnings, we can lose our innate goodness and become "morally depraved." The *Book of Documents* says: "The human mind is precarious, the moral mind is subtle."[45] The possibility that the human mind may stray from its natural and proper course has been a central problem for the Confucians. It is partly for this reason that the

Chinese history books are scrawled with the words "Confucian Virtues and Morality."

Confucians recognize that "morality is a life put to the test" in everyday moments; it acquires meaning only in a context that involves others. The fulfillment of moral responsibilities is the completion of the moral self and, at the same time, the way of arriving at a normative political order. In this perspective, there is no separation between what is required of the self and what the self genuinely "is," and relationships provide the strong binding power needed for a stable society. The *Great Learning,* one of the Confucian "Four Books," asserts that "peace throughout the world and order in the state depend on the family being regulated and the personal lives being cultivated."* A prevalent view during the May Fourth era was that the climate in the Chinese social realm had been well controlled to ensure a "good" reading, but the activists were deeply skeptical of the apparent order and harmony. They asked, Is this the way things really are? Is everything indeed well in our families and communities, or are we betrayed by what we think we see? In the "Diary," Lu Xun asked a pointedly "mad" question: Do the Chinese in fact secretly harbor the desire to "eat" their brothers and sisters, friends and neighbors?

In a Confucian environment the climate of emotions and desires is carefully regulated by a system of naming and evaluation designed specifically for relations. The most consequential theory of social relationships in China—"three bonds and six rules"—was formulated more than two thousand years ago during the Han dynasty. According to an important Confucian document of this period, *Discussion in the White Tiger Hall,* these bonds and rules "serve to order and regulate [relations between] superiors and inferiors, and *to arrange and adjust the way of mankind*"[46] (my italics). It is a theory "exclusively concerned with the establishment of order in all social groups from family to state."[47] As made explicit in the arrangement of the three bonds—subject and ruler, father and son, husband and wife—the way to order is predicated upon the willful subservience of the ruled, the young, and the female. Such theories have prompted Western historians and sociologists to come up with their own terms regarding the Chinese moral system. One is simply called "the ethic of submission." For Lu Xun and the new generation of moralists, the old Han theory eats people. Most have recognized that this simplified version of Confucian-

* The "Four Books" replaced the Five Classics as the basis of the civil sevice examination from 1313 until 1905.

ism was perverted, that it robbed the original teaching of its heart and spirit. Nonetheless, the morality that affects the everyday lives of ordinary people is this corpus of moral prescriptions that consume all that is living and pulsing.

What of the people—those who are "eager to eat people yet stealthily trying to keep up appearances, not daring to do it outright"? They do their eating under the pretext of morality. (So is it the morality itself or the person who utilizes the morality that is doing the eating?) The cannibals are slowly feeding on the flesh and spirit of the weak, the young, and the female; they eat to take away their particulars, to erase the essence of their being.

What of the children? The madman found them staring at him "strangely" while "their faces too were ghastly pale"; he was sure that they "have learned this from their parents," that they are obeying "the internal voices" and responding to "the moral signals," all of which have come from the family.[48] Yet the madman ends his diary with thoughts of children: "Perhaps there are still children who haven't eaten man. Save the children. . . ."[49] Even after "four thousand years of man-eating history," there is still hope. The madman's hope is, of course, Lu Xun's hope, which, when understood in the context of the May Fourth Movement, is built upon an idealized image of children. Children are receivers, within whom there is still space not yet filled. They have been taught moral lessons but have not used them as a pretext for cannibalism. Was Lu Xun correct in thinking that it is still possible to save the children because they are partially empty?

CHILDREN, TEXT, AND REALITY

Throughout human history, in China and in the West, children have been idealized. *Tabula rasa* and sacred symbols, such are the musings of poets and thinkers. Yet it was Yeats who wrote:

> Both nuns and mothers worship images,
> But those the candles light are not as those
> That animate a mother's reveries,
> But keep a marble or a bronze repose.
> And yet they too break hearts. . . .

"They" are the children. They are real—two natures, body and soul "blent . . . / Into the yolk and white of the one shell." Yeats was "Among School Children" when he wrote these lines; he was trying to come to terms with his own dualism.[50]

Children are not "Presences"—"that all heavenly glory symbolise." Yet they are special. How do we apprehend the mother's and our own reveries? Poets and thinkers have tried to understand, Wordsworth among them. In Book V of *The Prelude,* he sang of "A race of real children":

> . . . not too wise
> Too learned, or too good; but wanton, fresh,
> And bandied up and down by love and hate;
> Not unresentful where self-justified;
> Fierce, moody, patient, venturous, modest, shy;
> Mad at their sports like withered leaves in winds;
> Though doing wrong and suffering, and full oft
> Bending beneath our life's mysterious weight
> Of pain, and doubt, and fear, yet yielding not
> In happiness to the happiest upon earth.
> Simplicity in habit, truth in speech,
> Be these the daily strengtheners of their minds;
> May books and Nature be their early joy!
> And knowledge, rightly honored with that name—
> Knowledge not purchased by the loss of power!

These are the "real children" that "the candles light." And what secrets do they hold? Is it their knowledge of a soul—a purer life—from which they have recently parted?[51] Or is it the way that they comprehend "the essence of what a human being can manage to be"? Though "bandied up and down by love and hate" and often "bending beneath our life's mysterious weight," they do not yield. And their strength is gained through "simplicity in habit, truth in speech." Books and Nature are their "early joy," but their knowledge is not "purchased by the loss of power." In the "Diary," Lu Xun made no reference to children's strength, only to their "space." Their space, which is their hope, is not an emptiness waiting to be filled; it is a receptivity commanding strength. (Here one recalls Rilke's "flower-muscle"—"muscle of infinite reception / tensed in the still star of the blossom . . . you, resolve and strength of how many worlds!")[52] Simplicity and truthfulness are the daily strengtheners of the children's minds.

Many of the children whom Robert Coles came to know well revealed with piercing realism their unyielding resolve as they lay beneath "life's mysterious weight of pain, and doubt, and fear." (Caught up as they were in deep social prejudices and severe poverty, one wonders if the adjective "mysterious" is appropriate here.) We are moved and perplexed by their intense moral awareness and by their startling wisdom. Coles, borrowing a phrase from his wife, describes these children as "moralists, but with no pretense."[53] "No pretense"—is this why children are special? Is this the source of their strength? Is this what Wordsworth perceived?

In his reflections on his youthful education, Wordsworth mentioned specifically books, nature, and knowledge—the kind that gives one joy and does not take away one's potential to be. For a child who is fortunate to have an education, the knowledge he gains from reading and exploring the natural world does not stand apart from the knowledge he acquires experientially through his participation in a family, community, society, culture. The various kinds of knowledge combine and interact in ways that cannot be theorized about, but we glimpse the process when we listen to children talk.

All children in present-day China are required to go to school. Education is mandatory through junior high. In elementary school they learn mathematics, language, politics, science, hygiene, art, music, and, in some cases, English. In their language textbooks, there are stories of modern, revolutionary heroes and historical and folk heroes, fables from Aesop and fairy tales from the Brothers Grimm and Andersen, essays from the *Selected Works of Mao Ze-dong,* and vernacular renditions from passages of Mencius and Zhuang Zi. As education becomes compulsory and more children have direct access to texts, how do we understand the force that shapes their views?

A good part of the conscious life of children is habitual; in their judgments and activities they rely heavily on traditional assumptions. Yet as they work and play and learn, and when they are at home, or at school, or on the streets, they are "self-observers as well as observers of others," as Coles says. In China, many boys in their early teens told me that since they were in middle school they had to exercise more restraint in their speech and action. Why? One typical response was: "My parents tell me that that kind of adult carries more weight in society." So the internal voice that guides their thought and action clearly comes from their parents, who tell them how to prepare for character development and what is the sensible way to behave. Parents "are quite solid presences in a child's life"; they are a "psychological 'force' " with "everyday influence on the young."[54] Yet the child does not simply obey these internal voices. The same boys very often disagreed with their parents as to where this restraint should occur. One said: "My parents are too cautious. They ask me to do the same, not to express my opinions. I don't see anything wrong with saying what I want to say."

Learning to read and write obviously adds an extra dimension to a child's perception of herself and the world around her. In the past, for instance, she might not have thought of morality as a subject but will regard it as such after she has read *The Water Margin** and "thinks through" a given character in order to do her writing assignment. How a distilled response to a text helps to refine sensibilities is a complex question, and certainly not one that can be adequately explored here. But from listening to children, we know that it does happen. On many occasions I asked children their thoughts on "heroism" and specifically who were their heroes. Very often the children and I would spend a great deal of time on the subject of "character." Teng Hua-tao, a serious boy in Beijing, told me: "When I read biographies or novels, whenever I come upon a passage about the moral weakness of a person, I don't know why, but I have to read it several times. Sometimes I do this unconsciously. Usually on the first reading I don't understand it. Then I go back a second time, sometimes a third or a fourth time. Each time I understand it a little better." What compelled Teng Hua-tao to reread those passages that exposed others' moral weakness? At the time I did not ask him this question; there is no way of knowing what went on between him and the text, though I sensed it was a moral occasion for him.

In Chongqing the same topic of "heroes" and "heroism" came up when I discussed with children there how Chinese youths today perceive their culture and tradition. A pensive young man—his name was Fang Kan—first characterized China's thousands of years of history as "feudal" and then went on to say, "The feudal way of thinking is still deep-rooted within us. No one is *conscious* of it, but these feudal ideas keep creeping up on us from nowhere at all, and they are reflected in our conduct and in our daily lives." He cited specifically the Chinese notion of a hero: "When a person becomes a hero, we exalt him," and pointed out that many novels promoted "the idea of 'blind worship' "; "the main characters are depicted as being godlike." He insisted that "people in foreign countries are not like the Chinese," that they could even criticize their political leaders. His best friend Wang Lian simply said, "I

* This classic Chinese novel tells the story of Song Jiang and his band of outlaws, who have a hideout near the marshes of Liang Shan, in Shangdong province. They were supposed to have lived toward the close of the Northern Song (early 12th century). *The Water Margin* has enjoyed immense popularity since its publication in the Ming. The outlaws are looked on as folk heroes who try to undo the injustice prevalent in their time. In present-day China almost all children are familiar with the stories of the bandits from Liang Shan.

have no heroes. I have no idea who is a hero. History books tell us so-and-so was a hero, but do we know what he was really like? . . . We only know him as a perfect person, not as a real person, so can we really trust what we read?" Wang Lian was extraordinary among his peers; his thoughts were uncommon, and his relationship to texts was complex. He was doubting: he does not believe the words of the history books. Whence the uncertainty? Did it come from ideas embodied in other texts, or other ideas embodied in the same texts? Is it his age? Is it the cultural climate of the post-Mao era? Or is it a confluence of circumstances? Wang Lian and Fang Kan are not accurate representatives of their generation: they have done more thinking than most children I encountered. Yet one senses in their response that some form of critical spirit is in the making.

EDUCATION BEYOND TEXTS

Education is certainly not limited to the experience of texts. Most Chinese children are avid readers of books, magazines, and newspapers, though this is slowly changing as television becomes a standard item at home and as more varieties of program are offered. A few (all in elementary school) told me that they "don't like to read." Most "loved" to watch television, though their parents controlled how much they could watch. Aside from television there are movies and music, domestic and imported, which serve as occasions for "education." In addition, children frequently refer to news and information from acquaintances—relatives, relatives of classmates, or family friends—who have traveled abroad.

In the initial (December, 1978) issue of the young people's magazine *Today* (*Jintian*), the editors wrote in the preface: "As we open our eyes anew, we cannot just look back vertically to our cultural legacy over millennia. We must begin to gaze horizontally at other intellectual horizons around us. Only thus can we truly understand our own values."[55] To gaze is to encounter, and here we are reminded of Gadamer's metaphor, "the fusion of horizons." When horizons fuse, the perceiver, though still grounded in his own situation, has expanded his own vision. A fifteen-year-old related to me an experience during his first year in junior high when his school played host to a group of Japanese students. During one festive occasion, when everyone gathered in the school gym for a party, Lin Ting noticed a distinct difference between the two groups of students: "You could feel the liveliness on one side, and as for our side, . . . well, you couldn't really say that the atmosphere was heavy and serious, but certainly it was *solemn* and *dignified*." He said that his classmates looked like "little old men" when juxtaposed with their vivacious Japanese visitors. Lin Ting merely gazed across the gym that day, but he now understood something about China's cultural values.

"To understand truly our own values" does not have to be an experience in self-abnegation. The comparative perspective allows one to see oneself and others with more clarity and judge a situation with more objectivity. Often when gazing horizontally, one finds what is at home to be more desirable. Yao Chen-lin, a girl from Shanghai with whom I had a long conversation during my first trip and got to know well five years later during my second trip, told me that Chinese children rarely found their lives empty: "we are all so preoccupied with homework and exams." For her the intense academic work was a test of willpower; it gave her a sense of independence: "I acquire knowledge through my own effort . . . and I feel good about that." But she heard from her teachers that American children "feel listless, bored, and spiritually they are empty." She had "seen on television what it is like in America—the most comfortable conditions and the best facilities." What she could not understand was "why American children have the good fortune to be in a comfortable environment and yet they don't care to study." This irony strengthened her own resolve: she was even more "determined to study diligently" so that one day she could help "to build up our country."

When one encounters another horizon, often an inner transformation occurs as one's vision encompasses wider breadth and one's mind grasps greater understanding. There is a change in attitude, and one learns to assess one's own situation as well as others. During a round-table discussion in Hangzhou with a group of high school students, the subject turned to friendship and competition. Chang Pei-xun, a senior from Fujian Province, remembered the remarks of a professor from the Science and Technology University in Hefei: "as Wen Yuan-kai said, there are two types of jealousy. There is the Western type—if you are good, then I will be just as good. . . . But then there is also the Oriental type of jealousy—if you are good and I am not as good, then you can't be good either."* He believed that there was no point in becoming

* Wen Yuan-kai was an associate professor from the Science and Technology University in Hefei, Anhui, who along with his colleague Fang Li-zhi inspired the 1987 student movement in the PRC.

friends with the second type of person, and other students agreed.

I think what is afforded to the Chinese children in their education is more than *what* is perceived "vertically" and "horizontally." It is *how* one learns to assess oneself and others. Chang Pei-xun was not the same after his encounter with Wen Yuan-kai, and not because of what Wen had said, but because his words produced an echo in Chang's own response.

Students from this group in Hangzhou told me that the "Oriental type of jealousy" was more prevalent among adults, and they saw it as a product of the Cultural Revolution: "Before, people were simpler and purer, but after that experience, we became more complicated." But what are the circumstances occasioned by the Cultural Revolution that have particular significance for the children of the 1970s and 1980s? Memory and knowledge play a central role. The consequences of the revolution are before their eyes and worked into their lives—a quiet and withdrawn father, a sensible and prudent mother, both telling their children repeatedly the *virtue* and the *necessity* of "holding back."

CHILDREN AND POLITICS

For some Chinese, politics is woven into the texture of their lives at a very early age, in fact at the moment when their parents or grandparents decide on their names. They carry a political message if they are called "Red Army" (Hong-jun), "Inspiring Red" (Qi-hong), or just plain "Red" (Hong). There is politics in the colors they see and learn to distinguish around age three (often dazzling and distinct, with a lot of red); in the bedtime stories their parents and grandparents tell them; in the picture books they rent for a few fen an hour; in the songs and dances they perform at school; on the streets—the monuments, the posters, and the sound of radio broadcasts—where they walk to school every morning; in the games they play—Liberation heroes versus Guomingdang (KMT) agents.

From grammar school onward, politics becomes part of the regular curriculum. The children spend two to three hours of class time each week in "raising their political consciousness." They read mostly Marxist texts. As one high school student put it, "Other points of view might confuse my thought. Marxism is the orthodox doctrine." Yet the most immediate and pronounced influence does not come from these sessions of political indoctrination. "Political theories are to be memorized and then given back to the teachers," one student remarked. The children learn their politics primarily through what they witness in real life and through what they read between the lines. In language and history classes, for instance, they are forewarned explicitly by their parents and implicitly by their teachers and the school authorities about the danger of being "too frank"; what they reveal to others can be interpreted as evidence of "ideological problems." As the group of high school seniors in Hangzhou explained to me, "Sure, you can say whatever you want to say, but then they try to clamp you down. When anything happens, they will interrogate you first."

In Beijing I met Lan Hang, an elusive young man, yet honest in the most unexpected ways. He told me about the essay he had to write for the middle school entrance examination on "change": "We are all well prepared beforehand. This kind of topic, . . . like describing a person, we all write it this way. . . . We say that this person originally was not very good, and then something happened to him, and he became better. . . . That is the safest way to write. . . . I almost always follow the approved way of writing." To follow the approved way of writing will get one into a "key school" and perhaps into college, and set one on the right path toward a "bright future." Even Wang Lian, the young man who had no heroes and who recalled wistfully a childhood full of "wonder," admitted the need to conform: "Before college, there is really nothing for us to think about. But that's our ticket to better things, the only way we can realize some of our dreams." In writing his essays, Lan Hang was merely thinking realistically about his future and planning specific steps to get there. He understood clearly that in order to survive and thrive he had to make the correct political decisions along the way.

In class, students rarely disagreed with their teachers. Many children made this observation. Fang Kan was particularly unhappy about this: "We like to talk about things privately. We like to engage in big and empty talk. It all sounds so clear and logical when we do it privately. But when we are in class, nobody says anything that contradicts the teacher. I don't think this is very good practice." Ironically he was particularly sensible about making the correct political decisions for himself, yet insisted that when relating to others it was important "to keep something to yourself." He told me: "If you expose too much of yourself to others, then in case he attacks you, there is nothing you can do about it."

At home a child is no longer judged by her performance as a political being. There it does not matter whether she demonstrates ideological purity in her thought and speech and leadership in her action; no distinctions such as that between platoon leader and ordinary citizen exist. She is just her parents' child. Yet in this familiar setting, where she is most relaxed and at ease, the effects of politics are most profound. For there she observes the consequences of political movements and social revolutions on human lives. The way parents, relatives, neighbors, and family friends are offers the most telling evidences. Their remembrance of a recent past and their accounts of friends or friends of friends are deeply impressive. A boy in Beijing told me the story of Xu Hua-shui, which he had heard from a family friend who at one time had been a classmate of Xu Hua-shui. Xu was exiled to a labor camp in remote Xinjiang Province simply because his father was condemned as a Rightist. He left when he was a boy in his teens and did not return home to Beijing until twenty years later. In another child's memory, there were scenes of old scholars and old soldiers from the Red Army living in pigpens and feeding on chaff: "We were very small then. So we laughed at them, saying that they were dirty. . . . They were released just before the end of the Cultural Revolution."

During the revolution between 1966 and 1976, termed a "cultural" one, and especially during the years 1966–69, now remembered as the "Red Terror," there were full-scale attempts to overthrow cultural symbols—artifacts, customs, rituals—and to discredit China's traditional assumptions. Youths were the inquisitors, destroyers, and executioners, and it was their voices—frenzied and "mad"—that shook the Gate of Heavenly Peace vibrantly and violently. Now in these pages, again we hear the voices of children, but these are the children who live in the aftermath, the generation that has to think anew, after a turbulent ideological storm, of questions concerning culture, morality, and politics.

What is the aftermath like? Chinese children today do not seem like people crawling out from underneath the rubble. During the Cultural Revolution books were burned, ancient statues were disfigured, art objects were smashed, educational institutions were shut down, and parents were denounced by their children, yet one cannot say that all China's cultural symbols and cultural assumptions were reduced to ruins. They seem to be endowed with a life of their own. Gadamer says that "we belong to them before they belong to us." A youth of the present generation, Fang Kan, seems to agree, when he observes that the traditional cultural values "are reflected in our conduct and our daily lives." Their presence is felt in the nuances of the everyday. The power that allows them to transcend destruction did not come from above or beyond. It lies within and is intimately tied to the people's habits. But this does not mean that traditional values are static; they are responsive to change, and often adapt with enormous flexibility to a newly imposed sociopolitical order. When reconstituted, values do not lose their identity, yet one cannot say that they are the same as before.

As the Chinese experience since 1949 demonstrates, signed confessions and public self-denouncement—such as the Communist Party has required—do not fundamentally alter habits, perceptions, and prejudices, but the "new rules" that have become "rules of life" do. In present-day China 90 percent of women between the ages of twenty and forty-nine participate in the work force. This is a rule of life brought on by ideological orientations outside of China's tradition and carried out through the political system, and it has changed habits in Chinese homes and Chinese traditional perceptions of the husband-and-wife relationship. Chinese children, who are observers and at this point only partial participants of this transforming process, perform a most essential task for their culture.

The group of high school students I met in Hangzhou talked at length about this task, even though they were unaware of the weight of their charge, when they discussed the division of labor at home. Two girls spoke first about what they observed regarding their mothers. Zhu Yuan said, "My mama does a lot more . . . because she thinks taking good care of her family and her home is a woman's virtue." Everyone in the room laughed because such a notion seemed out-of-date. Li Ying's mother was different. She felt strongly that all women should work outside of their homes, and in her judgment those who chose to be homemakers were "no good." Yet, according to her daughter, she, too, did most of the household work. The boys were divided on this issue. Zheng Pu thought that husband and wife should be concerned for each other. In his family his mother usually worked long hours, and "things like cooking—my father often does them"; yet whenever his mother "comes home first, she does some of the chores that my father would normally do." He felt that with the reciprocity of feelings there would be domestic harmony. Another boy, Tian Ren-zhi—the only one in the group who was from a peasant family—had a different point of view. He was convinced that it was right for women to make sacrifices professionally because men had always demonstrated "more potential" at work. The question was immediately posed, what was the basis of his judgment? His response was: "But this is a common phenomenon, a common belief! . . . There must be a basis for this traditional view." All the women present, myself included, were agitated by his remarks. Nevertheless, we appreciated his honesty and courage, and I even tried to make allowances for his prejudice, blaming it on his peasant background. On a similar issue—the predicament of women in a peasant society—we heard Tian Ren-zhi's impassioned voice again, but this time his words did not provoke female indignation. He told us about his sister, who had just finished elementary school: "My mama told her, 'You can continue in school, but you have to do all the chores at home, too.' " His mother would punish his sister if the work was not done to her satisfaction, yet the same was not expected of him or of his brother. Tian Ren-zhi disapproved of this, and washed dishes whenever he could and tried to shield his sister from what he considered unjust punishment. He insisted that his views and actions have nothing to do with his relationship to his sister: "We argue all the time," he told me pointedly. This was how he perceived things and how he chose to act in spite of personal feelings.

Ancient rites and new rules, education through and beyond texts—these are the extrinsic forces that shape Chinese children as individuals. They form the basis of their judgment. But only when they have permeated an individual's unique moral sensitivity do they acquire a life, do they become living forces.

It was Emerson who told the graduating class of the Divinity College in Cambridge on July 15, 1838:

> I confess all attempts to project and establish a Cultus with new rites and forms, seem to me vain. . . . All attempts to contrive a system are as cold as the new worship introduced by the French to the goddess of Reason—to-day, pasteboard and filigree, and ending to-morrow in madness and murder. Rather let the breath of new life be breathed by you through the forms already existing. For if once you are alive, you shall find that they shall become plastic and new. . . . A whole popedom of forms one pulsation of virtue can uplift and vivify.[56]

Since Emerson's notion of the "Cultus" extends as far as the "new worship introduced by the French to the goddess of Reason," it can easily include the "system" contrived by the ideologists and the guards of the "Red" during the Cultural Revolution. That system, as Emerson would have predicted, has already collapsed. In China today the new finds expression through "the forms already existing" and is embodied by those who "are alive." One such person is Zheng Pu. His thoughts on the man-woman relationship represent the reconstituted values at their best. For him, domestic harmony is ultimately achieved through the concern that family members show to each other. Is this concern the same as the sincere intent which, Confucius says, humanizes a relationship? Are we once again faced with a *Confucian* perspective? I am not certain.

2

Creators of Bursting Colors

The Experimental School No. 2 in Beijing was the first school June and I visited in 1979. We had been told by friends and relatives in advance that this was one of the best schools in Beijing, a "model school" for outside observers. It boasted a "progressive" curriculum, and according to our sources, it also had better facilities and more well qualified teachers than the usual. The students were all screened for admittance. A child had to be "special" to get in, and special meant either that she had higher abilities or that she came from a "good background."

We were greeted at the front gate by the principal, a middle-aged woman, and several teachers. Our walk to the reception room gave us a glimpse of the schoolyard: a small garden ablaze with red cannas and a playground with a few simple pieces of equipment, such as swings, monkey bars, and basketball hoops.

The principal gave us facts and figures: how many teachers (83), how many students (980), and how many classes (22); where the students came from (five-sixths from the immediate residential community and one-sixth from elsewhere); the average age of the first-graders (six and a half); the subjects included in the school curriculum (math, language, politics, English, science and hygiene, art, music, and gym). Her remarks were informative and would have been important to us if we were after facts and figures, but we were not. When we did put forth our requests, we met with some resistance, but, on the whole, the principal was receptive to our "experiment."

Zhao Mei, Zhang Xiao-shun, and Zhang Chuan-guo are the first three children we talk with that day, and our encounter is plainly an auspicious beginning.

Zhao Mei, a pretty girl with a winning smile, volunteers to talk to us. She is not overly eager, just naturally exuberant. Her easy manner puts us in a comfortable position, thus making our conversation effortless. She is ten—a fourth-grader—and is the younger of two children in her family. Her brother—fifteen years old—is in the middle school. Her mother is an elementary school teacher, her father a cadre in a neighborhood revolutionary committee.

She first tells us about growing up.

When I was younger—before I started school—my nainai [paternal grandmother] took care of me. . . . No, Nainai didn't live with us. She lives in the country, not far from Beijing. I used to stay with her in her home. Since she was taking care of me, I didn't go to nursery school or kindergarten. I moved back to Beijing when I was six.

I like the country. In the country the air is fresher, and there are lots of things I can do there that I can't do in the city. When I was there, my yeye [paternal grandfather] was in charge of the cows and pigs for his work brigade, and I was allowed to go with him to tend the animals. My nainai also had her own pigs and chickens, and I helped her with the feeding.

Do you like living in the city?

In the city the conditions for education are better than in the countryside. Also I like living at home with my parents.

Now, during the summer and winter vacations, my gege [older brother] and I still go back to the country to visit. Often my parents come with us, but they usually can't stay long. When I was little, for a while my brother lived with me in the countryside. But most of the time that I was there, he was already back in Beijing with my parents.

When we visit our grandparents now, we still get up around six in the morning. First we help Nainai with the chores, and around eight we do our summer homework. That doesn't take long. Then I can go and play with the kids in the neighborhood—kids I grew up with. At twelve o'clock, we come home for lunch. In the afternoon I stay home most of the time, helping Nainai to clean up the house, wash the dishes, rinse the vegetables, and do some simple cooking. Sometimes I do the shopping for her. I also babysit for my aunts. My aunts—there are two—live with my grandparents. They each have children, a two-year-old and a three-year-old.

When I am there, I have a lot of fun playing with the neighborhood kids. Sometimes I go swimming with them. I don't really know how to swim, though. I just wade in the pond and splash the water. There are also little fish in a nearby reservoir. It's fun to try to catch them with your hands. . . . Sometimes you can. . . . I like to play with all sorts of animals on the farm. I also like to go to the fields with my yeye.

What is a regular school day like?

I usually get up around six and do some studying. Around seven I leave for school. I walk to school every day. My gege walks to school too, but it's a different school.

When we get to school, we first have study hall, then we all do morning exercises together. In the winter we also do exercises in the afternoon. That's because doing exercises warms us up. Class starts at eight o'clock. We have four classes in the morning and two classes in the afternoon. In between we have half an hour for lunch and about two hours for nap. School ends at four-thirty. When I get home, I do my homework first and then play with the neighborhood kids. I usually go to bed around nine or ten.

What kind of games do you like to play?

The girls like to tie rubber bands together in a chain and skip rubber bands. We also play a game [like jacks] with pig- or sheep-knuckle bones and a Ping-Pong ball. Sometimes we use pebbles. At home I play badminton with my brother and my parents in our yard. The boys like to play basketball and Ping-Pong.

Do the girls play with the boys?

Sometimes. But sometimes the boys look down on us. They think we're not good at certain games and they don't let us join in. Starting in third grade, boys and girls begin to play separately. And it gets worse when they get older.

Would you tell me about the red scarf you wear? Do you belong to a particular organization?

I am a Young Pioneer.

How do you become a Young Pioneer?

You can apply, beginning with first grade. If you are qualified, you can become a Young Pioneer. In the first grade, only about six or seven out of forty students get to become Young Pioneers. By the fourth grade, almost everybody is a Young Pioneer. . . . To be qualified, you must have good study habits, good behavior, a good working attitude, and good health. You also have to show love and respect for the Young Pioneers. Those who are selected are usually very happy. Their parents are also very proud of them. But those who are not yet members are not sore or jealous, and their parents usually spend more time working with them. They encourage their children to try harder.

Girls are admitted to the Young Pioneers earlier than boys because boys generally are more mischievous than girls. Boys are better at sports. Girls are better at studying.

The Young Pioneers is an organization for primary school children first formed in 1949 right after the Liberation. During the Cultural Revolution it was reorganized as the Little Red Soldiers. In 1978, the Central Committee decided that the Young Pioneers should be brought back to the elementary schools, replacing the Little Red Soldiers. The name change signifies a break with the Cultural Revolution era, but in terms of the organizational structure, much remains the same: there is a central corps with subdivisions of platoons and squads. The principal leadership comes from the corps committee, whose members are composed of representatives from each classroom or platoon. In 1979, we found that students had to be selected into the Young Pioneers, as they had been for the Little Red Soldiers; they were evaluated on the basis of how well their actions exemplified the "three goods" (san-hao)*—good in health, study, and work. In 1984 this was no longer true. All students in elementary schools were Young Pioneers. I was told that this was to discourage "elitism." "When all the students wear red scarves, no one feels inferior," several teachers explained to me. Although the induction* *process no longer existed, the organization was still governed by a hierarchy of leaders, deputy leaders, and committee members. Children were quick to point out who were the "cadres" among them.*

* * *

Zhang Xiao-shun is nine, a gentle-looking boy, small and thin with a light complexion. His family was originally from southern China, and he considers himself a native of Shanghai. His father died of cancer two years ago. His mother is the only wage earner in his family. They are financially pressed, and he is keenly aware of this.

First Zhang Xiao-shun tells me about his family.

I live with my mother and my meimei [younger sister]. Meimei is five. We play together a lot. . . . We don't fight. I help my mama take care of her. I pour water for her when she needs a drink, and when she can't reach something, I get it for her. In our neighborhood lots of brothers and sisters play together, and the older ones rarely bully their didi [younger brothers] and meimei. . . . My sister goes to kindergarten now for the whole day. She is only home in the mornings and evenings. . . . There are only three of us at home because my father has already passed away. My parents both came from the south. My lao-ye [maternal grandfather] lives in Nanjing, and on holidays he comes to visit. My nai-nai lives in Jiangsu Province. She is not used to the lifestyle of the North, and so she never comes here.

My meimei grew up in Shanghai. She lived with my aunt until she was four. She just moved back to Beijing last year. When she first got here, she was not too good with *pu-tong-hua* [standard Chinese], but now she speaks it well. I was in Shanghai one summer. I like the North better. It's too hot in the South, and they speak a different dialect in Shanghai. Luckily the two neighborhood kids I played with there understood *pu-tong-hua,* and so I didn't have any problem talking to them. But in Shanghai I couldn't go shopping by myself. My younger sister had to go with me. She understood the dialect, and so she was my interpreter.

When I was three or four I was in a nursery school. This was the kind where you stayed all week and only came home on Sundays. Then when I was around five, I started kindergarten. In kindergarten I got to come home after school. I liked that much better because I got to play with the kids at school and then come home to my mother in the evening.

What do you like to do when you are finished with homework?

I like to watch television, programs about enemy agents and wars during ancient times. But I haven't had a chance to see many because most of the time they are shown during the week, and I can only watch television on Saturday night. I also like to watch cartoons. We don't have a television at home. There are two other families in our courtyard, and they have televisions.

Sometimes during a summer night, I like to take a little mattress out in the yard, lie on it, and look at the moon. I look at the shadowy spots on the moon—the craters and mountains—and I imagine them to be rabbits and other little animals. Then I dream about going to the moon and playing with them. . . . I think a lot about traveling to the moon and other planets. It would be fun to go there. On the moon the gravitational force is weak, so a person can jump very high and then come down slowly. That sounds like a lot of fun.

Do you have any pets?

Not now, but once when I was about six, I had a sparrow. My baba [father] caught it when he was working in the country. We took care of it for a while, but then we just forgot about it. After a while it starved to death. Then last year we got a pet parakeet. The cage was the kind that was made of soft wooden sticks. If you bend one of the sticks just a little, it would break. One night we were in our neighbor's place watching television. After we came home, we forgot to take the cage in. The next morning I saw that my mama was looking for a cat. What happened was that a cat came and chewed the cage to pieces. The parakeet tried to get away but couldn't, and by the time my mother found it, it was already half dead. Its feathers were scattered all over the ground. There was nothing we could do, and so after a while it died.

When do you get a treat or a present?

My mother usually sets up these conditions before my exams: If I do well, she will get me a pen or maybe a magnet. And when it's around New Year, she gives me a little money to buy something I like to eat.

If your mother says that you can have a special present, what would you like to have?

A fountain pen. Sometimes I wish we could have a tape recorder or a television, but we can't afford these things now. In my family only my mother works. Every month she gets only about sixty-two yuan, and she has to send Nainai something out of that—that's my father's mother. So she really can't give us any spending money except on New Year, or when it's very hot so we can buy popsicles or sodas.

Zhang Chuan-guo is ten. His mother is a doctor and his father a professor of mathematics at a technical college. He has a thirteen-year-old sister, who he thinks is "bossy." He is direct and matter-of-fact when talking about family, friends, and himself. But he is also a gifted storyteller. He does not distract his listeners with emotions of his own, nor is he trying to entertain them. He loses himself in the telling: his eyes sparkle as his voice gathers intensity. He is best when the characters are Cao Cao, Zhou Yu, and Zhu-ge Liang and the setting is third-century China, when the three kingdoms of Shu Han, Wei, and Wu were battling for supremacy. He is able to recount a story from the Romance of the Three Kingdoms *almost without a break, pausing rarely to recall a name or a specific detail. His smooth narration often includes quotations from classical novels and local (Beijing) expressions. The use of regional phrases animates his stories and gives them a particular coloration.*

Do you play with your sister?

No, I don't. It's hard for us to play together. Whenever I want to do something, she doesn't want to. We played more when we were younger. Now sometimes we argue and we fight. She bosses me around all the time. She tells me what to do and how to behave. Whenever I get mad, I beat her up.

Do you do things with your parents?

No, they are too busy. My baba is usually home in the afternoons because he is a teacher. My mama, she is home much later, and sometimes she has to be on night duty. . . . When I was younger, my baba told me stories from the classical times, stories from the *Romance of the Three Kingdoms* and *The Journey to the West.* I was too young to read these books myself, and besides, at that time you couldn't find them in the bookstores. I like to listen to these stories, but sometimes when you hear them repeated so many times, it gets kind of boring.

*Would you tell us a story from the Three Kingdoms period?**

During this period Liu Bei [ruler of Shu Han] had two sworn brothers, Zhang Fei and [pauses]. . . Guan Yu. They were all fighting against the kingdom of Eastern Wu. At first Zhang Fei was trying to defeat Cao Cao [ruler of Wei], but he only cared about his front line and his battles with Cao Cao's army; he neglected the rear. Sun Quan [the ruler of Eastern Wu] and his men came from behind and overpowered Zhang Fei's troops. Zhang Fei was taken prisoner, but he refused to surrender to Sun Quan. Sun Quan finally had him killed. Liu Bei was enraged by this and wanted to avenge Zhang Fei's death. He took along a large army of men and horses and went to Eastern Wu. He laid siege to the capital. The people of Eastern Wu didn't dare make a move. They just sat there and guarded their kingdom. They were ready to defend it to the last. Meantime, those who were besieging the place, they had been trying for half a year. They were always attacking, and after a while, they couldn't care less. When Sun Quan saw that Liu Bei's soldiers were all exhausted and indifferent, he gathered up his army and launched a counterattack. He crushed his enemy in no time. At the end only Liu Bei managed to escape. When he got back home, he became very ill. Before he died, he looked at his son, and he said this to his chief counselor Zhu-ge Liang: "My son probably won't amount to anything. But in case he does, you are to protect him. If he doesn't, then you should proclaim yourself the ruler [of Shu Han]." After he said this, he died. Zhu-ge Liang did make Liu Bei's son the ruler. And he taught him how to fight, and then . . . [stops and shakes his head].

Who is your favorite character in the Romance of the Three Kingdoms?

Zhu-ge Liang. He is very clever. I've read the story "How Kong Ming Borrowed the Arrows" [chapter 46]. Kong Ming is the same person as Zhu-ge Liang. Now Zhu-ge Liang went to Sun Quan's camp and tried to make peace with him. He wanted to join forces with Sun Quan and together defeat Cao Cao. But Zhou Yu [Sun Quan's chief counselor] was very jealous of Zhu-ge Liang and wanted to make things difficult for him. So he said to him: "Soon we are going to be in a battle with Cao

* What follows is Zhang Chuan-guo's version. In the text itself, it is Zhang Fei's brother Guan Yu who is killed by Sun Quan. Zhang Fei intended to avenge his death, but while he is on his way to Sun Quan's camp, he is murdered by his own men. The murder is triggered by Zhang Fei's fiery temper.

Cao. If the battle is to be fought at sea, what would you say is the best kind of weapon?" Zhu-ge Liang answered, "Bows and arrows." Zhou Yu then said, "I feel the same way, but it just happens that we don't have enough arrows. May I entrust you with the responsibility of getting one hundred thousand arrows ready? And can you have them ready in ten days?" Zhu-ge Liang replied: "The battle will be fought any day now. If we have to wait ten days for the arrows, it would be too late. I can have them ready in three days." Zhou Yu could not believe what he heard. He said to Zhu-ge Liang: "You must be kidding, General!" Zhu-ge Liang said: "I dare to let you make it into a military order. If I don't have the arrows ready in three days, I am willing to accept your severest punishment."

After the banquet, Zhu-ge Liang went back to his camp. Lu Su [another advisor to Sun Quan] said to Zhou Yu: "In three days! He must be joking!" Zhou Yu replied: "I didn't force this on him. He asked for it himself."* He then asked Lu Su to go and find out how Zhu-ge Liang was going to pull this one off. Meanwhile he also ordered his men not to get ready the materials that Zhu-ge needed for making the arrows.

When Lu Su got to Zhu-ge Liang's place, Zhu-ge right away asked him to help. Lu Su said, "You brought this on yourself. How can I possibly help you?" Zhu-ge Liang said, "Let me borrow twenty ships from you, and on each ship I would like to have thirty soldiers and several thousand straw targets. I also need blue cloth to cover the ships and some heavy ropes." Lu Su agreed to it. Zhu-ge Liang also asked him not to reveal any of this to Zhou Yu. He warned that if Zhou Yu knew about it, there was no way he could get a hundred thousand arrows ready in three days.

When Lu Su returned to Zhou Yu, all he told him was that Zhu-ge Liang did not need feathers, glue, paint, or bamboo sticks—all the materials that were needed for making arrows. Zhou Yu was even more puzzled. He was sure that Zhu-ge Liang would get his punishment. In the meantime Lu Su got everything ready for Zhu-ge Liang as he had promised.

On the first day nothing happened. On the second day still nothing happened. On the third day, Zhu-ge Liang invited Lu Su to his ship, and he said to him: "Let's go and pick up the arrows." Lu Su asked: "But where are we going to pick up the arrows?" Zhu-ge replied, "Never mind about that! Just come along. When we get there, you will understand."

* Although Lu Su and Zhou Yu were both working for Sun Quan, Lu Su considered Zhou Yu unscrupulous and was sympathetic toward Zhu-ge Liang.

Lu Su boarded his ship and off they went. All twenty ships were tied together with heavy ropes, and they sailed toward Cao Cao's camp. When they got very close to the enemy, Zhu-ge Liang ordered the soldiers to beat thunderously on their drums and to roar with their voices as if in a battle. When Cao Cao heard this, he thought his enemy had come to attack them in the middle of the night. It happened that that night the fog was very heavy and Cao Cao couldn't make out what was going on; he could only see a long row of something moving toward them. He was sure it was a surprise attack. He ordered his men to aim their arrows in the direction of the ships. All the archers took up their bows and arrows and started shooting. There were altogether some six thousand archers.*

After this had gone on for a long time, Zhu-ge Liang ordered the ships to reverse direction and then to get even closer to Cao Cao's camp. Again the soldiers beat on their drums and roared as in a battle. This time Cao Cao was even more frightened. He ordered his archers to shoot even more arrows toward the ships. Finally when Zhu-ge Liang saw that there were enough arrows on the straw targets, he directed the ships quickly to retreat. As they were leaving, the soldiers shouted: "Thank you, prime minister, for the arrows!" By then Cao Cao realized the mistake he had made, but it was too late. When Zhu-ge Liang got back, he found that the straw targets were pierced with arrows and there were more than one hundred thousand. He then went to Zhou Yu to deliver what he had promised. When Zhou Yu saw the arrows, he was even more confused. Later, when Lu Su told Zhou Yu what had happened, Zhou came to have greater respect for Zhu-ge Liang.

Did your baba tell you this story?

No, not this one. I read it myself. My baba likes to tell me ordinary stories or funny stories.

Can you tell us one?

There was this person who was selling a painting. The painting has two mountains with a bridge in between, and on this bridge stands a man with a closed umbrella. The person met someone on the road and showed him this painting. Then they started talking. And while they

* The figures Zhang Chuan-guo quotes—twenty ships with thirty soldiers on each, one hundred thousand arrows, and six thousand archers—tally with those in the novel.

were talking, it started to rain. The first person took out his painting again and unrolled it. This time the man on the bridge is holding an open umbrella. The other person was very impressed because the umbrella in the painting had been closed when the weather was sunny and now it was open when it was raining. He bought the painting for a lot of money. He told many people about his painting. The weather was clear at first. After a couple of days it started to rain, but the umbrella in his painting didn't open. He knew then that he had been tricked. You see, the person who sold him the painting had two paintings, one with a closed umbrella and one with an open umbrella.

Does your mama share stories with you?

No. Only sometimes when she sees me playing for too long, she tells me what she was like when she was younger. She said that she studied a lot harder and that she wants me to do the same. Other than that she rarely tells us any stories.

When you have questions in your homework, do you go to your parents for help?

Usually I don't have any questions. My sister does. That's because she is in the middle school. What I am learning in school is not that hard, and so I don't have to go to my father for help.

What about personal problems? Let's say when you are upset about something.

There really isn't anything that makes me very upset. There are small things, like when I have an argument or when I get into a fight with someone, but that's no big deal.

Do you tell your parents about your fights and quarrels?

Sometimes, sometimes not, it depends. Not if it is a fight with my sister. That's because they usually turn around and give me a scolding. I do tell my parents what's going on in school, what new things I've learned, stuff like that.

Do you have a best friend?

I have many good friends, and I do have a best friend. His name is Lei Qiang. We have been playing together ever since we were in kindergarten. And at school we have been in the same class. Our homes are also close to one another.

What do you do together?

We do homework together and we play together. We play Ping-Pong, or we play some sort of a ball game. You see, we don't have much in our yard.

What do you do in the summer?

We play and we have homework to do. We have homework assignments every day. But I finish all of them at the beginning of the vacation. Then I'm free the rest of the time.

Have you been to other places outside of Beijing?

Not really. We hardly get to go anywhere. My laolao [maternal grandmother] lives in Tianjin [less than one hundred miles from Beijing], and we rarely visit her. My nainai lives in Tong-xian [in the suburb of Beijing]. Sometimes we go to see her. During the wintertime, she comes to stay with us. Nainai is blind. She lost her eyesight twenty years ago. When she is here, we all help to take care of her.

What other chores do you do for your parents?

I fetch the water, sweep the floor, hang up the curtains to dry when we wash them. And my sister and I take turns washing the dishes. We always argue about that because neither of us likes to do the dishes. And sometimes when Baba and Mama catch us arguing, they give us a scolding or a spanking. But usually I have ways to get out of doing the dishes. I say I have a lot of homework to do.

Do you have any pets?

Not in our house, but some of our neighbors have cats. Sometimes at night we like to chase them. We throw pebbles at them. I remember one year we had two sparrows in our house. We had caught them, and they were kept in a cage. We fed them rice and millet. Sometimes we tied strings around them and fastened them to a tree. One day when they were in the yard, the cats came along and ran off with both of them in their mouths. The birds died. So that night I beat up those cats. We are not allowed to have dogs in Beijing. But when my nai-nai was living in the Northeast, she had a dog. I used to play with that dog whenever I was visiting.

* * *

On a late August morning in 1984, I returned to the Experimental School No. 2 in Beijing. From the appearance of the schoolyard, little seemed to have changed—the iron gate, the raised beds with flaming cannas, the playground where the children had once played Frisbee with June and me. It had not been easy to arrange for my return. There was a new principal and the fall term had not yet begun. "If she could only wait until school opens"—this was the principal's message relayed through my contact, Mr. Wang. I could not wait, and I implored Mr. Wang to try again. He said he would try but he was not optimistic. The day before I was to leave Beijing, Experimental School No. 2 finally said I could come back to visit.

The new principal was a middle-aged man. He introduced me to five extraordinary children—four of whom were especially talented artistically. His choice was probably deliberate. As for me, I was simply glad I got to know Yu Sha, Wang Xiao-yun, Wang Wei, Teng Hua-tao, and Li Yi. We talked about their achievements but had more fun sharing stories of rabbits and crickets, birthdays and haircuts. I suppose they were all model students, yet there was nothing modellike about their behavior or thinking. They belong to that "race of real children": "not too wise, / Too learned, or too good; but wanton, fresh, / . . . Not unresentful where self-justified." And each carried his/her own colors, dyes, sounds, moods, and notions. Originally I had wanted to focus on their singularity; I wanted to write about our group conversation in such a way that it read as five separate interviews. After listening to the tapes several times, I decided that this was unnecessary and perhaps even unwise. Their individuality needed no rendering; it was there without special arrangement.

My first morning conversation was with the three girls, Yu Sha, Wang Xiao-yun, and Wang Wei. In the afternoon, the two boys were to come to my hotel; Mr. Wang had arranged for a car to pick them up at school.

When I went downstairs to meet them, I found four children. Wang Xiao-yun and Wang Wei had evidently overheard us discussing our plans for the afternoon: they waited at the school's front gate at the appointed time, and the driver picked up all four. They brought special gifts—photos and trinkets from their treasure piles—and more stories to share. "Anyway, we have nothing else to do this afternoon," they told me. I was warmly touched.

Before sitting down with the children in the morning, I had a long discussion with the principal about his school, which experiments with teaching methods and materials and makes recommendations to the ministry of education, textbook writers, and teachers at other schools. "All the recommendations are based on the teachers' actual experiences at school," he insisted. The following is an excerpt from what he told me:

"Our school experiments with methods which, we hope, will improve the students' learning abilities and develop their potentials. Since 1979, we have been making progress. For instance, one math period now can cover the same amount of material that formerly needed three periods to cover. In one semester, students spend thirty-three class hours learning the same material that formerly required ninety hours of class time, and they don't do additional homework. Our goal is to lessen the students' burden and at the same time increase their learning capacity. . . .

"Students do get graded from first grade onward. Giving them grades encourages them to do better and to continue to make progress. If they fall behind, they will know. They usually try to make extra efforts to catch up. The scoring encourages competition and excellence, but we don't want too much competition. It creates too much pressure for the students. We want to prevent this happening, and so we try to combine playing with learning; students can learn from playing. Half of the school day here is devoted to extracurricular activities: sports, dance, calligraphy, music, chess, crafts, and there are many others.

"Now the educational policy is not to give homework to first-graders. In fact the first-graders in this school are all very conscientious. Almost all students have scored ninety-eight percent or above in their math and language. . . . We encourage students to learn in a free and relaxed atmosphere. Children must find joy in learning in order for learning to be effective. In carrying out our educational reforms, we recognize the importance of self-motivation. The students have to take the initiative when it comes to acquiring knowledge. They are the principal players. The teachers are merely there to guide them. In class, for instance, the

teachers do very little lecturing. Very often, the teachers ask the students to do their reading assignments and form their own discussion groups. The representatives from the discussion groups then report to the teachers their views and conclusions. The teachers guide them and correct them when they make mistakes. We encourage the students to speak up during class. It doesn't matter if their ideas are right or not. We have been practicing this kind of teaching method since 1979, and we've had very good results. Students can even debate with their teachers if they don't agree. Confucius advocated that education be applied according to individual capacities and that it be comprehensive. We totally agree. I guess we can say that we are continuing this classical tradition of education."

The principal talked for about twenty minutes, and his remarks were not a prepared statement. I appreciated his generosity and openness. I asked a few questions but was eager to begin my interview with the three girls. The first question I asked them concerned their interests and activities outside of class. At the time I was unaware that these were girls with extraordinary talents.

Yu Sha has just turned twelve, but has already shown gifts in many areas.

Yu Sha (YS): I like to do Chinese painting. I learned it in the Youth Palace.* I also like to do calligraphy. Actually painting and calligraphy are from the same "family." I am also in the art group in our school. . . . Depending on what I paint, I use watercolors and sometimes just black ink. I like to paint animals, plants, children. I like chicks. They are woolly and soft. And they are also adorable. They are also full of life and vigor [*zhuang-qi-peng-bo-di*]. I also like to paint big roosters. For the comb and the wattles of the rooster, I use red paint, but the rest of the rooster is just different shades of black. I am the type who likes to do "splash-ink."† It's more daring to do splash-ink. I paint very fast. [Laughs softly.] It takes me about two minutes. But before actually starting, it takes me a long time to think, to concentrate. Right after I finish one, I go on to the next one.

* The Youth Palace, found in major cities, is a center that offers young people instruction in art, music, drama, and other extracurricular activities.

† Splash-ink, or *po-mo,* is monochrome painting in ink with bold, broad brush strokes, handled in a spontaneous but disciplined manner. The work should be an expression of the moment, and as the paper absorbs the ink, no changes can be made.

My father is a translator. My mother is a teacher. When I was younger, they both felt I was too lively. [Laughs.] They thought that practicing calligraphy would be a good way to cultivate my character, and so they sent me to the Youth Palace to learn. But I like to write huge characters with big brushes, and so practicing calligraphy does not really help to restrain me. Instead, it has made me even more daring than before.

Besides painting and calligraphy, Yu Sha also takes acting very seriously. She takes lessons at the Central Broadcasting Company and has starred in a movie. "I played the lead in that movie. The movie was shown on television a couple of years ago, but it was not very well known," she tells me. She has also traveled a great deal and has just finished a three-week trip to the Northeast with twenty other children from Beijing. "We were chosen on the basis of our talents," she informs me.

Wang Wei and Wang Xiao-yun are classmates and close friends. They are only a month apart in age (both are twelve), and, like Yu Sha, they have no brothers or sisters. Both sparkle. They are luminous and self-possessed, yet there are distinct differences in their personalities.

Wang Wei is very fond of her father. He tells her that children should be "lively and playful," and she is exactly that, as the smile on her round face shows plainly. According to her, she was happy even when she was alone with a whistle, a book of poems, and imaginary companions. She had hoped for real children to play with, but since it was not possible to have even one friend, she conjured up a whole troop and spent many joyful hours drilling them and teaching them Tang poems.

Wang Xiao-yun is a petite girl. Despite her small frame and delicate features, she projects a resolute presence. She is pensive but holds back nothing when expressing her thoughts. She speaks softly and slowly. Her voice is that of a child who feels weighed down. Her frowns are complex. She rarely smiles but communicates a rare kind of warmth with her eager and intense glances.

Wang Wei (WW): I like literature. My father used to be a high school language teacher. He has taught in several high schools. Now he gives seminars and lectures on child education. His classes are for teachers. He teaches them how to motivate and help children to learn—to read, to develop good study habits. . . . My father has helped me a lot. He wants me to develop a special talent, and so when I was only two, he taught me to recite Chairman Mao's poems. Then he taught me Tang poems.

Whenever I go to my mother's office, her colleagues always ask me to recite something for them. Just recently I recited a congratulatory message to the Olympic athletes from Beijing in the Great Hall of the People. . . . Before, when I was too young to go to school, after my parents left for work, nobody would be at home with me, and I had to play by myself. I was about five or six then, and at that time, in our yard—we have since moved—the youngest children were already in middle school, and I could never join them. I could only watch. I had no one to play with, and so I pretended there were small children around. I imagined I was the teacher and they were the students. Sometimes I was a gym teacher. I even had a small whistle. I would blow on my whistle and shout: "One, two, one, two." When my baba and mama came home, sometimes they would ask me: "What did you do today? Did you memorize those poems we taught you yesterday?" I would tell them: "I did. I did it with my students." It was great to have imaginary students. When I was teaching them, I was memorizing the poems myself. I played and I learned my poems.

I also copied classical poems on the pavement. I wrote with chalk. With words I didn't know, I asked my parents when they came home from work. At that time my parents had already taught me to write. And so before I started school, I knew how to write many characters already. I also had a book that had both the characters and their phonetic symbols.* With each lesson, I studied the new words first, and then I tried to memorize the text. I enjoyed doing this.

Anyway, there was nobody around. If there were someone to play with me, that would be even better, but there were no small children in our yard, and the older ones wouldn't play with me. Besides, they had to go to school. And so I had to play by myself, and that was fine. . . . At that time, my baba and mama both came home for lunch. In the afternoon, I was supposed to take a nap, but I didn't take naps. I didn't have that kind of habit. Now that I'll be going to sixth grade and I'll be taking the entrance exam next year, my mother has asked me to take naps again. She says that afterward I will have more energy to study. I still don't take naps. You see, she leaves after lunch, and she wouldn't know. . . .

Wang Xiao-yun (WXY): I have to take a nap. Otherwise I'll get a headache, and my eyes will ache too. The doctors said that I have some sort of disorder in my nervous system. I don't take any medicine. I just

* English alphabets using the Pinyin system of romanization.

have to make sure that I have good eating and sleeping habits. Usually I'm all right, but when I have a cold, the pain gets worse.

WW: I used not to be good at running. After lunch—we used to eat lunch at school—I would ask two classmates who were good runners to run laps around the schoolyard with me. I got better at running, but my teacher told my parents that I shouldn't be running after lunch, that I would get "a sagging [prolapsing] stomach" if I ran after a meal. So they didn't let me after that.

WXY: When I was in the first grade, I got sick quite often. I got scarlet fever and other things. I stayed home for months. Then that summer I started doing gymnastics. Since then I've had perfect attendance. I practiced gymnastics for four years. But when I got to fifth grade, my parents didn't let me go on. I had a lot more homework to do in fifth grade. I used to go to the gym in the Xi-cheng District Athlete Training School. I practiced on the balance beam, the uneven parallel bars, and the horse. I also did free-style gymnastics.

Did you want to continue?

WXY: It *was* a lot of hard work. [Laughs softly.] The gym was very far away. After school I had to take a bus there and practice for about three or four hours. When I got home, it was usually around eight. I do miss my coach and my friends there, but my parents want me to concentrate on my studies. . . . That first summer (right after first grade), I practiced at school. Then people from the Athlete Training School came to select students, and I was chosen, so I went there every day to practice. Once I had a bone fracture, but I didn't dare to tell my mama. Later she found out herself. She took me to the doctor, and the doctor said there had been a fracture that had evidently healed by itself. Now in the summer, when I have time, I like to go to the gym to watch my friends practice. They are all still there. In the summer, other than Sundays, they have to practice from eight to twelve in the mornings and then from two until the early evening.

We are talking about pets and small animals.

YS: We had cats, chickens, ducks, rabbits, everything. We bought them when they were babies but had to give them away when they got bigger.

WW: I had a kitten once. That was when I was in the first grade. My parents both had to work during the day, and no one was looking after her. She was thin, very thin, because very often we forgot to feed her. Then one day it ran away, and I think someone took her home. When she came back, she was blind. I felt very bad. I was too small then. I didn't know how to take care of her. I just knew to play with her. I think if I had a cat now, I'd be different. . . . At my laolao's place, in the country, there are all sorts of animals—chickens, roosters, ducks. When I was very young, around three or four, I used to stay with my laolao whenever my mama went on business trips and my baba was busy. I went back there last year. My laoye is there, too. He has just retired. He worked with electrical equipment. I like the scenery in the country. When you look at it from a distance, everywhere is green—the vegetable patches and the terraced fields. And there are ducks, geese, chickens, and pigs. I helped with the feeding. I didn't like to feed pigs, to pour the food into their troughs. I don't like pigs. They are dirty and big. But I was responsible for feeding all the chickens. I remember one morning I was helping my laolao do other chores and I didn't get a chance to feed the chickens. In the afternoon when I was taking the dirt out*—I carried it out in a bin—the chickens saw me, and they thought I was going to feed them. They all came toward me and encircled me. They wouldn't let me go, and so finally I had to put the bin down on the ground and let them see. Right away they started pecking. Then after a while, they realized that it wasn't food, and they left me alone.

In the courtyard where we used to live, there was an old grandma—actually she wasn't that old, she was in her fifties, and she was still teaching then. Anyway, she had a big cat and that cat gave birth to many kittens. One of the kittens was especially cute. She was like a woolly ball. Very often after dinner when we were all out in the yard to cool off, I liked to put her on a small table and tease her with a ball of yarn. Usually after a while, she would lose interest playing and try to run away. Of course I didn't let her. And when she ran, I ran after her and tried to catch her. When I did catch her, I grabbed her tightly by the neck and wouldn't let her go. I tried to force her to play with me. My mama, when she saw me doing that, told me to let her go. "You are going to kill the poor cat," she said to me.

* Since most Chinese houses and apartments have concrete floors, at the end of the day the dirt is swept up and dumped. Like taking out the garbage, it is a chore that most children can do.

WXY: My baba and mama do not allow me to have a pet, but I love small animals. When I was three or four, I lived in Nan-ko, in Beijing's suburb. Once I asked my laolao to find me a cat. She did. It was a yellow cat. I didn't know how to take care of it. I carried her on my back, and sometimes she was thrown to the ground. I even kicked her. I didn't know what I was doing. Then my baba thought it was too dirty to have her around the house, and he gave her away. I think he threw my cat away. I also like little chicks. I was also very curious. I remember using a knife to cut open a dead chick and a pencil to pull out its intestines to see what they looked like. I was pretty brave when I was small. I was also not afraid of rats. They all told me that rats carried disease. I didn't care. I just picked them up by their tails. . . .

This summer I went to my native town, the place where my baba came from, for the first time. It was in Hebei Province. When we got there, we went to visit my aunt. She had three dogs. They were very mean and fierce. They bite. We had three pancakes with us. Not long after we got there, two of the pancakes were gone. You see, I fed them to the dogs. [Laughs.] My yeye gave me a scolding. I guess now I am still fearless. I am not wild, just fearless. I am also not afraid of spiders, centipedes, and stuff like that. I was born here and raised here, and so I don't like Beijing so much. Children from other places, they long to see Tien-an-men Square. I'm a little tired of all that. I want to go to places with spaces that go on and on—wild fields, tall mountains, the open sea. . . .

This summer just before I left for my native town, my mama heard that someone was selling rabbits on the street. She took me out to see the rabbits. Once I saw the rabbits, I refused to leave. I kept pestering my mother to buy me some. She said, No. She thinks rabbits smell awful. She doesn't like small animals. Later I took some money and bought two rabbits behind her back. I put them in a grocery basket. I lined the basket with newspapers in case they peed. I also went to the kitchen and quietly took some vegetables for my rabbits. My mama later discovered them. She was so mad! She told me that when my baba came home I was really going to get it. I got scared. Then my nainai had an idea. She suggested that I give my rabbits to my xiaoyi [youngest maternal aunt]. Her child was about four. They always keep all sorts of animals at home, chicks, ducklings. I was always envious of them. But they are not that good to animals. Sometimes they mistreat them. My cousin liked to throw their cat on the ground, and he would do it over and over. That cat finally died. . . . My rabbits were black. At first, I was going to get white rabbits, but they seemed too delicate. Not long after I gave them to my xiaoyi, they died.

WW: Wang Xiao-yun gave me one of her rabbit's legs. It was so soft. I used to cuddle it when I went to bed at night.

Do you like to catch insects?

YS: Yes, all kinds of insects: locusts, crickets, dragonflies. . . .

WW: Children now like to catch field crickets [*you-hu-lu*]. They are black. Most don't have wings. The kids in my yard know all about catching field crickets. At night they put their ears to the brick wall and listen for their sound. The field crickets like to hide in the cracks. After they catch them, they put them in a jar and punch some holes through the lid so the crickets can breathe. After they are tired of playing with them, they dump them out. I don't like to catch field crickets. I'd much rather go to the fields and catch butterflies.

WXY: When I was in Hebei, in my native place, where we stayed was next to a high school. The school had a big field where a lot of wildflowers grew. I liked to pick wildflowers and put them in a vase. There were also a lot of mosquitoes and flies there. There was one kind of insect—they call them "kow-tow insects." If you squeeze their bodies, they will turn over and kow-tow. Some can even turn somersaults if you press their tails very hard.

WW: When I was in the country living with my laolao, there was this woodshed where they put the chicken feed and all kinds of junk. Sometimes birds got in. One day my laoye told me he was going to catch me some birds. When it got dark, he took a flashlight and went in the shed. He did grab a few birds for me and put them in a cage. The birds were very temperamental. They refused to eat, and at night, they flopped around the cage and woke everyone up. The next day, one bird died, and we threw it away. . . . My laoye also taught me a way to catch birds. This was in the country, and each family had a big yard. Anyway, you take a basket and turn it upside down, and then you hold the basket up with a stick and put some rice under it. The stick is attached with a string. You hold the other end of the string and hide in the house. When you see birds eating under the basket, you jerk the string, the basket will fall, and you will catch your birds. That day we waited and waited until it was dark, until I was tired of waiting. We didn't catch a single bird with the basket trick.

YS: One time I was in a dentist's office when suddenly a sparrow flew in by mistake. Everyone started shutting windows, but the sparrow just kept on flopping around. It banged against all sorts of things. After a while, it fell behind a cupboard and was trapped there. The doctor got it out and gave it to me. At first I was a little afraid of holding it. It was so small and my hands were shaking. Later a boy asked me to show it to him. As I was showing him, my hands let go a little, and it flew away.

WW: Once when I came home from school, I saw my baba holding a bird. He said that the bird had crashed into our front door. A boy in our yard had a cage, and we borrowed it. But the bird lived only for a few days—maybe it wasn't used to living in a cage. My laoye said you should only catch young birds and that after a while they'll get used to you. The more mature birds are more temperamental. They'd rather die than live in your home.

YS: My laoye had a yellow bird. It actually lived for several months. Then when we ran out of millet and forgot to feed it, it died of hunger. I even made a coffin for it. I built a little paper box. I glued the sides tightly together. Then I put the bird in, closed the top, and wrote "small bird" on the outside, and buried it.

WW: Once some kids near our yard had a small animal that died. I wasn't too sure what kind of animal it was. Anyway, when I saw them, they were burying it. They made a small earth mound, and on top of it, they placed a stick of incense. Then they all clasped their hands.

When I was small, a big boy gave me a dragonfly. I tied a string around the dragonfly, and then attached the other end to the side of my bed. I wanted it to catch mosquitoes. It had only a small area to catch mosquitoes, just around the bed, and so it didn't catch any. After a couple days the dragonfly died. . . . There was another time when I caught a cricket, but the cricket didn't make any sound. I asked my baba why my cricket refused to sing, but he couldn't answer me. He didn't know anything about crickets, and he wasn't interested in playing with crickets. And so I tried to figure it out myself. I examined it very carefully but still couldn't understand it. Finally I told the cricket: "You are a bad cricket!", and then started spanking it. I didn't kill it, but after the spanking, it was half dead. I was just so mad when other kids' crickets could sing but not mine. Afterward, I threw it away.

YS: At my nainai's place, my cousin once caught a dragonfly for me. He found it on a tree. I tied a string around its body and tried to force it to fly. I spun it around and around, but it could only fly very low. Suddenly a neighbor's cat sprang on it and ate it.

WW: I have been to Yuan-shi prefecture, in Hebei Province. That's where my father comes from. They have all kinds of animals there, even mules. When I was little, I was curious about everything. And so when I saw a mule, blindfolded, turning a mill, I thought: Now that's interesting; that's something new. The people who were working there all knew me. They liked to tease me. They told me: "You better go home and ask your father for some money first. See that mule. It is blindfolded, and it is giving you a performance. You better pay first if you want to watch a performance." I went home and told my father. He said that they were just teasing me. That was just a mule turning a mill. It wasn't any performance. [Laughs.]

Do you enjoy staying with your grandparents?

WW: Yes, but after staying there for a long time, it gets to be a little boring. In Beijing we don't have little animals to play with. On the farm everything is new and wonderful.

YS: My grandparents from both sides all live in Beijing. But at my nainai's place there is a large courtyard, and there are many kids there. In our building we have fourteen floors, but the children don't know each other, even those living on the same floor. We all stay home and have nothing to do.

In Beijing most of the older houses are arranged in small compounds (si-he-yuan). *A typical* si-he-yuan *has four housing units surrounding a central court.*

Why is that?

YS: Because a building usually has several floors, and on each floor there are seven or eight families, and nobody likes to run up and down the stairs to visit. If you live in a courtyard, you have a lot more contacts with neighbors. If you live in an apartment, after work or after school, you go back to your apartment, and you wouldn't try to make time to visit your neighbors.

WW: We live in a courtyard. In the evenings, all the children play together. We play card games, poker, and other games. But living in an apartment is different. I have visited friends who live in apartments. Once a person steps into his apartment and slams the door, it's locked. If you don't know your neighbors, it doesn't seem appropriate to knock on their doors. Also everyone has his own meter for gas and electricity. When we first moved into our new place, we didn't know anyone. But every family in the courtyard has to take turns adding up the gas and electricity bills each month. Then you have to talk to your neighbors. In an apartment building you don't have to do that. Each family takes care of its own bills. Many people choose to live in apartments because it's quieter.

Does everyone get along in a si-he-yuan*?*

WW: The adults get along, but the kids sometimes fight. We'd be playing, and for some reason or another we'd start fighting, and after a while everything would be all right again. Even though we are kids, we have our pride. Nobody wants to be the first to start a conversation after a fight. But if we really want to play again, we find some sort of excuse to make up. Once I had a fight with a friend, and neither of us wanted to talk to the other first. But I left my handkerchief at her house, and so I had to go there. I knocked on the door, and she asked: "Who is it?" I said, "It's me. I left my handkerchief at your house." While she was trying to find it, I was trying to figure out how to start a conversation again. When she returned with my handkerchief, I asked her: "Do you like the book that I lent you the other day?" She said, "It was good." And then we started talking again.

YS: One day I was drinking soybean milk for breakfast at my nainai's house, and my cousin blamed me for not closing the bottlecap tightly. I said to him: "So?" He was so mad. Then a little later, Nainai said that she wanted to take us to Beihai Park, and we were playing again.

WXY: This is how children play: they are fine one moment and squabble the next. You smell good one minute but stink the next. This is what the grownups say about us, about how we play together. [Everyone laughs.]

Tell me some of the mischievous things you do.

WW: I grew up with my xiaoyi. She lived in Shijiazhuang [about 250 kilometers from Beijing], but for a time she came here to live with us since my baba and mama both had to work. That was when I was younger. Even before that, once when I was visiting my grandparents, I thought I heard someone say something and what he said scared me. It was in the morning, and many old people were outside doing their exercises. Some were chatting as they were exercising. I thought I heard someone yell: "Xiao-wei [Little Wei] for sale! Two hundred dollars and you can buy Xiao-wei!" I was so scared because Xiao-wei is my nickname. I guess I went home and told everybody. After that my aunt liked to use that to scare me. She told me that there was an old man who wanted to sell me. So I was particularly afraid of old men. When she was taking care of me in Beijing, I always wanted to go out and play. She didn't want me to because she had to cook and do other things and couldn't keep an eye on me. And so she used that "old man" to scare me: She put a whisk broom behind the front door. She made it stand up and she put a hat on top of it. Then she told me, "If you go out, that old man will catch you." One day when she was busy working, I quietly crept up to the door to take a look at that "old man." I couldn't understand why he didn't stir. Then I quickly ran back because I was still afraid that he might catch me. After a while he still didn't move. I took a stick and poked him, but still nothing happened. Then I knew that it was all right, that he wasn't going to do anything to me. I hurried up and ran out. Afterward I wasn't afraid of old men anymore.

When I was little, I liked to play with boys. We always played war. We said we were the Liberation Army. But we needed guns and horses, and so I asked my mother to buy me a gun. And I borrowed a neighbor's cat to be my horse. I rode on the cat and when she didn't behave, I pulled her ears. One day my baba saw me riding the cat. He said: "*What* are you doing?" I told him I was riding a horse, that I was a soldier in the Liberation Army. He was not convinced. He said, "You'd better get off. Otherwise you are going to kill the cat. How would you like someone to ride on your back and pull your ears?" I listened to him because I didn't want to hurt the cat. I never rode on the cat again.

WXY: My parents are *very, very* strict. They are not at all open-minded. It's hard to be mischievous when they are so strict.

YS: One day I was playing with a water hose. I didn't know how to hold it, and so I sprayed water all over myself and a neighbor. Later when my cousin came by I sprayed water all over him. I did that on purpose.

What makes you angry?

WXY: I think . . . when you want to do something, and your parents don't approve, and they won't support you. . . .

WW: That's right! I agree. That time Wang Xiao-yun gave me a rabbit leg after her rabbit had died, my mother asked me: "Why do you want something like that?" I had to say something and so I said: "It's for dusting." She said: "All right, if it's for dusting, then use it for dusting." But I really didn't want to. I just liked to hold it. I liked to cuddle it when I went to bed. It was soft, and I liked to rub it against my face. Then one day suddenly I couldn't find my rabbit leg. I asked my mother. She told me she'd used it to dust the table, it had gotten very dirty and she threw it away. I was very angry. I cried and cried. . . .

Also my mother always wants to cut my hair. But I don't want to have my hair short because I want to have braids, and my hair never grows long enough to be put in braids because she is always cutting it. She tells me I look prettier with my hair short. One day my mother wanted to cut my hair again, and I said I didn't want to. Just then my laolao came to visit us. My mother turned around and asked her to cut my hair. I had these very short pigtails. They stuck up like this. [She held her hair up to show me.] My laolao, seeing that she was going to have a tough time convincing me, took a pair of scissors and chopped my pigtails off just like that. I was so mad. I cried. I threw a tantrum. I told them: "This looks so ugly!" When I was small I wanted to look pretty. [Laughs.] I was in a fit, and I wouldn't talk to my mama or my laolao. But after a while, you see, you have to eat dinner, and, therefore, you have to talk to them. And so that's what I did. I forgot about the whole thing.

YS: When I was staying with my nainai, they all wanted me to have short hair with two pigtails looking like two brushes. They always nagged me about getting a haircut. One day I got so fed up with them that I took a pair of scissors and cut my hair short, very short. All the grownups were so surprised.

That afternoon, when Wang Wei and Wang Xiao-yun come to my hotel room, they are joined by the two boys Teng Hua-tao and Li Yi. At school that morning Teng Hua-tao and Li Yi were most courteous, listening quietly to the girls and me chatting away, occasionally laughing or smiling when someone said something funny, but they kept their thoughts and comments to themselves, and never interrupted us. Now, after sitting down, the boys in chairs and the girls and I on my bed, we begin again, this time feeling more at ease.

Teng Hua-tao dominates the initial part of our conversation. He is handsome by Chinese standards, tall and thin; his face is shaped like a melon seed. He is approaching thirteen and his adolescent voice adds even more weight to an already serious and grave boy-man. He lives with his grandparents and rarely sees his parents, but when he does, he joins in their social circle. He is familiar with their writer and actor friends, and he listens to their conversations. "They tell stories and they pour out their grievances," he tells me. He is thoughtful and cautious with his judgment even when he discusses his father's films. The boy in him does occasionally peer out when the subject is "birthdays" or "how to avoid doing chores."

Teng Hua-tao (THT): Both my baba and my mama are film directors. They live in Xian because they are with the Xian Film Studio. They come to Beijing occasionally, and each time they don't stay very long. I have been living with my grandparents ever since I was born. I have spent very little time with my parents. They have made several films. Originally they were students of the Film Academy. After graduation, they were assigned to Xian Film Studio to work. Then they became directors. I have seen all their films.

What do you think of them?

I think they are not bad [seriously]. My baba's first film was a musical. Ever since he was a child, he loved music, and so as soon as he became a director, he made a musical. This was a film commemorating our premier [Zhou En-lai]. A better one, I think, is *A Village in the City*. He directed that one in 1982 or 1983. It was a movie about the workers in the Shanghai Shipyard. It was pretty good. My baba considers it his best. He also writes screenplays. He usually collaborates with someone else. Some of his movies were adapted from novels. My mother and my father always work together. They often disagree with each other and they argue. I am not particularly interested in making films. Because of my parents I have met many actors and actresses.

Are your friends envious of you?

That . . . I don't know. I don't think anything of it myself.

I like music. I like symphonies and piano pieces. I play a little piano. I have been playing for about four or five years. I like Beethoven the best. Bach is all right. I haven't played much of his music. It's too difficult. I have played a lot of Mozart, mostly his early compositions, those that he composed from age eight to age fifteen. His early music is very lively and beautiful. I have also played some of Bach's preludes, but they're too easy and I don't play them anymore. I like symphonic music, especially Beethoven's symphonies. The Ninth is my favorite. I don't understand the words in the chorus, but they sound beautiful. I understand that it was a poem composed by the German poet Schiller. Beethoven was an admirer of Schiller and had always wanted to set his poems to music. And when he added choral music to his Ninth Symphony, people during his time were shocked. . . . My father at one time was a conductor. He was trained as a conductor when he was a child. He studied in the same music school that I am studying in now. Then his interests changed. He liked to see plays and act in plays. When he was young, he was in several. Then he was accepted by the Film Academy. . . .

My piano teacher is from the Central Conservatory. My baba found the piano teacher for me. I have a piano at home. Now it's not too difficult to find a music teacher if you want to learn to play the piano or the violin. The Central Conservatory has lots of teachers and students, but it's hard to find a good teacher. My teacher is in his fifties or sixties. He is very experienced. He has been teaching since he was in his twenties. His name is Han Jian-ping. He is very strict with all his students. I study with him once a week for about an hour. When I am busy with my homework and don't have time to practice, I just go there and muddle through my lesson. . . . Someday I would like to have a career in music. I would like to become a concert pianist if possible.

Li Yi is a child compared to his classmate Teng Hua-tao. He is also shorter and rounder. He comes from a large family: he has two older sisters, and his extended family includes maternal grandparents, aunt, uncle, and four cousins—all thirteen live in the same house. There is a great deal of housework to be done, and very little space for privacy. His wants and needs are very different from those of the four other children. He longs to be alone and makes special efforts to come home late so that he can eat dinner by himself. He has little material comfort compared to his four classmates, yet he has fewer complaints. He speaks fondly of his parents and grandparents and of his grandfather's birthdays when "my uncles, aunts, and cousins all come, . . . there are more than thirty of us."

Li Yi (LY): My laoye plays the *gu-zheng* [the twenty-one- or twenty-five-stringed zither], and he plays it often. My grandparents live with us. My biaomei [girl cousins] are all learning to play the *gu-zheng* from him. At one time he was a music teacher and also a language teacher at school. I've studied a little bit with him—he is not at all strict.

WXY: My father plays the violin, but he doesn't play it well.

WW: My yeye likes to play the *er-hu* [two-stringed fiddle]. He is very good at it.

THT: My yeye likes to listen to the Beijing Opera.

And what about you?

THT: It's all right with me. [The other three shake their heads and say they don't like it.] I like to see it when there is a lot of acrobatic fighting. Older people like to see operas.

WW: My grandparents rarely visit us, and so when they do come, we have to go along with them and do the things that they like to do. And usually I have to see the Beijing operas with them. But I don't like to see operas that much. . . . My baba and mama once took me to the People's Theater to see one. At first I didn't know what was going on. Then my mama explained the story to me. Since it had a plot, I began to find it interesting. Sometimes in the theater they project the actors' lines on the wall to help the audience understand what they are singing. . . . I don't like Beijing operas that much, but I do like to do mime. When I was studying in the Youth Palace, we had lessons in mime. The teacher asked us to do a short sketch, like "Before Going to School," and we had to act out the things we did before going to school and also our moods without using any words. This was a little like acting in an opera.

What about plays? Are they popular?

WW: Most people like to see movies. . . .

THT: That's because with a play the story unfolds too slowly, and people are impatient. But older people still like operas better.

WXY: My lao-lao is different. She likes to watch ball games, sports, all kinds of sports. She is almost seventy now.

WW: I like to listen to storytellers chanting stories from the historical novels, like *The Water Margin, Romance of the Three Kingdoms, Biography of Yue Fei*. I've read some of them myself, but I don't like all those *zhi, hu, zhe, yie* [particles in classical Chinese]. When I was in the fifth grade, for a while the *Romance of the Three Kingdoms* was broadcast on the radio around noon. There was a storyteller chanting many of the stories from that book. Our teacher allowed us to bring radios to school, and we listened to the stories while we were resting.

THT: I don't like to listen to storytellers that much. I much prefer reading the novels myself. The storytellers have their own versions, and lots of times they can't quite express the intent of the author. I have read many historical novels already, *The Journey to the West* and *The Water Margin,* but I have not read the *Three Kingdoms.* I want to, but just don't have the time. It's impossible to do any outside reading when school starts. In the summer I already have a pile of books this high I mean to read. The *Three Kingdoms* would just make the pile higher.

When you read a novel or watch a play or a movie, very often there is a hero or a heroine in the story, sometimes more than one. And all of you are familiar with the revolutionary heroes of your country. What are your thoughts about heroes? Whom do you consider a hero?

LY: A hero, I feel, is a person who is able to lead and a person not only others *say* they admire but one that they truly admire in their hearts.

THT: I think a great deal about the character of a person. When I read biographies or novels, whenever I come upon a passage about the moral weakness of a person, I don't know why, but I have to read it several times. Sometimes I do this unconsciously. Usually on the first reading I don't understand it. Then I go back a second time, sometimes a third or a fourth time. Each time I understand it a little better.

The subject shifts. Teng Hua-tao tells me that he likes to listen to his parents' actor and writer friends chatting about the world and complaining about the way things are. He mentions one particular actor, Su Ye-shan.

THT: Su Ye-shan feels that people have degenerated, that they have become selfish and self-centered. He is too grumpy. He has too many grievances. Once he said that he had a classmate who was exiled to Xinjiang when he was a boy in his teens. He was told that he was sent there to do physical labor, but when he got there, he found the place was like a prison camp, surrounded by barbed wire and watched by prison guards. This classmate stayed there altogether for twenty years. He just returned. Right after he came back he played in several movies. We are all familiar with his movies. His name is Xu Hua-shui. His father was in fact a very learned man. I don't know exactly why Xu Hua-shui was imprisoned for so long. Life in Xinjiang was very, very hard. It was very cold there and at night they had no blankets, only their quilted jackets to keep them warm. When he came back to Beijing, his face was covered with a beard. He didn't recognize Beijing: "Is this Beijing? Am I really in Beijing?" he asked. He couldn't believe it. In fact he couldn't even find his way home. At the time Su Ye-shan was in Bei-yang Film Studio, and he recommended that Xu Hua-shui work there. They thought he was quite colorful. Because he lived in Xinjiang so long, he was reticent. He rarely spoke a word. He had a strong character. I think the reason [he stayed in Xinjiang so long] was that they had forgotten about him. . . . He was sent to Xinjiang before the Gang of Four.* At the time his father was condemned as a Rightist, but he didn't do anything wrong. He was only a boy in his teens. When he was sent there, he didn't expect it to be like that at all. But there was no way he could have come back. Nobody knew what had happened to his father.

And what are your thoughts about the Cultural Revolution?

WW: I wish it'll never happen again. . . .

THT: There is a very famous professor—his name is Wen Yuan-kai—who thinks that more people in China should be studying this disastrous period and Chinese history in general. He says that there are many people in Japan and in the United States who are studying Chinese history—her social history and her traditional culture. He thinks that in the future if we want to know what happened during the Cultural Revolution period we might have to go to these countries to obtain information.

The discussion comes back to the home, to the children's relationship to their parents. I ask them whether they would like to change their parents, and if so, how.

WW: My father gives seminars. His classes are for teachers. He teaches them ways to help children to learn. He has helped me a great deal. . . .

* The Gang of Four are the most reviled figures of China's recent past. The group, led by Mao Ze-dong's wife Jiang Qing, rose to power during the last years of the Cultural Revolution, when Mao's health was deteriorating. They were removed from their positions shortly after Mao's death in 1976 and subsequently brought to trial and sent to prison.

My mother . . . sometimes when she gets impatient with me, she screams and yells. I wish she could talk to me nicely.

LY: My father doesn't say much. He likes to keep things to himself. I wish that he'd talk to me more. My mother is very nice. She is very concerned about my "mental development." She is very caring. I just wish that she could help me more with my studies.

THT: My father never stops working. It has become a habit. He just never stops. He is making too many movies. His doctor tells him that he'd better slow down. I wish he would take a year or two off and just rest. And the same goes for my mother. On top of her work, she has family duties to take care of. . . . But I want to change too. I want to become quieter and more serious. A sign of maturity is being more pensive and more stable.

What about your environment?

LY: I want my environment to be quieter. [Laughs.]

THT: He is always saying that! That's all he wants.

LY: They tell me it's not good to be lonely, but I would like to be lonely for a change. I have such a large family that on my laoye's birthday, for instance, when my uncles, aunts, and cousins all come for the celebration, there are more than thirty of us. And we always try to take a family picture when we are all together.

I also wish we could have larger rooms and more tables. When school starts, sometimes at night, when we all have homework, we are short of tables. My parents are both teachers. They have to prepare for their classes too. Usually we have to hurry up and finish our homework so that others can use the table. Sometimes my mama waits until everybody is done and then she starts. And by that time it's pretty late. We never have enough space in our home.

WXY: I wish I could have my own room. I like to study alone. Our house has fifteen square meters, and it's pretty big, considering that this is Beijing. But still I wish for my own room, no matter how small. I want to have a little world of my own.

WW: I also want to have a room of my own. In the evening I could study there or just be alone. We do have a small room in our house, but my baba uses it at night. I can use it during the day, but once they are home I have to go to the larger room to study. I also like to eat my dinner alone, in the courtyard, by myself, and enjoy the food slowly.

Other wishes?

WW: I wish I could live forever. I wish I could be free to do whatever I want to do.

THT: I wish I could board a UFO someday. I also want to construct a spaceship myself. Then I have a small wish. [Laughs.] I wish that our men's volleyball team also wins a medal in the Olympics. It's always the women's team that's winning. . . .

WXY: I guess the men also want to bring some honor home.

Do you remember any particularly happy time with your family?

THT: Once I was with my baba in Xian. We were playing in the wheatfield. He took his sandals off, and when he wasn't looking, I hid them in the haystack. Finally when he couldn't find them, I told him where they were. He went looking for them but couldn't find them. I also tried. Finally he had to go home barefoot. [Laughs.] But now I hardly ever go to Xian. This was when I was smaller.

LY: When I was small, at night we used to turn off all the lights in our house because the lights were attracting mosquitoes. When the house was very dark, I liked to put a stool in the middle of the hallway and wait in a corner until someone came by and tripped over it. Every time I had a good laugh. It was such fun.

WW: I liked to play hide-and-go-seek when I was little. I always begged my baba to play with me, but at home we never had any good places to hide. Once we were at my laolao's in the country, where there were many places to hide. One day I was playing hide-and-go-seek with my baba again. I hid in the well. Sometimes the well water is very low. Even with a long rope, you sort of have to lean against the rim to scoop up the water. There were cemented bricks on the side of the well. They were like steps. Well, I climbed down and waited for my father to find me. He never showed up. He didn't know that I was that clever. When it was dinnertime, I was still down there. My baba thought I had long gone home and didn't even bother to go look for me. Finally I climbed out.

Do you help your parents with the chores at home?

WW: Now that I'm home in the summer, I do some chores for my parents. I do them because I want my mama to *praise* me. I cook the rice and I do some stir-frying, and when she comes home, she tells me: "You are such a good girl." [Laughs.]

WXY: I am an only child and so I am the laziest at home. I don't like to do chores.

Who does them, then?

WXY: My mother. Sometimes my father helps her a little. He is very lazy.

THT: I don't do any chores. I always try to find some sort of excuse to avoid them. If I really can't get away, if my nainai asks me to wash the clothes, I just dump them all into the washing machine, even if there are only a few shirts.

LY: I can't dodge the work at home. I have two older sisters, but one is already working, and sometimes she comes home late. The other sister is busy with her studies. When she was preparing for her high school entrance exam, my mother told me: "Your older sister should be spending more time studying, and so you are the next in line to carry out the responsibilities at home." I wash clothes, I sweep the floor, and I dump the dirt. I do a little cooking, but at home usually my laolao does the cooking. Since there are more than ten of us eating dinner every night, she is often very tired and so the food is not so great. Sometimes I purposely stay at school for a while and come home late. When I do get home, my baba will make some fried rice especially for me. It's quieter, and the food is better. [Laughs.] My mama is always terribly worried when I am late. She doesn't understand why I have to be at school. I have never told her the real reason.

THT: Fried rice with eggs is my yeye's specialty. He makes the best. A classmate of mine, once it was his birthday and he invited me to his house. He fried some rice for me, and it was very good. Before that, he was always bragging that he was a first-class chef, and I didn't believe him, but the rice did taste pretty good.

How do you celebrate your birthdays?

WXY: For my eleventh birthday, my mother asked someone to bake me a birthday cake. It was a beautiful cake.

THT: My birthday is most exciting because it's January first. Many people bring me cakes. Usually I end up with four or five. . . .

LY: I never get to have any of that. [Everyone laughs.] It's impossible to celebrate everybody's birthday in our family. When it's someone's birthday, she gets a bowl of noodles and a poached egg.

* * *

We met Wu Jin-song in Guangzhou (Canton) *in 1979. Guangzhou was our last stop before leaving for Hong Kong and then home. We had arrived the day before and had caught glimpses of this variegated city. We'd have liked to take a closer look and bring home more vivid colors of monuments and art objects and of lichees and mustard greens in baskets side by side, but we decided to spend our last day in China talking with Cantonese children.*

Wu Jin-song is a fourth-grader. In the three photos I have of her, whether she is alone or among her classmates, she stands perfectly erect with her hands behind her back, a forced smile on her tightly closed lips. Wu Jin-song brings to mind those images of children we find in the "model plays" (yang-ban-xi) *of the Cultural Revolution era; she is positive, willful, resolute, and proud. Each smile, each gesture, is a statement expressing an attitude. When she talks to us, very often she sounds like a platoon leader addressing her troops (actually she is one). Her voice—heavily nasal—is full of vigor and conviction. At the age of ten she seems to be singularly concerned with the moral behavior of others, citing several examples of the "good" and the "bad." But even with this "model child" who appears to be thoroughly indoctrinated, tendencies that are ordinary and "childlike" are plainly in her. She finds the sweets of Beijing tempting and the vending machines of Nanjing fascinating. She enjoys playing card games and "war" with other children.*

Wu Jin-song begins by telling me about her family.

At home there are four of us, Baba, Mama, Jiejie [older sister], and myself. My jiejie is sixteen. She is in the middle school. My father is a skilled worker. My mother is a biology teacher in Guangya Middle School. My parents are both natives of Jiangsu. My mama was from [the town of] Gaoyu and my baba was from Xinhua. Both my jiejie and I were born in Nanjing, but we grew up in Guangzhou.

What dialects do you speak at home?

My jiejie and I speak the Guangdong [Cantonese] dialect. My parents understand it, but they don't speak it. Actually my baba can speak a little, but his pronunciation is not accurate. So they answer us in *pu-tong-hua*. I am more used to speaking the Guangdong dialect. We talk to our friends in the Guangdong dialect. We hardly ever speak *pu-tong-hua*, only in class. But outside class even our teachers speak to us in the Guangdong dialect.

(*For someone who rarely speaks the* pu-tong-hua, *her pronunciation is very accurate.*)

What is your favorite subject in school?

English. That's because I am doing very well in English. My jiejie—we get along very well—sometimes helps me with words I have trouble pronouncing, but sometimes I have to help her with words that she has forgotten. And then there are words that I've learned but she hasn't. So I have to teach her. I also like my language class.

What do you do in your language class?

We read stories about the frontier guards and about people who do good deeds. After we read a story, we have to answer questions and tell the teacher the main theme of the story. We learn punctuation, and we take dictation. And once or twice we have to write compositions. Like last time we had to write about a schoolmate who studies diligently.

Do you remember what you wrote?

I wrote about Wang Gong-jian. He is in fourth grade, in class number three. He is also my next-door neighbor. I am not quite sure, but either this semester or last semester he was cited as a student of "three goods" [good in health, study, and work]. He was a committee member of his brigade, and he had an average of one hundred in his three major subjects. In my composition, I gave two examples to show how diligent he is. First, he studies English tirelessly. Even when he is walking, he tries to recall the vocabulary words he has just learned. This shows that he uses every minute, every second of his time to study. There was another example. One night I went to his house to watch television. He has a television at home, but I don't, and so sometimes when there is a good program, I go to his house to watch. That night, there was a special program. After I finished reviewing, I went to his house. He had not finished his homework and was still working. I knew that he wanted to watch the program, but at the same time he was afraid that he would not be able to finish his homework. Then he thought about the revolutionary martyrs who sacrificed their lives so that we could have the good life that we have today. He said that if we didn't study diligently we would be unworthy of what these martyrs had done for us. He also remembered that he was a cadre in his class. He said he should provide a good example for others.

How many cadres are there in each class?

There are nine cadres in each class. Five are committee members of the platoon. [Each classroom makes up a platoon.] Four are squad leaders. Of the five committee members, one is the platoon leader. She watches over the whole platoon. The committee is divided into four functions, and the remaining members are the heads of these four groups. The leader of the organization group is responsible for recruiting new members of the Young Pioneers. The head of the propaganda committee is responsible for writing and gathering propaganda materials. The chairman of the physical fitness committee watches over the health and hygiene of all the students in the class. The head of the study committee records everyone's learning attitudes.

Then each platoon is divided into two squads, girls in one squad and boys in another. Each squad has a leader and a deputy leader. The leader stands in front of the squad to maintain order. The deputy leader stands behind him; he is his assistant. I am the leader of my platoon. In my class, when anything happens, the committee members have to report to me.*

* Of the four subgroups, the study committee has replaced the labor committee, which, in the days of the Little Red Soldiers, was responsible for organizing activities on the farm and workshops attached to the schools. Cf. *Childhood in China*, pp. 132–135.

How many Young Pioneers are there in your class?

There are thirty, and we have forty-two students in our class. Originally there were forty-three, but one went to the United States. These thirty Young Pioneers make up a platoon, and I am their leader. If anyone does not behave, the leader of his squad has to report it to me, and I have to report it to the teacher. We also have to keep a record. Whoever is disruptive in class, we have to make a note of his name. Every week our teacher examines our record. Those who have violated the rules repeatedly have to have a talk with the teacher. If after the talk a student still refuses to reform, he will be punished. If he still doesn't change his ways, eventually he can be kicked out of the Young Pioneers. Any time he wants to rejoin, he has to reapply.

What kind of behavior is considered "violating the rules"?

In our class there is a girl who smokes. Everybody in her family is bad. She has many brothers and sisters, and they all smoke. Some are even thieves. Then there are other things that are considered bad behavior, like fighting, making a lot of noise in class, not listening to the teacher, not handing in homework on time. . . .

Why are certain students not allowed to join the Young Pioneers?

That's because they don't pay attention in class or they don't do well in their studies. Their names are all in our record. We also keep a record of all our classmates.

Do the Young Pioneers organize any special activities among themselves?

This summer the committee members of all the platoons and all the squad leaders will get to go to summer camp. The deputy leaders have to pass a test first before they are allowed to go. Also every Monday morning between eight and nine-thirty, the members of each squad do some activities together, like reviewing their schoolwork, drawing, reading, or performing some good deed.

Do the cadres themselves ever do anything wrong? And do they ever make mistakes in judging others?

Hardly ever. The girl who went to America, she did something wrong once. Once somebody brought candies to class. This girl searched her and took the candies from her. She ended up eating the candies herself. Others found out about it and pointed out her shortcoming. The Young Pioneers can do that to their leaders.

Whenever there is a dispute between a cadre and a noncadre, whom does the teacher listen to?

The cadre. But the teacher can also question other students.

The subject changes from the Young Pioneers to herself:
If you had a day all to yourself, what would you like to do?

First I finish my homework. Then I help my mother with the chores. Then maybe I'll watch some television. In the afternoon I will take a nap. After my nap, I'll help my mother fold the laundry. Then some reading and more reviewing. At night if there is a good program, I'll watch some television.

What if your mother tells you that you don't have to do any chores?

I'll still do my homework first because that's most important. Then some review. Then I'll go and try to find some neighborhood kids to play with. There are lots of kids in our neighborhood. In our building originally there were two other girls, but they moved away to Hong Kong. Then a new girl came. And next door to us there are two boys. We always play with the boys. We play cards. Then there is another game we like to play: we have two teams with two on each team. First one team has to send out a person to start the game. If that person gets caught by the other team, she is put in jail. But she can take three steps from her jail, and while she is taking the three steps, her teammate must try to save her. When he touches her like this [she taps my arm], she can start running. If she is caught again, she goes back to jail. If not, she can return to her team. . . . Then there is another game called Five Bullets. You start the game with five bullets, two hand grenades, and a gun. Then there is another person who tries to catch you. As you try to run away from him, you can either fire a shot or throw a hand grenade. When you have emptied all your shots and thrown both of your hand grenades, you have to run to a particular place to pick up ammunition.

If you can do that before someone catches you, then you are safe, and you can start firing again. If you get caught, you have to be "it."

You said your family was originally from Jiangsu Province. Have you gone back there to visit?

Last year in August. It was the fifteenth. No, no. We started out on the fifteenth. By the time we got to Gaoyu, it was the eighteenth. My gonggong [paternal grandfather*] was very sick—he is dead now—so we went to see him. We also stopped by other cities along the way, just to have a look. We were in Shanghai, Nanjing, and Xinhua. I like Nanjing. There, the environment is better, and so many things are automated. One day I was out with my mother, and there was this machine that sells different kinds of drinks. I don't remember the names of these drinks, but one was ice milk. Anyway, the machine tells how much a drink costs. After you put in the money, a cup appears and your drink is automatically poured into your cup. That was neat! I like Shanghai too. There you can find all sorts of things and there is a lot going on in the markets and on the streets. I think the people there are better. They are not like the people here. In Guangzhou most people are very crafty. Usually they don't care about anyone else other than themselves. And if you, for some reason or another, offend them, they will remember it forever, and they will never let you forget it either.

Two other girls were present as she talked, both natives of Guangzhou. They did not rebuke her. They seemed uncomfortable but remained silent.

Are there any places that you would like to visit?

I would like to spend a winter in the North. I like to play in the snow. There are lots of fun things to do in Beijing and lots of goodies to eat. There are pastries and ices. I saw them on television. They look so good.

But the place that I would like to visit the most is the United States. There the science and technology are very advanced. If I go and study there, I could gain so much scientific knowledge. The place that I don't want to go is Hong Kong. A lot of people say that Hong Kong is good. I don't see why. I saw a program on television recently. It was a movie,

* In southern China some people refer to their paternal grandfather as "gonggong" instead of "yeye."

but we learned a lot about what it is like in Hong Kong. There many people are poor, and life for them is hard and tiring. Very often they have to hold many jobs. Otherwise you and your family won't have enough to eat. Then there are some who are very rich, and all they do is gamble all day long.

What would you like to study in the future?

I want to learn English well, and I want to be an elementary school teacher.

What would you like to teach?

Whatever *they* want me to teach. In whatever area there is a need for me. But I prefer to teach the three major subjects—math, language, and English.

* * *

I did not have a chance to speak to Li Dong-wu the first time I saw her, which was in Beijing in 1984. I was at a friend's apartment, and she was one of several neighborhood children who had come at my friend's invitation. That morning I only had enough time to talk to two, but they all filled out my simple questionnaire. During lunch as I was sifting through their responses, I came upon this:

Family name: The fourth one in the Book of Family Names
Given name: Dong-wu
Sex: If not a boy, then it must be a girl
*Place of Birth: Capital of the Qin dynasty**
Siblings: Brother—Six years older than me
His school: The best university in China

Li Dong-wu had given me a quiz, and it was my turn to respond to her, so I asked my friend to bring her around to see me. One evening the two showed up in my hotel lobby. They had been riding more than an hour on their bikes, burrowing their way through the Beijing

* 221–206 B.C.

traffic, and I was sure they were exhausted. But they said, "No," and they were laughing.

Li Dong-wu likes to laugh. She slaps her thigh when she laughs. She tells me: "My parents never tell me to behave like a girl. There is no need! They know I won't go too far." Her parents are also not anxious about her studies. "I have always been a good student" was her explanation. She has a special relationship with her brother. They argued and fought constantly when they were younger because she was a "tag-along" but resented her brother treating her like one. But now they can "really talk."

My friend, Zhao Xin, had worked with peasants in the fields of rural Shanxi for four years during the time of the Cultural Revolution. We occasionally hear her voice in the background.

Li Dong-wu begins by telling me about her relationship with her brother.

We get along very well now, but when we were small, we fought all the time. The fights were *so bad*—I mean, *so bad*. He teased me and was so bossy. And so what I did was I went to my baba and mama and I told on him. I told on him all the time. Every time I did that, he warned me not to do it again. I wasn't going to listen to him, and so the next day I would tell on him again. [Laughs.] But now we are fine. Once we got older, we stopped fighting. This was when I was around nine or ten. Now occasionally we still have "contradictions," small "contradictions," like if I slam the door too hard, he'll say, "Hey! Go easy, all right?" In the past we fought because he was bossy and he thought I was a squirt. I remember that when he went out, he didn't take me along; he locked me inside our house. But now my brother is going to be a junior in college.

Zhao Xin: I never see your brother.

Li Dong-wu (LDW): It's true. In our yard very few people have seen him. He rarely appears in our neighborhood except when he comes home and he has to pass through the courtyard or when he goes to visit his friend Xiao Liang. In the summer he stays in his room all day long. We have been living on that courtyard for three years but very few people know him. When I tell my neighbors I have a brother at home, they want to know what he looks like. [Laughs.] He keeps others wondering about him. My friends come to our apartment to play, and they never get to see him. He is always in his room, studying, reading, or playing the harmonica. He taught himself to play the harmonica. I did, too. Before he wasn't interested in music. He has a good voice, but he always sings out of tune. One day he read an article somewhere and it said that music can improve one's intelligence. Soon after, whenever he had a chance, he asked me to practice singing with him—to get the right pitch and tone. He also wanted me to learn the harmonica with him. This was about a year ago. Actually my gege is already very smart, but he wants to be even smarter. He has lots of "hidden potentials." In a year's time he is already playing the harmonica very well. Usually after listening to a song just once, he can play the melody on his harmonica.

Zhao Xin: Everybody in the neighborhood knows her [points to Dong-wu], but not her brother.

LDW: They know he exists but just haven't seen his face. . . . Now my gege and I, we chat a lot. He likes to tell me what's going on in his school, but he's still not serious when he talks to me. . . . Once he and his friends went biking all the way to Yunshui Cave.* It was very far from Beijing. On the way someone deserted the group: he turned back. Later my brother told me he had no respect for that sort of person. He said that he lacked willpower.

I like to play pranks on people. Like this afternoon [laughs], I was in Zhao Xin's office. . . .

Zhao Xin: I stepped out for a moment, and when I came back I couldn't find her. Just as I was wondering where she was, she jumped out from behind the safe and went, "Boo!" She scared the wits out of me.

LDW: But my brother, he never plays tricks on me. I just realized this the other day. He would never trick me, deceive me, or tell a lie. He is very honest, very truthful. But me, I am different. [Laughs.] But still he is quite an example for me. . . . When I see that he is in a good mood, I like to play pranks on him, and he has no idea what I am up to. I think it's so funny. Nowadays no matter what I do he just doesn't get mad at me anymore. Once when he was just getting ready to sit down, I challenged him. I said: "I dare you to sit down." Well, he did sit down, and, of course, I pulled the chair away. He went plop and landed right on the

* Yunshui Cave is in Fangshan County, about twenty kilometers southwest of Beijing.

floor. [Laughs.] Now whenever he sits down, he always makes sure first that there is a chair behind him.

Does your brother have many friends?

He does, but all from school. In our yard he has only one friend, Xiao Liang. Xiao Liang moved here from Haidian District, which was our old neighborhood. His friends from college rarely come, because Qinghua University is quite a distance from here. Besides, since he started college, he has been studying so hard, so much harder than before.

Tell me about your relationship with your parents.

I was very naughty when I was small. My parents didn't try to impose a lot of rules on me. They let me be most of the time.

What about your studies? Did they watch very closely to see how you were doing in school?

No, because I have always done well in school. [Laughs.] My mother doesn't watch over my shoulder, but she always gives me problems to solve. There is this one workbook I have, which is called *A Thousand Questions,* and it's this thick. [She shows me.] It was written in "unsimplified characters," and I couldn't recognize many of the words in it. And so my baba helped me along: he would say, "Now which character do you think this one looks like?" and I would just make a wild guess. I was about eight or nine then.

Do you have time to play after you finish your homework every day?

Usually when I finish, it's the middle of the night already. How can I play? Even if I finish my homework at school, when I come home, I help with the chores. After dinner, it's dark outside. Who will play with you? Sometimes I watch some television, but usually there is nothing good to watch. I do all my playing at school. At night I think more clearly, and I like to do my homework then. During recess most of the time I have nothing to do. If I try to work on my homework, my teacher would chase me outside. I do have team sports during gym class and after school. Our class organized our own soccer team. It's usually boys against girls. It's quite chaotic when we play. You have the forwards in front, but most of the time the fullbacks don't know what they are doing—they all somehow get in front where the forwards are. And they run out of bounds and don't even know it. [Laughs.] In the midst of all the confusion, someone scores a goal. The umpire blows the whistle and asks us to stop. He makes an arbitrary decision, and one team is very angry. The argument continues even when we are back in. Then after class, the boys tell us: "Forget it! What do you girls know about soccer?" We say to them: "How good do you think you are? Don't you know we're better than you?" Then we start to list all the good players on our team. There is Shen Yen, short but with such developed muscles! Once she missed the ball and kicked me and then tripped me. Boy, that hurt! My leg was purple and blue. She was tough, tougher than the boys.

We also play basketball with the boys. We play mixed teams. The boys teach us. The basketballs belong to us. We won them in the intramural games we played. The school usually locks up all the gym equipment. . . . The boys and girls in our class do a lot of things together. Maybe it's just our class, but we are very close. We have a good group. I'll be starting my third year in junior high. So far the boy-girl relationship in junior high is very good. In elementary school it was different. It was awful. Boys and girls started to play separately in the fourth grade. . . .

Zhao Xin: Each class has its own style, its own tendencies. The relationship depends on that. And when you have a spoiler, then that's it. There will be bad feelings.

What makes you particularly angry or happy?

Nowadays I try to be generous-spirited and broad-minded (*kuan-hung-da-liang*). Like today, my friend Xiao Hua was fooling around with me. She dragged me from my bed to the floor. I didn't want to get my dress dirty. I had put on my best dress to get ready to come here, and I didn't want to change again. So I screamed: "My dress! My dress!" But she didn't understand me. She pinned me to the floor. I was much stronger, and so I managed to get up. My dress did get dirty. But I thought, "So it got dirty. That's no big deal." I wasn't like this before. I used to bottle up all my anger. The rage filled up my body, and it came all the way up to my throat and sometimes it got stuck there. I could feel it. That was when I was nine or ten. . . . I like to cry and laugh. Crying and laughing are good for your health. Once I start to cry, I can't stop. I cried so much when I was little. I think even now I have swollen eyes from crying too much then. It's true. Look at my eyes. Do you see it? From the time when I was very little, just beginning to understand things, if anyone touched me or if something frustrated me, I cried and cried. Of course, I didn't dare to cry in front of guests, but certainly in front of my family and people whom I knew well. I stood in a corner and cried. At that time I didn't like to laugh that much. But now I laugh a lot, sometimes for no reason at all. [Laughs.] But I still cry a lot. Several times I cried in school. I don't even remember why. I know that it had nothing to do with schoolwork or conflicts with my classmates. The last time I cried was when the Chinese women's volleyball team was playing against the American team during the Olympics. I was listening to the radio in my baba's office. The Chinese team had just lost three games. At first I thought that they were just playing three games, which meant that this was *it*. I just couldn't control my tears, but there were a lot of people around, and so I ran out of the office and toward the library. I grabbed a book, held it in front of me, and went out. Someone stopped me and said that I hadn't checked out the book. The two teams did play a fourth game, and the Chinese team lost again. . . . Also when a movie gets to an emotional part, I cry. Sometimes people sitting around me stare at me. Then I have to restrain myself, but when they're not looking, I start again.

*You put down on the questionnaire that you were born in the capital of the Qin dynasty. Xian?**

Yes. I was giving you an IQ test. [Laughs.] My parents were sent to Xian for reeducation. I was born there. We didn't come back to Beijing until 1980. But whenever my mother was on a business trip, I went with her. I wandered everywhere. I remember well the place where I grew up. I can even draw you a map. We lived in the suburb of Xian. We had to take the bus to go to the city. I was there for about nine years. I didn't know much about the country—how the peasants worked and lived, but I do recall what it was like living there. I also remember the environment: the mountains, the rivers, what paths to take, the kinds of trees on the mountains. Whenever I think of Xian, I think of these things. The place that we stayed was in a small factory town, but it was surrounded by country. It had a large factory and a three-story building. What is most vivid in my memory is the times I went to the fields to dig for wild vegetables. This was not because of famine. The wild vegetables were used to make *jiao-zi* [dumplings] and soup. Really good. Why don't you come again? Next time when you're here, I'll show you where to dig wild vegetables. You can find them in Beijing too. . . .

* Actually, the Qin capital was Xianyang, a city to the northwest of Xian.

When I was little, I liked to dress up in a military uniform. I wanted to look like a Red soldier. When I got home from school, I didn't like to do my homework, and so I would pick up a trowel and go out to the field and dig for wild vegetables. I always put them in my pockets, but when I got home, they were usually crushed. You couldn't eat them, but some were all right. I liked to cook them myself.

Some children in my school were from the country. It was a school for the children of the factory workers. When I first went to school, the principal thought I was too young, but he still put me in the second grade because he thought that I had the ability. My baba at the time was a teacher in that school. I stayed in the second grade for two months. Then I was put back to first grade because I had not learned the phonic rules [of the Pinyin system], which were very important. Six months later I was back in second grade. During all these complications, my baba thought that the school didn't know what it was doing, and so he had me transferred to a school in the country. I was in that school for only a day. The gang of children at school was *so wild,* very wild. The clothes they wore were not as neat and tidy as ours. I kind of looked down on them, but I didn't show it. I was a child, and it was easy for me to get to know other children. Just when I had made a few friends, they told me to come back to my old school. Now I don't even remember what my classmates looked like.

When I was at school in Xian, I was on the athletic team. Once we went mountain climbing. At first the teacher thought I was too young to go with them, but my baba gave me permission to go, and so I went. I was very fit then. When we were climbing, I didn't even pant. But I was not so brave when it came to spooky things. At the foot of the mountain there was a grave mound. I was so scared, but thank goodness there were other people there. So I ran past it without stopping and started climbing. I didn't even dare to look back. Once I was on the mountain, I was so happy. I was skipping and running. I had such a good time. The place was full of mountain dates. They are red and prickly. We picked and picked, and I filled my pockets with them.

I also liked to play in the wheatfields, especially hide-and-go-seek. I am sure that I destroyed a lot of wheat plants. But I was light, and whenever I stepped on them, I always straightened them up. They looked all right. You could also pick wild vegetables and berries in the wheat fields.

. . .

Zhao Xin: I am in my thirties. The only times that I have been awakened by my own laughter, in the middle of the night, was when I was living in the country. Ever since I left, I have not experienced again the same kind of happiness—a sort of ultimate happiness. In the countryside, I was working with older and very experienced peasants (*lao-ba-shi*). It's sort of my personality to go all the way, to put all my effort into doing something. I was the same way when I was working in the field. I preferred to work with those *lao-ba-shi*, plowing the land and doing real work. These *lao-ba-shi* were older men in their forties and fifties. I was just a teenager. They were very funny, and I called them "old masters." I want to go back to Shanxi and find them someday. I was one of those "fervent youths" who volunteered to go to the country and work on the production teams. We were told that we were going to a place with "green hills and blue waters." But what we found were "desolate hills and barren peaks," "bare mountains and dried-up rivers." [Laughs.]

LDW: The place where I lived, the water is so clear you can see the bottom, and at the bottom are green and red stones—they are so beautiful. There were also water rats in the river and little fish. I loved to catch fish. I used a net—the kind you filter milk with. I put the net in the water, and when I saw a fish swimming by, I quickly scooped it up. But the fish always managed to slip out as soon as I scooped it up. I tried so many times but didn't catch any. Then my gege taught me a way. He tried to grab them with his hands. We caught several that way, and we put the fish in a jar. Then I said. "Not good enough. Let's go and catch some big fish." We went to a place where the river was deeper. My gege and his friends used *ga-shi*—we call it *ga-shi*. They are sort of like limestones. When you put them in the water, they fizz and give off bubbles. Actually the odor is not good for us to breathe. They put the *ga-shi* into the river to poison the big fish. After a while all the big fish floated up to the surface. They picked up the dead fish and waited until the water cleared up before jumping in to swim. The water was deeper than me, and so I didn't dare go in. I stood on the bank and watched. They also tried to find fish in the crevices. They dug with their fingers. Sometimes they could dig out a river crab. One day as they were digging, suddenly something large and black dashed out from the rocks. That was a river rat, and it gave them a scare. They all rushed to shore, and nobody dared go in again. The rat swam toward a crevice, its body swaying back and forth in the water. My brother and his friends used a bamboo stick to poke at the crevice, but the stick didn't go very far.

The water was near our house and our school. It was a big river. Now as we are talking, suddenly I remember so much, so many things one after another. In that same year, once we followed the river downstream. My gege and his friends, they walked very fast, and I was running most of the time, trying to catch up. This was far away from the bridge—the place where we caught all those fish. It was in the spring, and the frogs were laying eggs. The eggs were floating on the river in a huge patch, sticky and slimy. I didn't know what made me trip, but I fell suddenly and touched the eggs. Later I took some home. The eggs hatched into little tadpoles, but the tadpoles all died after a while.

* * *

Meeting Zheng Gao-xing in 1984 was an extra. On an especially hot and humid day, my family and I arrived in Hangzhou in the morning, and planned to do some sightseeing in the afternoon. After lunch we ventured out to the West Lake, where we met an American who spoke Chinese. Our conversation, a mixture of both languages, caught the attention of Zheng Gao-xing, who stopped to listen and didn't seem in a hurry to leave. So my husband and I persuaded him to stay and chat with us. I think he was just as eager to find out about us as we were to learn about him.

Zheng Gao-xing is an affable, cheery fifteen-year-old. Everything about him is lucent: no irony in his smile or doubts in his voice. He speaks to me in pu-tong-hua, *which, judging from his accent, must be quite an effort. Himself not a native of Hangzhou, he is here to visit a friend from his village. He tells me more about himself:*

My friend attends college in Hangzhou. He is a student of Zhejiang Institute of Technology. I am staying with him because it's summer vacation and there are empty beds in his dorm. There is also someone else from our village who goes to Zhejiang University [also in Hangzhou]. . . .

I'm from Haiyen, which is not far from here. There are four in my family. Other than my baba and mama, I also have an older sister. She is sixteen. . . . We have about a little more than four hectares of land.* We plant a lot of wheat on our land. We also plant watermelons, potatoes, and beans. Once or twice a week, my mama and baba take the watermelons, beans, and potatoes to the free market to sell. We don't

*1 hectare = 2.471 acres.

sell the wheat. We eat it ourselves or feed it to the farm animals. We also sell a portion to the government. When my parents take the watermelons and vegetables to the free market, they either carry them on the back of their bikes or load them onto a cart and pull them to the market. Usually my mama works in the fields. Sometimes my baba helps. My baba was a mason, but now he owns a small store. He sells cigarettes, candy, soy sauce, and just about everything. He has to mind the store and so my mama does most of the farming. My baba had to have permission from the government to open up the store. Now many people are doing things like this. You can open up a store in your own home as long as you build an extra room for it. That's what my father did. Someone else from our village did the same thing. In the summer I sometimes watch the store for my baba. I rarely go to the fields to work. I don't know anything about planting or farming. My parents don't let me go to the fields. They think I am too young. My older sister helps them. She just finished junior high, but she didn't take the entrance exam for high school. She plans to become a seamstress.

Did you grow up in the country?

No, by the sea, by Hangzhou Bay. When I was little, my friends and I always went swimming in the sea. We took fishing poles and nets with us to catch fish and blue crabs. Each time we could catch about three to four catties [about four to five pounds] of fish. There were so many fish that you could grab them with your hands. We looked for them among the rocks and in the crevices. They are small, but you can eat them. You sprinkle them with salt and other seasoning and then pan-fry them. They taste delicious!

When I was younger, I also liked to catch cicadas. We hung a small bag on a pole. The pole was long and could reach the cicadas in the trees. We tried to get the cicadas to fall into the bag through the tiny opening. Once it was in the bag, it couldn't get out. We also used spider webs. We wrapped them around the end of a pole and tried to get the cicadas glued onto the webs. . . .

There are also lots of small animals around where I live: chickens, ducks, pigs. And we can have cats and dogs as pets. We have a cat at home. If you want to have a dog, the dog has to get shots. That's because there is rabies in the mountainous areas around us and we don't want it to spread into our village. . . . When my baba was young, he had a dog. The dog didn't die until I was about seven or eight. She lived more than twenty years. When she died, we buried her on the beach. I was very close to that dog. I took her with me when I had to guard the melon fields or when I played war with other kids. . . . When we play war, there are two teams—each tries to escape from the other. When you are captured, you become a prisoner of the other team, and the kids on your team have to save you. When I had my dog with me, our team used her to scare the other team. We let her stand guard while we ran and hid. My dog would just keep on barking while we scrambled to find a place to hide. The other team didn't dare go near her. That's how we got away. Now I only have a cat. The cat catches mice and sparrows. We like to find sparrows, and we always take my cat with us. Sometimes we find baby sparrows, and we take them home with us and put them in a cage. Usually they don't live long, never more than ten days. We also raise chickens and pigs. Sometimes we eat the eggs, and sometimes we sell them at the free market. We don't eat chickens except during New Year's. All together we have eight chickens and a pig, a young pig. Every three or four months we take our grown pig to the market and sell it. We raise the pig until it's ready to be slaughtered—when it weighs about 150 catties [around 200 pounds]—and then we sell it and buy another young one. The government has set dates each month for buying and selling pigs: the eighth, eighteenth, and twenty-eighth. . . . I have seen people slaughtering pigs before—two persons, one holding the pig from behind and another holding her mouth and a third person jabbing a knife right in here [points to his throat]. Then the meat is either sold to the people there or to the commune store.

He tells me about his education.

I was seven when I went to first grade. I was in primary school for five years. Now I am in Penghu Junior High. Originally I was to go to Haiyen Junior High, but my father got me transferred to Penghu. He talked to the principal there, and since my entrance exam score was high enough for me to go to Penghu, he admitted me. My father wanted me to go to Penghu because it is a boarding school. In a boarding school I can concentrate on my studies and don't have to worry about doing chores and other things that I normally have to do if I am home. The distance between home and school is about eight or nine kilometers. I go home every Saturday afternoon after school finishes and come back Sunday noon. I have to study very hard at school. There are many subjects—geometry, algebra, physics, chemistry, language, politics, and English. I like language the best. In language classes we write essays—

something memorable from our childhood or our views about what's going on in our society. No, we don't ever write stories we create ourselves. . . . In our studies we put emphasis on math, language, physics, politics, and English—the subjects we'll be tested on in our entrance exam.

Do you like living at school?

Since I can't live at home, I guess living at school is all right. . . . At school we have to get up at five. After we get up, we study a little. At seven-ten, we have our morning study period. We start our formal classes at eight. We have six classes a day. We finish around four-thirty. After resting a little, we have dinner at five. From six to eight we have our study time. At eight-thirty, the light is turned off.

When do you have time to play?

We have a ten-minute recess after each class. We have two hours of lunch, and that's when we play, or talk, or do something we like. Then around dinner we have a little time to play or relax. I like living at school because our life is well ordered. We don't lose our direction. I remember when I first got there I missed my parents very much—every day I was looking forward to Saturdays and Sundays. It took me about half a semester to get used to it. I have been there for two years now.

In the future I want to go to college. Everyone at home wants me to go to college. I am anywhere between the first and fifth place in my class. When I finish college, I want to be a builder. I want to build houses and buildings in my native place so that it'll be as beautiful as Hangzhou. . . . There are about three thousand people in our village, and more than thirty of them are either in college now or have been to college. Each year we have about five to six kids passing the college entrance exam. They get into all sorts of schools, like Fudan University, Hangzhou University, Beijing University, the foreign language institutes. . . . Many are studying engineering.

What are some of the things that you do with your parents?

In the summer, when I am at home, sometimes I have to go to the market to sell watermelons with my father. I don't like doing that. I much prefer watching the store for him. I do like to go to the field to dig potatoes with my mother. Each time we can dig about three hundred catties [about 400 pounds] of potatoes. We haul them back in a cart. We feed some to the pigs and sell others either at the market or to the government. We don't like to eat potatoes. We are tired of eating them. We boil them in soy sauce until they are reddish-brown. They taste good when you eat them occasionally, but not every day. We eat a lot of fish—small fish, bream and large carp—but also pork, vegetables, and jellyfish. The jellyfish . . . usually the fishermen go out to sea to net them. Sometimes they catch so much that their boats are filled to the top and they even have to dump some back into the sea. We always rub jellyfish with salt and wash them first before putting them in a tightly covered jar with more salt, and alum. Usually after about three or four months, we take them out, soak them in water for a while and eat them with soy sauce. It's very good.

He describes his home for me.

We are the first family in our village to have a two-story house. My baba, who is a mason, and a couple of other masons built the house. There are six rooms. My parents sleep in one, and my sister and I each have our own room. There is also a storage room. My nainai has four sons, and she stays with a different son each month. My baba is the third son. His younger brother has a movie theater. He has five rooms in his house. His oldest brother is a teacher. He has four rooms in his place. They all live in the same village.

He tells me about New Year and other holidays.

All the relatives get together to eat New Year's Eve dinner. We light candles and pay respect to our ancestors. We wear new clothes and grownups give us money. There are also firecrackers and fireworks. Usually the celebration lasts about ten days. We also celebrate the Dragon Boat Festival and the Mid-Autumn Festival. And then there is something else my friends and I like to do. We go out to the fields and have a cookout. It's called a "meal from a hundred families." We set up a small tent in someone's fields and start a fire. We cook and eat and chat. That's a lot of fun!

* * *

It was Dong Dong's uncle who took me to see her. My husband and I were buying tea on top of the Longjing Mountain near Hangzhou when *he approached us and told us that he had something better at home—tea of the highest grade, leaves that were picked right after Pure Brightness (Qing-ming).* His home was only a short way down the mountain, and he could take us there. With a small band of children trailing behind us,† we walked along a path lined with the houses of Longjing tea farmers.*

The tea farmer who led the way was in a talkative mood; he had much to say about many things, from tea to politics to his experience during the Cultural Revolution. His tea—stored in an earthen jar—was expensive, his house—a newly built two-story with six rooms and a large storage space and certainly the best on the block—was impressive, and his company was wonderful. Although we had wanted to see many other places that afternoon, suddenly we were not in a hurry: adults talked, and children were invited in to watch the Olympic games. And when my husband asked him whether we might talk to any of the children in his family, he took us to his niece. Dong Dong was a tall, slender girl, soft-spoken and shy but with strong ideas about her own future. We did not really have a chat; I asked questions and she responded. But since her answers were straightforward and honest, I was quite certain that her formal manner had little to do with the tape recorder or my strangeness.

Dong Dong and I sit in a working room—a place where her uncle dries and roasts tea leaves. The door opens to the outside. Occasionally family members and neighbors peer in with curiosity. Dong Dong seems a little uneasy when that happens, but when they leave, she has much more to share. We did not close the door. Somehow it does not seem natural to block out the sounds of children and animals in the yard.

She first tells me what her day is like.

I go to Xihu [West Lake] Middle School. School lasts about six hours each day. After I get home around three-thirty, I start cooking. I have to prepare dinner every night. I have a younger brother. He is nine. He goes to a school around here. I used to do the same, but the entrance exam placed me in Xihu Middle School, which is in the city [Hangzhou]. Actually there is no middle school in Longjing. . . . After I finish preparing dinner, I have to wash clothes, all the clothes in the family. And then after dinner, I have to do the dishes. Sometimes my brother helps me. When all the chores are done, then I can do my homework.

* A solar period around the beginning of April when the Chinese sweep their family graves and pay respect to the deceased.

† There were altogether five children—my two plus the three Hangzhou children we took along on our outing. See below, pp. 203–11.

Usually that takes about two to three hours. I go to bed around eight-thirty.

In the summer, after breakfast, I help my waipo to do chores. My waigong [maternal grandfather] also lives with us. In the morning we pick vegetables from the garden and bring them to my nainai and my shushu [uncle]. They both live in Kunliao, which is very near here. It takes about half an hour to walk there. . . . My waipo is a devout Buddhist. She was a Buddhist even during the Cultural Revolution. She doesn't go to the temple anymore because she can't walk that far.

She says more about her family.

My mother picks tea leaves. She has been picking tea leaves since she was fifteen. She carries baskets of leaves home, and my uncle fires them. He roasts the leaves in a large pan. He has to constantly turn the leaves with his hands. He then dries them. Most of the time women pick tea leaves, and men roast them. Men are also responsible for watering the tea plants. They have to carry water to the hills where the tea plants grow. It doesn't take too long to climb up the hills, about fifteen minutes. We sell half the tea we harvest to the government. We get to keep the other half ourselves, and we sell it from our homes.

My baba works in an industrial acid factory in Hangzhou. He collects money. He is like a cashier. Originally he was not from this region. He came from Ningpo [about a hundred kilometers west of Hangzhou], but still we have a lot of relatives around here. . . . My didi and I get along pretty well. Sometimes we argue. He likes to play with matches and gets angry when I tell him not to do dangerous things. But still I look after him and help him with his homework.

As you grow older, do you feel that your relationship with your parents is changing?

When I was little, I had very few chores to do. I washed vegetables, and that was about it. But now they ask me to do a lot more at home. Also since I have gotten older, they are more concerned about my studies and are stricter with me. I was well behaved when I was younger, but not anymore.

At this point her older cousin who has been standing at the door asks Dong Dong something in Hangzhou dialect, which makes her seem uncomfortable about continuing the subject. We decide to talk about something else, but as soon as her cousin leaves, she tells me more about her present relationship with her parents.

If my parents want me to do something and I don't want to, I just go into my room and do my homework or something else. . . . They want me to become a factory worker. But I think what they want most is that I pass the college entrance exam. Only if I can't get into a university, then they'll want me to become a factory worker.

And what about yourself? What would you like to do in the future?

I want to be an athlete, a runner. I was in a provincial competition last year, and I came in fourth. I run every morning with a friend. I want to run faster; I want to get better. Also I want to study medicine. I want to become a doctor. I am not that good at science, but I am going to keep on trying.

3

Weaving and Weaving Many Feathers

In 1984, I visited a community on top of a hill in the city of Chongqing. The place, comprising office buildings and living quarters, was connected with the Institute of Scientific and Technical Information. The Institute publishes the Chinese version of Scientific American, *and it was Gerard Piel who had arranged for me to be there; he had telexed his associates in Chongqing weeks in advance, telling them about my visit and asking them to help me to make contact with the children in their community. This was how I came to know Fang Kan, who at the time was sixteen; both his parents worked as translators at the institute.*

It was a late morning in August, and we were in the formal reception room of the institute. Fang Kan had two friends with him, Li Ji and Zhang Jing, but it was he who dominated the conversation. He was articulate and fluent in pu-tong-hua, *unusual for a native of Sichuan. At the end of our session, I invited Fang Kan to lunch with me at my hotel. (I was to return to the institute that afternoon to talk to another group of children.) A driver from the institute offered us a ride. The car spiraled down the hill and then plunged out onto a wide avenue. It was around noon; the most populous city in China was seething with activity.*

We continued our conversation in the car and in the dining room. Later in my hotel room, with my tape recorder turned on to catch every phrase, we chatted for another hour.

On the return trip, a city bus dropped us off at the gate of the institute compound. But to get back to the building with the formal reception room, we had to follow a complicated passage that tunneled up through the staff houses, up hundreds of steps, and by the time we reached the top of the hill, I was quite out of breath. Fang Kan turned and said with a smile, "That was my short cut!"

We went straight to the reception room, where a group of high school students was already waiting for me. Fang Kan recognized a few and nodded to them, but he was eager to talk to one particular boy. The two stood in a corner and chatted quietly, absorbed in their conversation and in each other. I overheard Fang Kan saying to the other boy in Sichuan dialect: "I didn't know you were going to be here." Later they told me they were best friends.

That afternoon in Chongqing was special for me because of these two boys—and the affection between them. The next day I was determined to see them again. I took the bus back to the gate at the bottom of the hill. Guided by only a general sense of where Fang Kan's house was (the day before he had told me it was near the building where we met), I started ascending "the stairs to heaven." The long short cut stretched even longer as I made several wrong turns. When I finally found my way to the basketball court in front of the familiar building, someone directed me to Fang Kan's home, on the ground level of a recently constructed two-story building. He was well known in the neighborhood because he was class president, first in his class, and a recipient of numerous awards.

Fang Kan was surprised to see me. He introduced me to his older brother, a friendly person who asked me to stay and chat. They took me to what I believe was their study, a small room with wooden desks and chairs. Perhaps it was also used as a living room—I wasn't sure. His brother told me he knew all about my eventful day with Fang Kan, and this time he dominated the conversation, talking very fast and moving quickly from topic to topic. Fang Kan, who had had so much to say the day before, was very quiet, though he smiled and watched us as his brother chatted away. It was very clear that he loved his brother greatly.

Afterward, Fang Kan and I walked to Wang Lian's home. Along the way, he showed me where he used to live. "We were all crammed into a single room," he told me, "but it was all right. I didn't mind it at all."

Wang Lian's home was in an older section of the residential com-

pound, and, according to Fang Kan, it was a good deal smaller. Wang Lian was even less prepared for my appearance than Fang Kan had been. A table in the living room where he was working on math homework was piled with papers and books, and the chaos was in marked contrast to Fang Kan's clean and orderly study. Fang Kan, helping him to tidy up the living room, seemed rather embarrassed by the fact that his friend was in shorts: "Go and change," he said to him quietly, "and get something to drink for Chin A-yi [*Auntie Chin*]*." Wang Lian disappeared briefly and came back with orange sodas, but he hadn't changed.*

I hadn't brought along my tape recorder this time—it hadn't seemed necessary. I had ventured out that morning simply because I had felt that I had to find my friends and talk to them one more time. We did talk, about childhood and growing up, about dreams and more dreams. Thoughts and memories were all that mattered that morning. Fang Kan sat in a chair next to the table; Wang Lian stood or sat close by—I don't now remember which—and both were facing me. I bent forward on my bamboo chair to listen. Sometimes I would just gaze at them, from one to the other; their faces were illuminated by a soft, dim light. At that moment I understood clearly why I had to be there. Now, as I reflect upon that day, I ask: Is this what Lytton Strachey meant by "to come close to life"?—"To look at it, not through the eyes of Poets and Novelists, with their beautifying arrangements or their selected realisms, but simply as one actually does look at it, when it happens. . . . To do that even with a bit of it—with no more than a single day—. . . surely that might be no less marvellous than a novel or even a poem, and still more illuminating, perhaps!"

When it was time to go, they accompanied me down the hill. We made a detour to their school, which they said they wanted to show me. I took a picture of them standing on the soccer field as the August sun poured down its radiance on their tall, slender figures. Their image in print gives a fixity to things that in my memory are sometimes vividly clear, sometimes baffled.

The following transcriptions are based on tapes of my conversations on the first day, together with my notes of events and other talk on the second.

"Learning" is the first topic.

Fang Kan (FK): When I was small, I was very lively, very naughty. I used to lead a group of kids, and we ran around and amused ourselves with all sorts of things. I treated learning like this: as long as I did all the assigned homework, that was enough. In tests, I got high marks, but come to think of it, I don't think it was a very creative or flexible kind of learning. In areas where I should have developed myself, I didn't—they were left uncultivated. In junior high school I began to realize something else: the students came from different areas; they were all top achievers, and the competition suddenly became more intense. Under that kind of pressure, I was at first more passive—I was forced to work hard—but after a while, after putting in some effort, I began to establish my lead as a top student in my class. Then I felt more relaxed, and learning became more interesting. It became more natural. I no longer felt I was forced into doing anything. I was more at ease and confident, and learning was more fun.

In Wang Lian's living room the next day, Fang Kan tells me:

We were very happy when we were children. We were without cares and we were wild. We played war all the time. I had fun being a child. Then things started to change when I got to junior high. We became serious, our workload became heavier, and our goals were more or less decided for us. We were to go to college.

Wang Lian (WL): Before college, there is really nothing for us to think about. But that's our ticket to better things, the only way we can realize some of our dreams.

FK: When we were young, we had no toys and so we made swords and guns and we invented games, very creative games. Now that we are older, pressure from exams doesn't allow us to develop ourselves in that way. We've learned too much theoretical knowledge and not enough practical knowledge. We hardly work with our hands. Our parents are even worse, if they are intellectuals. We lack the materials and equipment to learn practical knowledge. . . .

This sudden awareness [of the pleasures of learning] . . . I think it happened because I was doing well in class. I had more confidence. Psychologically I was more secure. I was able to get rid of whatever burden had been there before. Also, our class teacher was very concerned about what we thought. He taught us better ways of studying. Whenever he came across something in the newspaper about examples of how others were able to achieve because of their rational and systematic study habits, he read them to us. We could always compare ourselves with these examples and incorporate their methods with our own. This was very different from elementary school, when we had to memorize everything. We came to understand that learning is not just memorizing what the teachers and the books say. After the class we have to think about these problems and practice some more.

Tell me more about your elementary school education.

FK: It was very rigid. The teachers taught us things in class, afterwards we did exercises, and that was all. We were very young, our minds were open; if someone taught us something meaningful, it was very easy for us to absorb it and remember it. But no one did that. We didn't have any activities outside the classroom, either. I think extracurricular activities are very important. After school, when we got home, there wasn't any space for us to run around, and so we got together in gangs and roamed around the neighborhood. There was no way that we could develop our talents and abilities, like in sports or in writing. Primary schools put too much emphasis on test scores. They only care about getting us to score high on exams and not about developing our abilities. It seems that many students who get high marks in elementary school somehow start to slip when they get to middle school. I think it's because their way of learning is too rigid. On the other hand, there are students who didn't do all that well at first—maybe their scores were in the eighties and that's because they made careless mistakes on tests—but because their way of thinking was more flexible, they could put their minds to use as soon as they got to junior high. Junior high allows you to do that—it requires you to do more thinking. A lot of my friends agree that primary school shouldn't put too much stress on the scores, that there should be more school activities to help the students to develop their minds. Kids that age like to play. They are bouncy and lively. Their way of thinking is simple. They need teachers to give them a start. There is no way they can understand so many different problems! If students very early on can understand the actual purpose of learning and acquire real interests, their abilities can be more fully cultivated.

Li Ji, a year older and a grade higher than Fang Kan, is seventeen and will be a senior in high school. He and Fang Kan attended the same middle school and seem to know each other well. He comes from an "intellectual" family. His parents, too, are translators in the Institute of Scientific and Technical Information. His older brother also works in Chongqing as an industrial engineer in a research laboratory.

Li Ji (LJ): Yes. When I was in elementary school, it was still under the Gang of Four. The atmosphere at school was terrible. Every day the teachers taught us just a little bit. When we got home, we had very little homework to do, so we played most of the time. We didn't do much for those five years. We learned very little in first and second grade. I think it wouldn't have made any difference if I skipped them altogether. [Laughs.] The Gang of Four was toppled when I was in fourth grade.

Did you learn anything from those years of playing?

LJ: We liked to make models. I am sure that we learned something from doing that. We also like to play war games. Those games teach you about loyalty, especially to friends.

We discuss the parents' role in a child's decisions about his future. I ask, as you were growing up, were you trained to be independent?

FK: Parents mainly want us to create our future through our own efforts. They don't want us to be dependent on them. And so it's important for us to learn to make choices for ourselves. Parents can only inform us about what's going on outside—give us some references. But you have to do your own thinking and make your own decisions.

I was trained to be independent. Ever since I was little, I've always done things myself. I didn't need my parents to wash my clothes, help me get dressed, or to keep a watch on my studies. I've always looked after myself. Many kids need their parents to be next to them when they are studying. I don't. My parents are very busy with their jobs. They have to work long hours, even at night. So not only don't they have time to give me individual attention but also I don't want their help. Because I feel that if I study myself—dig into things myself—it's more interesting. If I am pressured to study and do well in school, then the learning is more passive. In learning I like to take the initiative. Only when I come upon difficult problems that I cannot solve myself, I go to my parents and ask them for help. I have always tried to do my homework, my own studying myself. Ever since I was in junior high, I've pushed myself to do my own learning.

LJ: When I was little, I always listened to my parents. Now I have my own ideas, but I still discuss all sorts of issues with them. I can talk to both of them about almost everything. We spend a lot of time chatting and talking and arguing about my studies, society, and just everyday things.

FK: My mother . . . is more cautious and is more concerned with trivial things. I like to talk to her about everyday matters. My father is busier with his work. He is a quiet person, not very sociable. I talk to him about science, problems in math or science that are hard to solve. But not everyday things. He doesn't care about them, anyway.

What about the relationship between parents?

FK: We have seen parents quarreling, but we don't talk about it with our friends. In our country, parents quarrel but after a while everything is all right. [Laughs softly.] Sometimes the argument gets to be pretty bad, but somehow the problem eventually seems to get solved by itself. The arguments have a lot to do with the family's financial problems and also with how to divide the chores up at home. Because wages are low, money becomes tight when there is the added responsibility of supporting other family members. [Laughs again.]

How does this affect the children?

FK: We study, and it's our responsibility to study well, to create our own futures. Of course, we also understand the situation at home. We all know that our parents have worked very hard to raise us, to support us. We all understand the situation and we try to be frugal. And usually we don't have any big requests. There is also tremendous pressure for us to do well on our exams. If we don't, then we feel we haven't lived up to their expectations. Even during vacations we don't feel at ease.

What about more personal problems? Do you talk to anyone about them?

FK: I like to talk to my gege about them. It seems that it's easier to talk to people closer to your own age. My parents were born in the nineteen thirties. As for the way we think, nothing gets through to them—there is no real communication between us. They always try to contradict whatever we think is right. And so we don't say much. When we young people get together, we are carefree, and there is nothing we can't say to each other. But when we talk to our parents . . . well, in our country, we attach a great deal of importance to age—the difference between the older and the younger in a family—so we have to talk to them respectfully, and we can't be at ease. . . . To older persons, you have to be respectful and observe distinctions. In a conversation you have to watch out what you say. If the wording isn't right, you get scolded.

LJ: I don't feel that with my parents I have to be careful of what I am saying. I say whatever is on my mind, and that's all right with them.

The boys agree that Fang Kan's relationship to his parents is more "typical."

What are some of the important values your parents have passed down to you?

FK: Mostly how to handle affairs, how to resolve conflicts when dealing with other people.

Which one of your parents has influenced you more?

FK: My mother. She always consults my baba on important matters. But when something happens, she is always the one who represents the family. My baba is a sort of lifeless, spiritless person. [Laughs.] . . . When it comes to handling things, my mother's pet phrase is: "You should not harm others, but be careful and don't let others harm you." The reason is, she says, that there are all kinds of people out there. And no matter whom you are dealing with—friends or enemies—you should not have any bad intent. Your conscience must be clear. If the other person wants to attack you for some reason or another, he will think twice, because you have never caused him any harm. . . . People in my parents' generation are cautious. That's because they have experienced the Cultural Revolution. They are very sensitive. They have all kinds of suspicions about the most trivial things. But we are young and we are different. We are ready to accept whatever happens. We are not so hesitant. We don't have too many apprehensions about the future.

To Fang Kan, experience is a way of explaining his parents' sensitivity and suspicions. During the Cultural Revolution, I learn, both his mother and his father were sent, at different times, to reeducation camps to do manual labor. And his maternal grandfather had starved to death during the 1961 famine. Fang Kan tells me more about him.

FK: At one time he was a high school teacher, but later he had a little business; he sold snacks and soybean milk. He started doing this even before the Liberation. After the Liberation, he couldn't make a living, and, not only that, he was also attacked. His little business was considered private ownership, and so he was publicly criticized and denounced. Actually, the central government wasn't like this—it allowed a certain amount of small private ownership—but the people on the lower level wanted to show how "left" they were. They misinterpreted things. They thought that anything private was bad, and things got out of hand. The central government did not know what was happening at the lower level. The situation really got out of hand.

Both you and Li Ji have older brothers. Do tell me more about them.

LJ: My elder brother is now twenty-seven. He was an "educated youth" during the Cultural Revolution: he was sent to the countryside to work with the peasants. He was there for three years. He had a lot more tempering than me. He passed the college entrance the first year it was offered again [1977]. When he came back from the countryside, I was still very little. He said that the work had been hard and that the life there wasn't easy. He told us very little about those three years. Now we talk more about the present and the future. . . . When he was away during the Cultural Revolution, he came home only about twice a year, and we hardly spent any time together. But now he lives at home, we have lots of time together.

FK: My brother is a junior in Xinan Normal College. After college, he will be assigned to a teaching position in a high school or a technical college. He'd like to teach in a college. He studies mathematics—mainly computer science, and he wants to teach in a college because very few high schools have computer facilities.

I would not have known much more about Fang Kan's brother, except for these few facts, had I not gone to see them the second day. Being with the two of them, I could make some sense of what they shared. His brother told me more about himself:

I grew up during the Cultural Revolution era. At that time school was a joke. We did nothing but play until we were in junior high. We skipped school and did as we pleased. We didn't have any foundation to speak of. I wasn't at all like what my brother is now. He has a broad knowledge of things, in math, science, and language. We were stuffed like ducks during our junior year in high school, to get ready for college entrance. But there was no foundation to build on. Now that I'm in college, I'm not really interested in what I'm doing except maybe the computer science courses I've taken. But what choices do I have? Even with computer science, my school is short of good teachers and facilities. We don't have the same learning conditions as the students at Qinghua University. Then after college we're assigned to work units according to "need." There's no choice involved. In this society, it's difficult to make changes. You just have to adjust to your environment. My brother and the kids from his generation are too idealistic. Life out there is not the way they perceive it.

Fang Kan is a keen observer and an avid conversationalist. Though he is prudent and thoughtful, he is also eager to tell his story. He recognizes the merit of reticence, but words pour from him. He has much to say about socialism and capitalism, China's immediate and distant past, youths and peasants, heroes and the Chairman.

We first encounter Fang Kan's thoughts on history and tradition:

FK: In our minds, China has a long history and thousands of years of culture. Although we have a long and superior cultural tradition, the history—the feudal history—is not necessarily a glorious one. This long feudal history has made us ignorant. The feudal way of thinking is still deep-rooted within us. No one is *conscious* of it, but these feudal ideas keep creeping up on us from nowhere at all, and they are reflected in our conduct and in our daily lives.

What kind of feudal ideas are you referring to?

FK: For example, many writers today talk about reforms. But some of their writings only give the appearance of being concerned with the present; actually they long for the past. It gives you a feeling . . . a feeling that they are not revealing clearly what they truly want to say. Now a lot of people like to read martial-art novels. You'll find many feudal ideas in them—the idea of brotherhood and loyalty (*yi-qi*) and the idea of "blind worship" (*mang-mu chong-bai*). Also in many novels, the main characters are depicted as being godlike. To be godlike . . . I think every person's abilities are limited, but to laud someone to the sky. . . . I think people in foreign countries are not like the Chinese. For you, it doesn't matter who you are, even if you're the president, people can still criticize you. But our country is different. It came from a feudal state. Feudal ideas are still going strong, like the relationship between ruler and ministers. . . .

When a person becomes a hero, we exalt him. I think everyone in a society, no matter what he does, is a part of that society. Each of us simply makes a different contribution to our society.

Who, then, do you think is a hero?

LJ: A person who can bail out his country, his people, during a crisis. I think *that* person is a hero. No matter how much time passes, people of later generations will praise you. I think this kind of person is a hero. No matter how time changes and ideologies change, people will consider your accomplishments as glorious. That's the kind of person. . . .

During the Cultural Revolution young people looked upon Chairman Mao as their Red Sun. He was the source of their being and well-being, and they worshipped him. How do kids of your generation view him now?

FK: Now, I think, we're more realistic about who he was. We no longer regard him as a great man without faults. Anyone who knows anything about politics and philosophy knows that no one is perfect. Of course, we all realize that Chairman Mao in the past made many contributions. He liberated the peasants and the workers in the shortest time possible. He transformed China into a safe and stable socialist state. But later in his life, especially during the 1960s, he did things that were very wrong. Everyone feels this way. Some have gone to an extreme and they say that Chairman Mao was the worst kind of person, that he made absolutely no contributions to Chinese society. These are students in junior high and primary schools. They are younger, not like us. We are more knowledgeable and more experienced. Those kids lack analytical abilities, and they are influenced by what others tell them. . . . Of course during those years, life was hard and people had a lot of gripes. And the kids hear complaints from the older people. But we all know that Chairman Mao led us during the Liberation and during the 1950s he made more contributions. We also know that the mistakes he made later on were very serious ones. If he had not made these mistakes, our country would have been more progressive and prosperous. There were errors in his guiding ideology. He was too impractical. We all agree on this view, and we can say it to anyone. No more misgivings.

I think it's natural to judge Chairman Mao this way, because he was a man and not a god. So is there anything we can't say about him? Our country should be like other countries. Everything should be open to discussion. Nothing secretive. Now we say what we want to say about Chairman Mao. But a few years ago, when the central government had not decided about how to appraise him, the trend was to attack him and to deny his accomplishments. Sometimes in class, when a teacher mentioned his name or his writings, all the students would start jeering. But ever since the central government decided on a "correct appraisal" of him, many students have changed their attitudes. We still read his essays and poems, the ones he wrote earlier in his life.

During the 1960s, there was a leader, Tao Zhu, who said that every man has defects just as the sun has black spots. Some insisted that he was alluding to Chairman Mao. They said that Chairman Mao had no black spots, that he was the brightest sun. Tao Zhu was severely criticized and in the end was beaten to death. This was after several years of imprisonment. . . .

Have your parents told you what happened in Chongqing during the violent period of the Cultural Revolution?

FK: There was a lot of fighting in Chongqing because there was a large armory here. There was no force from outside that came in and tried to bring things under control. And so the fighting got worse. I was just born then. That was in 1968. That was the worst year. Later it got better. At night stray bullets were flying everywhere. That was quite scary. Once there were two sides fighting near Yangjiajun [a suburb of Chongqing], and more than a hundred people were killed. For several days, the dead were left there unburied and the smell was terrible. The passersby were frightened. Nobody dared claim the bodies. Finally the Liberation Army moved in and buried the dead. There were two sides. Most of them were youths, high school students. Intellectuals also took part. They were all full of courage and vigor. Each side claimed they were protecting the revolution's "fruits of victory," and each attacked the other. The fighting lasted for more than a year. People here stayed home most of the time. They only dared go out during the day, not at night. In the beginning, people used knives, sticks, and then they used guns. Many opened fire for fun, and the bullets could accidentally hit you. There was no way to protect yourself. They even sank a ship in the Yangtze River. At one point they even set up cannons on ships and pretended that they were on battleships.

Do you think that young people nowadays are capable of the same behavior?

FK: I think that because young people in general are more malleable, they are also more easily influenced. If the influence is bad, they will go on the wrong path. Plus, they are emotional and energetic. They don't take everything into consideration. Once they are aroused, it's hard to . . . Anyway it's easy to manipulate them. If you use them in the right way, they can do a lot of good. If not, they can do a lot of harm. Youths today use their minds a lot more, not like then, which wasn't long after the Liberation, and young people were more immature. They lived during the transitional period between the old and the new societies. They had just come to know the happiness of the new society, and they cherished this happiness, so when they heard that so-and-so dared to insult the revolution, they were very angry. Kids today think much more carefully before they act.

During the 1960s, there was a famine. That was when my grandfather died. At the time we were paying back loans to the Soviets and there was a mass famine in Sichuan. Many died. In the cities it was a little better, but in the countryside it was . . . Many peasants ate a kind of white mud—I have never seen it—that could temporarily fill their stomachs. But if you eat too much of it, it's no good: you can't go to the bathroom. But to survive, you had to eat it. Sichuan was a lot worse than other places. Many people fled from Sichuan. Then in 1974, 1975, there was another famine. We all went to the [institute's] dining hall to eat because there was nothing to eat at home. In the dining hall you could get a bowl of clear broth.

Fang Kan's brother: Dried sweet potatoes were sent to us from Shandong, the Northeast, and Beijing. The people there got so fed up with the people in Sichuan that they put notes in the sweet potato sacks, calling us "Sichuan rats." They said that we were stealing food from them, that we were too dependent on them.

FK: I think no matter who is in power, his government should first think about the common people. If the people are forced to do something desperate, that's no good. . . .

During the Cultural Revolution many intellectuals were criticized, but my parents' work unit was directly under the central government, and so their situation was better. There was no full-scale criticism; nevertheless, certain people *had* to be attacked. In fact, several old cadres—some from the Red Army—and those who had "foreign connections" were imprisoned. Some of them had come from Taiwan or had been in the air force in Taiwan. Some had relatives overseas. Some were old scholars. They were all considered suspects. They were all put in pigpens. We were very small then. So we laughed at them, saying that they were dirty. They were eating chaff. We didn't hit them. We didn't understand anything then. Our parents told us that they raised pigs. We didn't understand it, but we knew that they slept there in the pens. We liked to go there and play. Most people were sympathetic toward them. They were released just before the end of the Cultural Revolution. A lot were old soldiers from the Red Army.

LJ: My older brother who was sent to the countryside during the Cultural Revolution told me that the good peasants were very good to the youths sent there, that they were very concerned about them. There wasn't much food, but they ate a lot, and the peasants always gave them enough to eat.

How do young people nowadays view the peasants?

LJ: Young people in the cities are not very concerned about the peasants.

FK: We feel that . . . Our country, during thousands of years of feudal rule and being an agricultural country all that time, the peasants in the past were always oppressed. And because of these historical circumstances, the peasants have "the mentality of a small producer." They care only about having a peaceful environment where they can farm and live. But they don't know how to create such an environment for themselves. In the past, whenever there was a peasant revolt, the leaders were usually not real peasants, but were disguised as peasants. Peasants only care about satisfying their basic needs—food, clothing, and shelter. They should struggle for something higher. We students feel that the peasants should be better educated. They should be awakened. They should understand that they must work not only for their livelihood but also for their society. Many people think that peasants are low-class and ignorant. I don't think that way. Because our country in the past was a feudal state, the peasants were not properly educated.

For instance, there is electricity in the cities. At night, we watch television and listen to tape recorders. The peasants don't have electricity. Around seven, it's already dark, they chat a little and then they go to bed at eight, and the next day they have to get up and do another day of work. They have no cultural life. Only the peasants living near the cities can watch television. But it's very important to have a cultural life! Through television you can understand what's going on in the outside world. You can understand your society in general and keep up with the times.

What about the children from peasant families? Don't they want to become better educated?

FK: Yes, but most of them are the ones who live near the cities. The peasants living in remote mountainous regions are still very backward. Our country has also created a feudal way of thinking: no college graduate wants to go to the mountainous or frontier regions because life is hard in those places. No one wants to go, and the people there are already backward. Plus, the outside world is developing so fast, and so now the gap is becoming even wider. The government now encourages students to go to these places, but the college graduates . . . [Laughs softly.] Many people are not willing to go because the quality of the material and cultural life in these regions is so poor. We also don't understand the languages or customs of the minority peoples. And, the pay isn't good, and the climate is hard to get used to. Many parents simply don't want their children to go to these areas. I think I don't have any problems with it.

Many urban people still look down on the peasants. Young people look down on them perhaps because they are uneducated and don't understand the developing trends in our society. They have the manners of a "small producer": they like to bargain when they buy things, and that annoys people. They think that peasants are petty, that they care too much about money and trivial things.

LJ: This sort of bias is very widespread. Young people don't care to learn about the peasants or their way of life. When my brother and other students were sent to the countryside, they had a much better understanding of peasant life.

Do you feel that because students spend so much time on book learning, they might ignore other aspects of life, for instance, learning to relate to others on a larger scale beyond family and friends?

FK: When you enter society, you have to relate to all sorts of people. If you have good relations with people at work, there is harmony.

Otherwise, there will be a lot of contradictions. It also will affect your performance at work.

Young people nowadays are willing to . . . actually, they're going through changes in this direction. We are all more aware of the question of how to become a part of society. We try to go forward. It's not like several years ago when we were only concerned with book learning, when we knew nothing about human relations and the ways of the world. Now we are more in touch with society, and we begin to understand certain social phenomena and problems. We pay more attention to these things. It's very important to do this. If you get along with people, it's more likely for you to have a more even relationship with everyone.

In our class, it's impossible to be good friends with everyone, but we always greet each other with a nod. Relations are always harmonious. We might not be good friends with everybody, but at least we show basic courtesy to each other. And because we do, it's easier to ask a favor from someone even though you don't know him well. Otherwise, it would be hard to open your mouth and ask if you have never talked to that person before. In general, we pay attention to these things. We try to maintain harmony and try to avoid direct conflicts.

Which relationship is most important to you?

FK: I feel . . . I feel the relationship between brothers is more open and direct, but our relationship to our parents is more important. With brothers, there is nothing you can't say to each other. You can say what your view of things is, and even though it might be different from his, it's all right. It's not going to hurt you in the future. But if you talk to people outside your family and you don't know them well, and you talk about problems you shouldn't, then you are exposing too much of yourself. If he attacks you, there's nothing you can do about it. Talking to parents brings results—greater results. When you have voiced your opinions, they can give you suggestions based on their own experience. But with those in the same generation—your brothers and sisters—you share similar views. Talking to them is not the same as talking to your parents.

And what about your best friends? When you talk to them, do you have to be on guard?

FK: No. You can say anything to your best friend. He is like your brother. But if you meet someone casually and the conversation seems to be going well . . . but if you don't really know his character, it's best to keep certain things to yourself. You should not let yourself be completely exposed. You can have a brotherly relationship with a friend, but you must first understand him, and your interests and views must be similar.

You speak of a brotherly relationship that you have with your friends. What about your relationship with girls? In your middle school, do girls and boys do things together?

FK: We go on outings in groups. In our society we don't encourage individual activities between girls and boys. It's not that it is not allowed; but when a girl is too open and at ease with boys, she invites other people's attention and it's not appropriate. In high school our teachers disapprove of any closeness between boys and girls, even when they are in groups. And so there isn't much understanding between us.

Actually I don't know what's the matter with girls. They're not interested in sports, in keeping their bodies fit. They don't care much about current events. They study very hard and they read novels and that's about all they do. Their interests are very limited. You can't get them involved in any kind of heated debate because they are not interested and they don't care. Maybe this is society's doing. This is an element of the feudal society that has passed down to us. Girls are even more protected and dependent than we are. And mothers—they are very caring but maybe too caring. They are tedious, but still we are very devoted to them.

LJ: I think men and women are more equal in China than in other countries. At home, both my parents do the chores; there is no difference between them, and I think this is right. But in the country, I understand, it's different. Usually the peasants prefer to have boys, and the women work in the fields and then also have to do most of the chores at home. In the city, men do more chores than women. [Laughs.]

FK: I think men and women should be equal in society. But not in every way. Some work men can do but women cannot. Other work, women can do but men cannot. I hope that in a family men and women are equal. In society, they should also be equal. But too much equality is not a good thing either. [Laughs.]

Fang Kan reflects on living in a socialist state:

We can't say that there is absolute equality in the society we live in, and that what happened during the Cultural Revolution was not our Party's fault. The Party was wrong in not stopping the extremist tendencies right away. It did not intend to have things happen the way they did. People on the lower level violated the Party's directives. But now our country has made a good start in industry and agriculture. In other areas we are not the most backward country. We live in a stable and secure society that has been good to its people, but this is not enough. We are still quite far from our goal. All people have food to eat but we don't eat well. We have security, but our living standards are still low. We have to improve in these areas. In other words, our socialist society is still in its childhood stage. It is not yet fully developed. Therefore we need to adopt technologies and methods from outside to help us establish a sound economic foundation. Only then we can arrive at our goal.

In the process of economic expansion, do you think that people might care too much about material gains and consequently forget about the socialist ideals?

FK: Yes, that is a problem. In recent years, since our economic situation has improved, people have become more selfish. Each thinks for himself. I hope the trend will not continue to be like this. I know it's impossible to get rid of selfishness completely, but people should not go too far. When the country is in trouble, everyone should help.

How do you feel about capitalism?

LJ: Some of my friends feel that systems in other countries are better and their standards of living are higher. They say that here we work eight hours a day, but we are not efficient; in other countries they are more efficient and after work they have more time to play and relax. But we have to work and after work to do house chores, and because of inefficiency, we don't get enough work done and we don't get to play. So we lose both ways.

Most foreign countries allow private ownership. I am talking about large companies and capitalists. In order to earn more money, the capitalists have to improve the workers' conditions. This way, their productivity rises, and it's also possible to create more advanced technologies. But here we all "eat in the canteen, from the same large pot." It makes no difference at all whether you work hard or not. And so we think that the policy of "eating from the same large pot" doesn't really work.

FK: Our society is going through a lot of changes. Take Shenzhen. It has done very well, and so our government is opening up fourteen more cities. The enterprises in Shenzhen are just like those in a capitalist society, how wages and benefits for the workers are determined, for instance. But within the factories socialist principles still prevail. This way we can avoid excessive competition among factories and bankruptcies will not occur. We avoid being an exact copy of capitalism, but there is more incentive for the workers. Our present policy encourages advanced technology as a capitalist system does, but we also preserve the equality that we find in a socialist system, and our progress is planned and more balanced.

LJ: Our inefficiency and indifference have something to do with job assignments. After college, we think it's better for us to look for our own jobs rather than to be assigned to work units. That way we can handle our own affairs.

FK: There are some colleges that allow students to look for jobs themselves. Shenzhen University is one. When factories or companies come to recruit, the teachers make recommendations according to the students' special fields and abilities. Then, if you're recommended, you have to go to that company to take a test. If you don't pass the test, you have to stay in school. This way, the competition among students is more intense. Now when a person gets into a college, very often he feels that he has gotten into a "safe" (*bao-xian-ku*). The government guarantees his food and board. After college he'll have a job. It's like having a "golden rice bowl." No one can break it. But the new policy will make students work harder. Even if they get into a college, they'll have to do well or they won't get a job and will have to stay back one more year. In this way, our society can progress and living standards can become better. Young people today are getting more and more open-minded. They are willing to learn from capitalist societies.

What about other influences from capitalist societies, music for instance?

FK: A lot of kids love the popular songs from Hong Kong. I think that's because we've been isolated from the rest of the world for so long and once we begin to open up, everything from outside seems strange and wonderful. We've never seen these things before and we think that they're better than what we have. But that is not necessarily true. Like the electronic instruments that seem to sound better than the *er-hu*.

There are more feelings expressed in Western music, but Chinese music is deeper and more graceful. People are tired of "model operas." But actually we have not given full expression to our traditional art and culture. . . . Most of the kids do not appreciate Peking operas. Our taste in art and music is not so hot. Our master performers all look the same and sound the same to us. We can't appreciate why they're so good. Also the operas are so long! It takes them hours to finish; those last few lines, last few words, especially seem to go on and on and on. [Laughs.] We just don't have the patience or the time to listen. We have our studies to do. . . . Several years ago we blindly loved anything that came from the West, no matter whether it was good or bad. This year our government started to do some cleaning up, and the situation is getting better. Of course we don't want the clean-up to mean no outside influence at all; it is just the bad elements like pornographic songs from Hong Kong. Patriotic songs and songs that express our love for our native land are more suitable for us. They do not corrupt our minds and they still retain some of the Hong Kong flavor. . . . Anyway, our taste in music is very different from our parents'. Whenever we turn on the radio, they start complaining: "Not that kind of music again!"

What about kids who create problems? Do you know anything about them?

FK: There are kids who come from families that have very little discipline. The parents just let their children do anything. Or they come from divorced families where neither parent looks after them. Some of these kids have learning problems, and the pressure from home is so great that they finally give up and fool around all the time. They don't go to school in the morning, but they go home at the regular time, and no one at home knows where they've been all day. Most of them are from working-class families. You see, in a working-class family parents are more "unrestrained." They do and say things as they please. They scream and yell and break things. They have little control when they are angry. The children are influenced by their parents' behavior. They catch on fast.

A good friend of mine in Shanghai, the son of a factory worker but himself an intellectual, had a different view of this matter. In a long evening conversation he told me rather emotionally about the children of factory workers: "There is a great deal of prejudice on the part of intellectuals and their children against these kids. They think they have discipline problems, that they commit crimes, the reasons being that they can't communicate with their parents and their parents can't help them with their schoolwork. But sometimes it is precisely because of these factors that these children achieve more individual development. About half my classmates who did well academically are in fact children of factory workers. Because their parents did not watch them closely, they had to be self-motivated." A high school student in Beijing who came from an intellectual family made the same observation to me about his working-class classmates, whom he found to be "more creative" because "less confined."

Fang Kan comments further on those youths who have broken the law:

Most of the criminals who are sentenced to death are in their twenties and thirties. These are people who have committed robbery, murder, or rape. Early this year about a hundred and forty people were executed. Each month more than ten are executed in Chongqing. We have very strict rules and regulations. This is the law: those who deserve to die will be executed; those who are borderline cases will also be executed. This is the way to ensure order. In the last couple of years, after some "rectification," the streets are much safer. Before, in 1981 and 1982, the problems were a lot worse, young people carrying weapons—knives. I think this was due to the Hong Kong influence. Kids were blind in their admiration for the kind of freedom found in a capitalist society. They thought that the social trend was toward more freedom and that this meant "anything is possible." Now, after the rectification, crimes are down. All the executions are done in public. All the criminals are ignorant and uneducated—peasants and transient workers. They don't know what the laws are. Some are also victims of the Cultural Revolution, people who didn't get an education. They commit crimes for the most ridiculous reasons—for little bits of money. They must not be acting rationally.

At the end Fang Kan talks about his future:

At this point I am not really sure what I want to do years from now. I'd like to do work that is more creative—computer science, business administration, biological engineering. These are the more advanced technologies and they're also more practical. Like in computer science, you have to design your own software. I think that's more interesting. . . . But when I am finished with school, I do want to come back here to Chongqing. I believe that Chongqing has a lot of potential for development. Many new policies started here. I think eventually Chongqing will be like Shenzhen, developing at a very fast rate. I have high hopes for Chongqing. Also my relatives are all here. I will be nearer them. We are very attached to our native places, especially Sichuan people. We are used to the climate here, our kind of food, and our dialect.

When I talk with Wang Lian, others share their thoughts with us, and while each in a special way makes this afternoon in Chongqing richer and fuller, it is Wang Lian who makes it especially memorable. His standpoint is not quite that of an ordinary Chinese fifteen-year-old: he positions himself outside the reality that conditioned him and affords us a view that is "fresh" and "wonderful" (two of his favorite words). He has startling things to say on many subjects, from family to heroes. His often introspective responses are at the same time so direct and honest that they make his listeners laugh. He is also the only one who insists on speaking to me in Sichuan dialect (which makes the transcription a painfully slow but highly instructive experience). Thanks to him, my ears are now better trained to catch distinctively Sichuan words and phrases.

Wang Lian tells me about his preschool years:

WL: Before I started school, I lived with my nainai in another town. This was in Sichuan. . . . My mother came to see me all the time, but my father was working in Beijing then. When I was about five, my baba came home; he was transferred back to Chongqing. I don't remember much about Nainai. She died soon after I left her. I guess I was close to her, but I really don't remember. She was illiterate, originally a peasant from the country. Famine forced her to come to the city. But that was when she was very young. My yeye was from the city. . . . I don't remember my nainai or my baba or my mama telling me much about their pasts.

What about peasant life in general? Do you know much about it? How do you see your relationship to the peasants?

Xiao Di, a classmate of Wang Lian, answers first; he talks slowly and calmly. He has an older brother who is already working and a younger brother in grammar school.

Xiao Di (XD): I lived in the country with my nainai when I was very young. She was a peasant and had to work in the field. This was in the

Northeast, in Heilongjiang Province. I remember living in the country wasn't so bad. It was sort of carefree.

WL: Our understanding of peasant life comes from radio, television, and newspapers, so we don't know much. But still we are very concerned about it. . . . I think we are most concerned about land reforms. Peasant life has been improved since the Sino-Japanese War, but the peasants are still bound by their traditions. They lack knowledge and understanding of socialist ideology. The peasants whom we know live in the suburbs of large cities. Our contacts with them are mainly from buying vegetables from them. From the way they dress, the way they talk and act, we feel there is something "dirty" about them. Yes, we still discriminate against them. . . . But now that their lives have been improved, we city-dwellers are glad. We are concerned about the peasants because they are the foundation of our country.

During the Cultural Revolution, youths at your age were sent to the country to learn from peasants. If you were asked to do the same now, would you be happy to go?

All: No. [Laugh.]

WL: I think the tempering doesn't amount to anything. We don't have to live with the peasants in order to understand them. . . . In the past, intellectuals were sent to the countryside to do physical labor. I really don't see that as necessary. But if we were to bring knowledge to them, that's different. I guess if I were assigned to go, I'd go.

But do you want to go?

WL: Of course not. [He says this quickly and emphatically and everyone laughs.] Even to bring them technology, only a few of us are willing to do that. If we're sent, there is nothing we can do about it. But no one would choose to go.

XD: If you are able to go to college and if you are able to go on to graduate school and get a Ph.D., you should be allowed to take the examinations and continue your studies. But if you don't have the ability and you are assigned to work with the peasants, then you should go.

Tao Lu, another classmate of Wang Lian's, is an unreserved and unaffected girl with a broad build and a full voice. Her mother is a physician working in a maternity and child care center, her father an editor for a scientific journal. She has a younger sister in junior high.

Tao Lu (TL): In our class we conducted a survey to find out what we want to do in the future. We were asked to write down our goals in life, what we want to do after college, and also the reasons. No one said they wanted to do work in the countryside, not a single person! Most said that the peasants were still using the kind of hoes that had been used several thousand years ago. They said that that sort of work was . . . anyway, very primitive. If they could drive tractors instead of using hoes to do the plowing, they might consider. Then it might not be so bad.

Did your parents ever say this to you: that it would probably do you some good to go to the countryside and get a taste of what it's like?

XD, TL: No.

WL: My father did. [All laugh.] He thinks I should be sent to the country. According to him, I need some toughening up because I lack the "will of sustaining hardship." I don't want to go. . . . We have relatives in the country. Maybe next summer I'll go there. . . . It's true, though, most of us are bookworms, and I don't think that's right. We learn that young people from other countries are more motivated to do work with their hands. Not us, though. They're much more practical, but we're so bad at applying our knowledge. And even if we want to work with our hands, we have other problems. Let's say we want to build a bookshelf: we don't have the tools or the materials. We want to learn, but we can't.

It was Fang Kan's brother who tells me with a great deal of frustration that Chinese youths, unlike their American counterparts, can find neither summer jobs nor any sort of part-time job to help out with the family finances: "There are already too many people and not enough jobs in our society. Of course we want to test ourselves and become more independent. But our environment does not allow us to do that. We stay home and we study and that's about it."

I ask, what about helping around the house?

WL: We do a little. In general there is still a great deal of dependency. I don't know why. I guess we simply don't like to do chores. If parents do them, we are certainly not going to volunteer to do them.

Do your parents require you to do certain chores?

WL: Are you kidding? Of course they do. [Laughs.] I won't do them on my own. I think they're the ones who should be doing them, but if they ask me, I have no choice. Otherwise . . . I think that if you are doing something, you should like what you are doing.

XD: My parents always make sure that the chores they assign me won't interfere with my studies. Like sweeping the floor, washing dishes, shopping, cooking. . . .

What about going out with friends, going hiking, for instance? Is it easy for you to get permission from your parents to do that sort of thing?

WL: Parents in general still worry a lot, especially when we do something that might be dangerous. They worry, but we think it's our business and we don't want them to interfere. So there we have a conflict. . . . In general, we want to be less and less influenced by them, but the process is very slow. It takes a long time, but still we want *very much* to be independent. The desire is very strong . . . but no matter what, our parents are always concerned. They are always telling us what to do.

TL: I feel the same way. Usually when we plan to go somewhere, we first have to get the teachers' approval. And if it involves the slightest risk, they will say, "No." They will say, "You have to ask your parents." So usually we have to deal with both the parents and the teachers.

A student in Hangzhou told me that when she had a conflict with her mother the hardest thing to take was her mother's tears; she would soften her stand when her mother started crying. Do you find that to be true in your relationship with your mother?

WL: My mother doesn't cry. She just gets *angry*. [Everyone laughs.] We are all so stubborn. . . . And my parents get very mad and unhappy, and then I just feel awful. . . . Anything we do, we feel that we must be responsible to them. But when we do what they want, we feel that we have done so at a loss. Yes, most definitely. . . . We are very curious about the outside world. We find ideas from other countries new and strange. When we read how people in foreign countries live, we know, of course, that we can't do the same. We read that Americans learn to be independent from childhood, and we want to be independent too. Maybe things will change in a few years, because foreign ideas are gradually finding their way into the masses.

When you have a conflict with your parents, how do you vent your anger?

WL: We don't go that far. It's not in our nature to vent our anger. We just bear it. Maybe in the past when we were younger we threw a tantrum, but now we have to be *totally* obedient (*dao-guo-lai ko-guo-lai de yi-fu*). We have to follow the feudal idea of filial piety and loyalty: if you are not obedient, then you are not filial. [Laughs.]

Then you don't have real confrontations with your parents?

XD: Not real ones. . . .

WL: I wouldn't say that. I have confrontations with them lots of times. I argue with them, especially when I think that I am right. But I don't do anything to vent my anger. I hold my anger in and afterward I reflect on what has happened. I think to myself what's right and wrong and I keep it all to myself.

And do you talk about it with your friends?

XD: No, not really. We don't talk about our angry moments with our friends. Usually we talk about happy things, important issues. . . . Anger is something personal, and we have to deal with it ourselves. Maybe if we're just chatting and we're in a good mood, we might mention some unhappy incident that already happened a long time ago, but even that's rare.

TL: I think girls are different. We can take a lot more. We have more tolerance when we are angry, but it's hard for us to keep things to ourselves. We are quicker with our mouths. Somehow we always manage to tell everything to a friend. This doesn't mean that we tell everything right after something has happened. But after a while. . . . It's easier for us to reveal our feelings and emotions.

WL: What we [boys] like to talk about are *other* things, but personal things. . . . No, we simply don't talk about them.

The subject shifts from home to school.

WL: Most of the time in class we listen to the teacher lecture. Sometimes we raise questions, but they are insignificant. Usually we discuss the material among ourselves after class.

What kind of teachers do you like best?

WL: Those with a sense of humor. I think the Chinese have a better sense of humor than the Westerners. [Laughs.] The Westerners use a lot of action to make you laugh. The Chinese are subtler. They . . . I can't quite explain it, but this is how I feel. Also young people have a better sense of humor than their parents. Parents are more serious and *solemn.*

What about competition in a class?

WL: If someone else and I are about the same level in school and if on a test I didn't do as well as him, of course I wouldn't feel good.

If that someone else is your friend, does the competition have an impact on your friendship?

WL: *Absolutely not!* I'll just have to do better on the next test. But we still help each other with our studies.

When I see Fang Kan and Wang Lian together the next day, Fang Kan speaks intimately of their friendship:

We have been good friends since first grade. Before that we knew each other, but Wang Lian's home was far from mine, and so we weren't really friends. Plus, he was so quiet, always deep in thought, but I was very active, full of mischief, very extroverted. I was the leader of the kids in my neighborhood. And so we didn't make any effort to become friends. But when we got to first grade, we were in the same class and he moved closer to where I lived, and so we became friends. We were in the same class from that time until last year when they finally separated us. We're still in the same school, just in different classes. We made a pact, always to try to go to the same school. We have done it up to this point. We have our minds set on going to the same college in the Nanjing area. It'll be harder, though, to try to get into the same college. I have another friend there. He used to live here, but he moved when he was in the second grade. We still write to each other. That has something to do with the fact that I want to go to Nanjing. Wang Lian probably doesn't remember him. He didn't hang out with him.

After Fang Kan finishes, Wang Lian has nothing to add, but gazes at his friend and smiles a little.

What do you do in the summer?

TL: We review our schoolwork and we read novels.

WL: We also exercise a lot. We play soccer and basketball, and we swim.

TL: Parents usually don't allow girls to swim because they think it's dangerous. They read in the papers that so-and-so was drowned in the swimming pool, and they get scared. They never go to the swimming pool and see for themselves whether swimming is dangerous or not. There is no way I can convince my parents. No matter what I say, they won't listen. Parents are stricter with girls, and we are more inclined to listen to them.

WL: There are a lot more girls now in the pool, a lot more than before. But they all stay in the shallow end. [Laughs.]

TL: We're not active. We don't like to get out and do things. The only thing we are concerned about is not gaining weight. [Laughs.] We don't care if we are physically fit or not. As long as we don't get sick, then it's all right.

Tao Lu's comments seem to confirm Fang Kan's observation about girls that "They're not interested in sports, in keeping their bodies fit." He said more, of course. In his view, the girls' sheltered existence and lack of curiosity is society's doing, a remaining feudal element. This opinion is shared by a number of the boys I interviewed. This is why I particularly appreciate the presence of the girls when the issue is raised, not only Tao Lu but also Hong Li.

Hong Li is sixteen and does not go to the same middle school as the rest of the group. She says little, and each time she does speak, it is about her parents, both of whom are associated with the institute. She is unhappy about their high-handedness. She has an older sister who works at a printing house.

XD: Boys are bolder. They have more to say in class. If the teachers don't call on students by name, usually it's the boys who are more willing to speak up.

TL: I disagree. In our class girls always initiate things, and the boys follow us. It's the girls who are always taking charge.

What about the relationship between boys and girls?

WL: We have different interests. We hardly do anything together. It's impossible for boys and girls to become good friends. We are not at ease when we talk to girls. We don't feel free. It's just not fun. Yes, we talk to them, but there is not much to say, and we never say more than what is necessary, nothing superfluous. . . . In primary school we played hide-and-seek with them and that was fun. But then we go through stages. . . .

XD: In junior high we had a lot more to talk about, but not in senior high.

TL: I think it's our traditional view that there should be a distance between boys and girls.

What about your plans for the future?

WL: I really don't know what I want to be. . . . Now we are just building foundations. I am interested in astronomy and oceanography, and I like to read books in these areas, but I like to get a broad base, to explore many areas.

Wang Lian tells me later that he cannot think beyond passing the college entrance exam. Ideals and dreams have to be postponed until after.

XD: I feel the same way. I read a lot. Books, newspapers, magazines, they're influences in my life. Now I can only think about acquiring broad knowledge. I haven't thought about specializing. I'm more interested in the natural sciences than in the humanities, but I also like to read works of literature. I think nowadays it takes us longer to decide what we really want to do.

TL: In junior high I was very interested in literature. But in high school when we had to decide which area to go into, science or humanities, my parents told me I should study medicine. So now there is no more chance for me to study literature. I started out liking both chemistry and literature. Now I have only chemistry left. I like chemistry very much, but I can't say this is what I want to specialize in. When I take the college entrance exam, I'll have to consult my parents. My mother is a doctor, and she wants me to study medicine, but I'm not all that interested in medicine. If I have my way, I will choose chemistry. But I always have to obey my parents even if I want to do something else. Yes, I will follow their wish because there is no way that I can go against them.

Hong Li (HL): I put down agriculture as my first choice for college. My parents weren't happy about it, and my relatives also opposed the idea, but I wasn't going to yield to their wishes. It is my career and my life, and I have the right to choose what I want to study and to decide what course I want to take in life. They disagree with me, but I don't care. . . . My mother thinks that doing work in agriculture will be too hard on me. It would mean going to the field to work. She thinks that it's more sensible to do something theoretical.

If you could change your parents, how would you change them?

WL: If I could change my father, I would wish that he would be born again, born into our time so that he could appreciate our way of looking at things. I know we have very little experience in relating to others and in handling practical matters, but our vision has more depth. We can see things with more clarity. My father may have more experience in certain matters, but he doesn't quite grasp the essence of things. He does not have a sense of priority. We may not have as much information, but we know what we know more directly and more clearly. Middle-aged people do many things at the same time. They are so diffused, and everything gets so complicated for them! If they could only go back to our age, it would be wonderful! When we encounter something new, we are so excited, so enthusiastic because we find it fresh and novel. So we examine it more closely, with more sensitive eyes. Maybe grownups have seen too much and so everything seems commonplace. They are not as observant. Things just don't seem strange and wonderful to them.

Because our mind is a blank space, we are more responsive, more sensitive to the world around us. . . .

Actually I would like to return to the time when I was even younger. My feelings and impressions from that time are beginning to lose their colors. They are becoming hazier. Maybe things are changing. . . . I want to be even younger because I remember seeing things even more clearly then, and the world was full of wonder. . . .

My mother? There is no way of changing her. [Laughs.] She didn't have much education, and so she reads very little. I wish that she'd do some reading, starting from the beginning.

(*Wang Lian's mother is a health inspector in a food company. His father works in the Information Center. He is a civil engineer—a designer.*)

XD: How to change my father. . . . Maybe it's the age difference, maybe the time he lived in when he was young was so different from ours—anyway, he feels that what I think is not important. I wish he would let me be, that he would not give me so much help and advice except in situations when it's absolutely necessary. What he requires from me is too strict. I wish he'd let go a little. . . . As for my mother, I wish she'd let me take care of some of the responsibilities at home. She tends to monopolize everything, always telling me that her views and opinions are correct.

HL: Parents are so weighed down by their views and opinions that they no longer develop their analytical abilities. . . . I think my father should change his way of educating children. He is too anxious for his children to become great talents. You have to do everything as he wishes. If you don't, he gets very unhappy. He imposes his will on us and doesn't try to understand us. For instance, he insists that we do our homework at a certain time. During that time, he doesn't let us watch television or even brush our teeth. He doesn't care if we can concentrate or not. We have to sit there even though our minds may be drifting and we are not studying effectively. He thinks he knows the best study methods, the best time to do homework. But what he thinks is best is not necessarily best for others.

TL: I wish my father were not so authoritarian. If he says "one," then you'd better not say "two." Since he decides everything, he would never let me do things as I want to do them no matter how wrong he might be. I wish that sometimes he would see things from my point of view. Some things he feels are insignificant, not worth the time and energy to learn them. But I may find those very same things to be very interesting; I may be charged up about learning or doing them. But if he doesn't feel the same way as I do, he insists they are dull. He never tries to understand. . . . I wish my mother would take more interest in learning, in acquiring knowledge so that she has more to share with us. Every day she comes home and does the housework. She doesn't let you help and she doesn't talk to you about what's happening in the world. She sees patients and does housework. She's not interested in anything other than medicine. My father is more interested in new things. If we say something about something he doesn't know, he'll ask us where we got our information. Then he goes to the source and tries to find out as much as he can so that we can have another discussion about it.

In what ways would you like to change yourself?

WL: To change myself. . . . [I think] that depends on the environment. The environment dictates our lives. I don't see how we can change ourselves purely by raising our consciousness. Sure, we must first have an awareness, but once that is entangled with the circumstances in our environment, it is lost, gone. . . . Yes, when we want to change our character, we must first have an awakening, but . . . anyway, I feel that physical conditions determine a lot of things. Some people will say that we are completely dependent on material conditions, that material conditions determine everything. I don't think that's completely true. Awareness is of a higher level. At the end, changes are brought on by people with strong wills. But then how are characters formed? That again depends on environment. Environment shapes a perception, which turns around and brings change to the same environment. . . . The Chinese as a whole are more introverted. At this point I am more open, but I want to be more reflective [he already was!], and so I want to be more introverted, to be calmer and more sober. When a person is open and extroverted, he seems fluffy and frivolous. And so I want to change. But no matter how hard I try, I just can't do it. And I know that I shouldn't do anything forcibly. So I just let myself be myself and let things follow their natural course.

What about the persons you admire, persons whom you consider as "heroes." Who are they?

WL: I have no heroes. I have no idea who is a hero. History books tell us so-and-so was a hero, but do we know what he was really like?

Historians tell us his strengths but not his weaknesses. We only know him as a perfect person, not as a real person, so can we trust what we read? When I think of heroes, I don't think of any specific people. I think of the "hero" in many persons, and they may be workers, peasants. I think of various heroic qualities that many persons have. Perhaps if you put all these qualities together, you'd have a perfect hero, but that's not possible. . . .

XD: "Hero" is just an image, an abstract idea.

WL: It is a collective idea. . . . Therefore to worship any one person as a hero is not necessary, I think. During the Cultural Revolution, young people were blind. My parents told me about how they fought and how absurd everything was. I don't think that will happen again. Now we have an open-door policy. Ideas from the outside world have given us a different perspective.

Any historical personages that you would like to meet?

WL: The way historical figures are portrayed is definitely one-sided. They all seem to be great. I bet if I were to meet them and to get to know them, I'd find that they were not really so great. I think they were probably just ordinary persons. I feel that we should try to understand what people were really like—no matter how great they appear to be, no matter whether they're scientists or other famous people. If I were to meet Edison or Einstein, I'd want to know all about their background—how they grew up and so on. The way they were—their thought and action—had everything to do with their environment. The biographies we have are very limited. Only very few tell you what these people really were like.

Now I have a whimsical question. If you could be an animal, which would you be?

WL: It's meaningless, wanting to be another animal. Animals only care for their survival. We humans think that they are noble, but animals don't know if they are noble. . . .

I remind him that I'm not asking him to consider seriously the possibility of a metamorphosis, that my question is a lighthearted one. Wang Lian does not seem to understand—perhaps he is not listening to—what I am saying. His thoughts remain on the same track.

WL: Animals labor for their survival. They live to adapt to their environment. If someone tells me I can change to another animal, I'll say to him: "No thanks, I am not interested." Animals do not have the ability to think. Without that life is meaningless. We humans have consciousness and thought.

Also misery and unhappiness?

WL: Of course, but they make our lives more interesting. That's what makes us different from other animals.

* * *

Yang Zhi-cong was the official interpreter for the Essermans and the Piels on our 1979 trip. She was an intelligent and savvy woman who understood the rules well and knew how to interpret them flexibly. She accompanied us throughout our journey, and when we said good-by in Guangzhou, we knew we would see her again. We did, in New York City, two years later, at a reunion that Eleanor and Gerard Piel arranged. By then she was a graduate student at the University of Michigan, where she was doing research in population control. In 1984, when the Piels and I saw her again in Beijing, I remembered what she had told me five years before, that she had a son—"a very naughty boy"—in elementary school, and I beseeched her for a meeting with him. She laughed and said, "All right. He is a young man now and likes to talk. I think you'll have a good time with him." She was right about her son and about our meeting.

Tall and lean and fifteen, Lin Ting is no longer mischievous, but he can be very funny. I am not sure whether he is aware of this. He seems serious enough, with a cultivated voice and stylized gestures, but these merely reinforce the humor, adding drama to it. He uses a great deal of ideological language but most of the time with a twist. In translation, the irony is perhaps lost, for it is wedded to the dynamics in his voice and to the particularities of the Chinese language.

Our conversation is primarily about school. His mother joins in occasionally.

Lin Ting (LT): In class most of the time the teacher lectures, but we do have some chance to speak. In primary school, students are more eager to respond. When a teacher asks: "Who can answer this question?," you see all the hands go up. But it's just the opposite in middle school: when the teacher asks a question, students are reluctant to raise their hands. I think the older we get, the less inclined we are to test ourselves in front of others. We are not so spontaneous. Even when we know the answer, we only mutter it to ourselves. We don't want to say it out loud. Why? I think it's just vanity. We think it's embarrassing to give wrong answers.

But it's different when it comes to discussions—there are plenty of discussions in language classes. Let's say we are studying a Tang poem. Usually those poems have little relevance to our lives. [Muses.] Anyway, the students have to prepare ahead of time. They come to class with their own interpretations. The teacher corrects us when she feels a different explanation is more appropriate. There are very few disagreements—usually over a word or a phrase but not about anything fundamental. And most of the time we feel that the teacher is more knowledgeable and better prepared and so we listen to her. At the very end of our discussion, when we come to the summary, the teacher often says this: "Now your interpretation on the whole is pretty good, but . . ." [Laughs.] Then she adds her own comments. She usually gives us a broader perspective on things, and her choice of words is more *tactful*.

In the class on politics, things are a bit different. The teacher explains an issue and points out the most important theories about it. We listen and take notes, but we have very little *in-class* discussion though a lot of *after-class* discussion, especially during lunch. Boys and girls all join in. . . . We finish our morning class around 11:45. That's when we have lunch. At our usual speed, we should be able to finish lunch by 12:15, but if we get into one of those discussions, by 1:15 we're still not finished. [Laughs.] Some of the boys in our class, me included [laughs], when we get together, we can sometimes argue for hours over a single issue. I remember just before graduating, in our final essays and in our farewell parties, many of us reminisced about the wonderful times we had spent together debating and contradicting each other.

Why do you have less discussion in politics class?

LT: The teacher has his schedule, certain set requirements that he has to fulfill. If we debate endlessly, it's hard for him to control the schedule and cover all the material. Also, we students feel there are certain things we can't say to our teachers so directly. There is a generation gap.

Teachers and students understand problems differently. Many of us fear that our views may be wrong. But we *have* to express them, and so we tell each other. . . . According to a recent survey in *Chinese Youth*, ninety-five percent of the high school students in Beijing do not like their politics class. The figure is very high! Kids don't like politics classes because they are mechanical. You have to memorize everything. Actually it's not that students don't like to memorize, it's just that they feel constrained. They want to express their views in their own words, and they want to be able to question the existing views. The same article mentioned a student who took a chance on one of his exams: he didn't memorize a thing and answered all the questions according to his views, using his own words and expressions. His teachers criticized him, and even his parents thought he was crazy. Most students wouldn't dare do such things. They don't think it's necessary to take this kind of risk. We discuss politics after class. The tests are easy to cope with. They are fairly mechanical: you memorize the answers and then you give them back.

What are some of the topics that you study in politics?

LT: The history of social development. We learn about productive forces, the relations of production, and things like that. We also learn something about law, for instance, the constitutional rights of citizens. I think students are more interested in studying the constitution. We even talked about what is considered "self-defense" in case someone tries to attack you. Our teacher gave us concrete examples, specific cases, in which self-defense had been applied. Now that was interesting! We all sat up and listened for a change.

His mother: What they are doing in class has a lot to do with the recent campaign to heighten young people's awareness about the importance of laws. During the Cultural Revolution they had no idea what laws were. Our constitution was enacted in 1982, and since then many penal laws have been passed. The newspapers have been doing a lot of propaganda. They are trying to educate the masses about our constitution and our laws.

You've just taken your entrance exam to senior high. What was the past year like?

LT: It was pretty good. At the beginning, we all thought that we'd be doing nothing but studying. Actually that was not possible. In our class, the good students still carried on their normal lives, doing what they liked to do. There was this one classmate of mine, he likes to collect stamps. Many kids like to collect stamps, but he is a serious collector. He knows everything about all the stamps he has—their history and value. So he went on collecting his stamps. We had sports events, singing contests, talent shows, and we put on plays. I'm the kind who likes to have a good time, and so I went on outings and participated in the talent show and in plays. I really like doing those things. Yes, I had a good year.

His mother: He's just like me. [Laughs.] When I was in school, I was a student leader, involved in everything.

LT: Most people feel that extracurricular activities and learning cancel each other out. But I don't think so, and I think most of my classmates agree. The two are actually the same thing, and they reinforce each other. Most of us, no matter under what sort of situation, still try to pursue our interests.

The students you refer to, are they good students, students confident about their abilities?

LT: I think most students in China are quite modest. They all feel that they are inadequate in many areas. After all, nobody's perfect. . . . I think having confidence has nothing to do with how well one is doing in school. A so-called good student might not have much confidence in himself.

How can you tell?

LT: We talk—I mean the kids in my class—and I'm one of those who does a lot of talking. [Laughs.] I can tell, just from talking to someone, whether he has confidence or not. Some kids who aren't doing all that well academically—they don't have any special talents and they don't stand out in any particular area—are still very secure. In fact the person who sat next to me made the same observation just before the end of school. "Look at so-and-so," he said. "Most people don't think much of him, yet he has lots of confidence in what he's doing and what he can accomplish in the future." Maybe confidence has something to do with personality. Some are secure by nature. Others have to build up their sense of security.

During the second semester of our third year, we had to study a lot harder. By that time we had already covered all the required work, and so what we did was review and practice. I was not good in chemistry, and so I spent more time memorizing periodic numbers and chemical equations. (I prefer history, but it was not one of the six subjects we were tested on. We don't even study history during the third year.) Most of the time we concentrated on reviewing physics, chemistry, and math. In middle school we only get enough history to cope with the regular exams, but I don't think that's adequate. In language we study excerpts from historical texts, but that's all. Classical Chinese is fine, but it has to be in simplified characters. It kills me if I have to read the complex characters.

What was the topic of your essay question on your entrance exam?

LT: We had to write a review of an essay called "Yesterday, Today, Tomorrow." The essay was pretty good. The author talked about the meaning that yesterday has for the present. But yesterday is still in the past; it does not return. Tomorrow is full of hope, but it is in the future. For him, today is most important, yet most people fail to grasp the present. I think he's right. Most kids today are only concerned with the future. Their goal is somewhere in the future. The future gives them the drive to work harder.

What about you?

LT: Perhaps I'm like that, too. The efforts I make now, today, are for some goal in the future.

His mother: I think this attitude has a lot to do with our environment and the present circumstance of the Chinese people. There are so many people in China, and we are competing fiercely to get the best education. Let's say tomorrow I have an exam in politics, but I don't like the subject, I don't like memorization, and I'd much rather spend my time doing something that interests me. Do I really have a choice? No. If I don't do what is required, I will fail the exam, and that has other consequences. If there were other ways for us to succeed, then it would be easier to say, "I'll do as I please." But these choices don't exist in China. Children have to be in schools, in good schools, in order to get anywhere. When I was younger, we were the same—we struggled for a goal. Without a goal there is no motivation, no drive.

LT: What's more, the entrance exams are used to measure the teachers' abilities, too. "Good teachers" are those who are good at predicting the exam questions. If a teacher gets it right, he is considered brilliant. Not long ago we—the kids in my class—had a private talk about our teachers. Some were very unhappy with one particular teacher because he had guessed all the questions wrong on our entrance exam. Others defended him, saying he was an open, frank, inspiring teacher. . . . If a math teacher has shown us in class the exact steps in solving a given problem, and if a similar problem appears on the entrance exam, well, that teacher has it made! He is praised as a *good* teacher, a *great* teacher. He is *hot!* All it is is that he guessed accurately. But the students don't feel that way. They feel the accurate guess is the result of his teaching experience. I don't think that's right, though.

The subject changes from teachers to students. Lin Ting talks about his classmates. He begins with a particular experience in seventh grade.

That year our school played host to a group of Japanese students. These kids were all seventeen- and eighteen-year-olds. We were thirteen- and fourteen-year-olds. Yet compared to them, we seemed like little old men. We had a party for them in the gym. You could feel the liveliness on one side, and as for our side, . . . well, you couldn't really say that the atmosphere was heavy and serious, but certainly it was *solemn* and *dignified*. Now that's really no good. . . .

His mother: He likes things to be lively. [Laughs.]

LT: And when they started dancing, I mean they were really dancing! A friend and I were doing pantomime to entertain them. This friend said to me: "Look at those seventeen- and eighteen-year-olds. They could be thirteen and fourteen. But our seventeen- and eighteen-year-olds are like twenty-seven and twenty-eight." We were so stiff, and they were so alive. They'd tell us this or that, and we'd just nod our heads a little and mumble "Mm, mm." You could feel the difference! It doesn't mean that on this side we all grew beards. It's just that the feeling was so different.

Most students are a little cautious about being spontaneous. Under certain circumstances, it's all right, but in other situations you'll be criticized [softly]. Others will form an opinion of you, and we all care a lot about how others see us and judge us. The image everyone wants to project is of this quiet, pensive, and serious person. Actually, what most of us really *want* is to be lively, spontaneous, and just happy. For example, when we have a "happy get-together" [*lian-huan-hui*]—a party—nobody is really "happy" [*huan*] or jovial during the party. Let's say a New Year's party. We make *jiao-zi,* and we talk and have fun. But the happiest time for us is not during the party but at the party *after* the official party, when the teachers have gone home and the Communist Youth League members and the cadres have also left. Then we begin *our* party. We turn on our tape recorders. We say whatever we want to say, and we play games. That's when we are really having a good time. Usually what we remember best is the party after the party. So most of us do love to play and to have fun.

His mother: We really have too much discipline in our country. Parents and teachers are always telling you what is proper and what is not. These are the feudal elements that have been passed down to us.

LT: We like to talk about "decorum" (*ti-tong*). Very often, for no reason at all, we point to someone and say: "Now you're losing your sense of propriety" (*you-shi-ti-tong*). [Laughs.] When you talk to your teacher, if you sit like this with your legs crossed, he'll say that you are outrageous and unruly. But how can that be outrageous and unruly? It's just comfortable! The teachers themselves like to sit with their legs crossed. Still, most students conform to school rules, though they may not like them. Some even criticize their classmates for not behaving properly. I'm one of those whom the teachers often call "lax in discipline" or "not setting strict demands on himself."

His mother: I recall that when I was in the United States, once in a movie theater I saw a father with three daughters and they all had their feet up on the seats in front of them. I thought that was funny. I cannot imagine the same scene in China. In China, when a father brings his daughters to the theater, they would be all sitting like this. [Straightens her back and puts her hands on her lap.] But in the theater I saw all those little feet resting on the seats in front of them! [Laughs.] The two cultures are so different. . . . But I think when foreigners come to visit China, they often get an inaccurate view of Chinese children. The children they see, in schools and nurseries, seem much more rigid than they really are. When the visitors arrive, all the children are instructed to behave, even the nursery school and kindergarten children. Actually *before* they arrive, the teachers are busy wiping the children's noses and making sure their clothes are clean and neat. I think that this is the Chinese perception, this is what they consider "good children."

* * *

In 1984 we visited Xian, a place where one can find vestiges of both the first emperor who unified China and the only woman who ruled China. Stored in the city's Forest of Steles are also images of the Former Han (202 B.C.–A.D. 9) carved on stone slabs and, in the Pagoda of the Great Goose, sutras the celebrated monk Xuan-zang brought back from India more than thirteen hundred years ago. Xian (formerly known as Changan) is a treasure house, the site of a resplendent past, the capital of the Former Han and Tang dynasties.

In Xian my husband was invited to give a seminar at a major science and technology university, the Jiaotong Daxue. The vice-president there heard I'd been interviewing children in China and, as a gesture of good will, asked a student from the university to take me to the swimming pool in the university residential quarters, where I would find a "community of children."

At the gate, the attendants at first were reluctant to let me approach the children. "Many of them here are from the country. You can't let her talk to them," they told my guide. She assured them that it was all right; that this was the wish of the university administrators. After some persuasion, we were let in. At the pool the children were darting in and out of the water, splashing and kicking. Their joy seemed complete—and the air rang with the sounds of laughing, screaming, and yelling. I have never seen so many Chinese children so totally involved in playing. The sight and sound overwhelmed me. I stood there immobile, realizing how intrusive my presence was. How could I simply pick a child out of this and persuade him to drop out of the fun and abandon his friends so that I could record his story? I felt irresolute and awkward. Then I saw Bai Lan standing nearby on a patch of grass, shaded by a tree. She was about fifteen and was wearing regular clothes, not a swimsuit. She was waiting for her younger brother and cousin to finish their afternoon swim, I learned, and was very willing to talk to me. Her little brother, Bai Hao, and a cousin, Dai Li-xin, and a friend of theirs eventually joined us and we all went to a nearby park.

There on a stone bench we begin to chat:

Bai Lan (BL): I am going to be a sophomore in the fall. I live with my yeye and nainai, right here in the university housing. They are already retired. I grew up with them. My baba and mama work in the suburbs. My mama teaches elementary school. My baba is an engineer. I go home to my parents only during summer and winter breaks. My mother sometimes comes here during the summer. My cousin here lives with us. He is the son of my dajiu [oldest maternal uncle]. My dajiu has two kids, and he is the older one. He has been living with our grandparents since he was three. I've spent more time with him than with my own brother. When he first got here, my grandmother fell and broke her leg, so he had to go to kindergarten, even though he was only three and was too young to go to school. So they put down on the application that he was four. He started first grade when he was only five and a half.

My grandmother was a seamstress because the family needed money. She originally came from a wealthy family. Her father was a merchant but didn't really have to work for a living because the family was so rich, and he just stayed around the house most of the time. My yeye was from the country—their families were both from Jiangsu Province—and he was an accountant in the printing house that belongs to Jiaoda (Jiaotong University).

I was raised here in Xian. During the Cultural Revolution I went to Beijing and Inner Mongolia. I was too young then and so I don't remember anything about the trip. My father at the time was stationed in Inner Mongolia with the army, and my mother took me there to visit him.

Bai Hao, who has decided to hang around with us instead of with the two other boys, occasionally interjects a question or a comment. He is nine and lives at home with their parents.

Bai Hao (BH): My jiejie has been to many places, but I haven't been to any place except for Xian.

BL: When my father volunteered for the army, my parents were separated—I don't know for how long. But ever since I can remember things, my parents have been living together. When the Gang of Four was overthrown, I was in first grade. I don't recall what our life was like before that. My nainai tells me that life was very difficult then for my mother and her brothers and sisters, especially for my erjiu [second uncle]. He had to go out and cut a kind of grass that was used to feed pigs. That was the only way he could earn some money and go to school. My grandparents have too many children and my yeye was the only one who was earning money.

Do you like living at home or with your grandparents?

I like it here better. I've got lots of friends here. At my mother's place, I don't know anyone.

Then, looking at her cousin, who at this point is having great difficulty filling out the questionnaire I have given him, Bai Lan suddenly changes the subject. Dai Li-xin, the cousin, like Bai Hao is nine and tells me he has a five-year-old brother who lives at home with their parents. He is playful and very verbal. At one point, the three boys are telling me how to make their favorite snack, "oil cake," and Dai Li-xin adds that one can buy them on the street. "They sell them for a mao [ten cents] a piece." "That's pretty cheap," I say. "Did you say pretty cheap?" he asks quickly, mocking my ignorance. "It's terrible! So expensive! Definitely not worth it." His directness makes me laugh.

BL: My cousin is doing very poorly in school. Maybe it's because my grandparents are old now. Even if they watch over him, it's no use. This past year I was preparing for my entrance exam. I stayed with my yifu [uncle—husband of her mother's sister], who also lives here on campus. He is a professor at Jiaoda and helps me with my studies. And while I was away, my cousin fell even more behind. My yeye didn't understand his textbooks, and he didn't know how to teach him. Plus, my cousin has no self-motivation. He is very slow. When I am home, sometimes I help him. I don't know why he's doing so poorly. My mama has tried all kinds of ways to make him do better in school. She even threatens him. She says to him: "If you don't finish your homework, you can't watch television tonight or you don't get to eat that" (which is usually something that he likes). But he doesn't listen, and he doesn't care. It's no use. My jiujiu—his father—is the director of the Sang-shu-ping Mining Company. His mother is an engineer in the same company. They live very far from here. They have to take a train to get here. They come quite often to see him. My uncle is very busy. . . .

BH: Dajiu gets telephone calls even at three o'clock in the morning.

BL: His mother comes here more often than his father.

I'm surprised to hear that Dai Li-xin is a slow learner, but his cousin appears to be right: he is unable to fill out most of the very simple questionnaire. Among Chinese children of similar circumstances this appears to be uncommon.

How is your relationship with your parents?

BL: It's all right. My baba and mama get along very well, though. They are not like some married couples, arguing all the time. I have never seen them quarrel. My mother is a teacher, and she knows how to bring us up and how to educate us. She knows there are times when she has to be especially affectionate to us, and times when she has to be tough. I don't live with them most of the time, and so our relationship is fine. It probably would be different if I were at home.

Among my aunts and uncles, they all fight with their husbands or wives. I think the reason that my parents get along so well is because my father has a very good temper. My mother has a heart condition. When she is irritable because of her work or her students, my baba always tries to tease her and make her laugh. And very quickly my mama forgets her frustrations, and she is fine. The doctor says that my mother's heart condition is not serious. Last year my parents were invited to so many dinners. According to the doctor, she probably drank a little too much then. He said that alcohol poison might have caused her heart condition. Now she shouldn't be too excited or too angry. My baba, with the kind of temperament he has, is very good for her. . . . Here in general the relationship between husband and wife is all right. But they do argue, and they do fight, sometimes over trivial things. In my [extended] family, my aunts and uncles fight, and very often they turn around and get very angry at their children. There are seven children in my [extended] family, and six of them are boys. When the parents dump all their anger and frustration out on my cousins, I feel so sorry for them.

My father is an engineer, but working in the factory, I feel, has destroyed all his professional ambition. Before, both my parents had high aspirations. My mother went to a normal school, and she was only eighteen when she graduated. She wanted to make a career. She wanted to devote herself to educating children, but her school . . . anyway she is not that confident anymore. My father is the same way. He was an airplane mechanic when he was in the army, but when he came out, he was assigned to do design work in a rectifier plant. It's a completely different kind of work.

During the Cultural Revolution my parents didn't have a bad time because of political reasons, but [pointing to the third boy there] his father was sent to the cowshed. I don't know why. His father is much older than my father. His sister is a classmate of mine.

What do you do during the summer?

My friends and I—talk, sometimes about our studies and sometimes about our view of life. We have our own ideas about our society.

What sort of ideas?

BL: Once we had to write an essay on "human relationships." We said to each other that even though human relationships in our society are in a big mess, we have to write something different. We have to say that everything is all right. They tell us that in a capitalist society relationships are based on money. We said to each other that in a socialist society this is even more so. [Laughs.] Of course, we were just talking nonsense. When it came to putting it down on paper, we all had to write it differently. What we write and what we think are not the same.

Do you discuss differences in the classroom?

BL: We never disagree with our teachers. Our ideas may be different, but we never say what they are out loud. There is a small group of kids who always raise their hands in class—mostly boys. They like to talk in class, but mostly about schoolwork and homework assignments. In our class girls don't like to speak out. If you do, all the other kids will say that you like to show off. There is one boy in our class who talks all the time. We all think that he is a show-off. But our teacher likes him the best. When she lectures, she is lecturing to him. Boys and girls in our class don't talk to each other.

We girls like to chat with our language teacher. She told us about her experiences in the women's college she went to. We all envy her. We'd all like to go to a women's college someday. Now is not like in the past. Our society is more chaotic. Boys will come to talk to you for no reason at all. But if we could go to a girls' school and later to a women's college, that would be wonderful. We could live together and not worry about anything.

The same language teacher, just to get us to disagree with her, sometimes will purposely say something and then she asks us: "Do you agree?" The boys all yell, "No!" "If you don't think it's right," she challenges us, "then tell me the reasons." Then the boys start to explain. We girls laugh at them. We tell them: "What's the point? No matter what you say, the teacher will insist that she's right." Usually this is the case. The teacher always tries to refute you. If she doesn't, she feels she's lost face. And this is our language teacher, the only one who lets us disagree with her in class! Other teachers are so serious and self-righteous. They never smile. Just looking at them is enough to make us feel scared.

You mentioned that there are boys who like to bother the girls. . . .

They like to tease you and call your name from outside the classroom. But if the teacher is there, they don't dare to do it. Sometimes they'll shout your name at you when you are walking on the street. They don't dare get close. It's just very annoying. That's all. One girl from our school was beaten up by some boys right at an intersection—there were eight of them beating up this one girl—but this rarely happens. About a year ago we had three special classes for students who didn't pass the entrance exam for high school. Now we don't have them anymore. Students like that didn't study. They were just troublemakers. Now they're not around anymore. I remember that during that time my mother didn't allow me to go out at night.

Do you talk to your parents about these things?

Yes, a lot. When I was in junior high, there was one boy who liked to bother me. I didn't know what he meant to do. I went home and told my parents. Most parents don't understand their children. They say that if you are serious, why should anyone want to bother you? They blame you for what has happened. But my parents are different. They just told me not to pay any attention to him. They said that the more I was afraid of him, the more he would try to annoy me. I also spoke to my teacher about it. She had a talk with him, and he stopped. He didn't pass the high school entrance exam. He's going into the army. I hear that he got in "through the back door" (*zou-hou-men*). His yeye is an old cadre. You figure that someone who is the grandson of a high official would be better brought up.

Were you nervous getting ready for the high school entrance?

My school is a "key school"—we have two different exams, one for those who are already in the school and one for students who want to get in. The standard for our own students is lower. Most of my classmates have passed.

What subjects do you like best?

History, ancient history, especially Tang history. In the future I'd like to do research in history. My baba wants me to become a reporter. He tells me that it's important that we write well. . . .

BH: My baba is a good writer himself.

BL: He is good in everything, math, science, and literature. He encourages us to keep diaries. He doesn't set any requirements. He just tells us to write. Even if it's just something very routine—"I got up this morning and brushed my teeth. I had breakfast at seven"—that's all right too. My didi also keeps a diary.

What do you and your grandparents talk about?

Sometimes about when my mother was little, but mostly about how hard life was in the past. My yeye also tells me about my erjiu. He was very smart and a very good student in school, but he was also very naughty, a real troublemaker. One day he was sitting in the back of the classroom, and he pulled this girl's pigtails. I guess she complained. The teacher scolded him, and when he got home, he got another lecture from my nainai. From then on he refused to talk to any girls, and he actually didn't, until he got to college. He was only in the third or fourth grade when this happened. Of course, he talked to his sisters. He and my other uncles were very protective of their sisters. They wouldn't let anyone hurt them. . . .

Why do you call your maternal grandparents "yeye" and "nainai"? Aren't they your laoye and laolao?

That's because my real yeye and nainai died a long time ago.

4

Gathered from Cradles, Singsongs, and Green Heroes

In 1984 my family and I came to Zhongxin Elementary School in Shanghai, where I had visited before. The principal and a number of the teachers had been replaced, but by chance the only teacher in school when our contact telephoned for me was a Mr. Li, the English teacher who had received June Esserman and me years before, and he was happy to help me again.

This morning, when we first arrived, a group of children from the neighborhood was waiting for us in the reception room, all of them students of this school—their families all residents of Putuo District. In the afternoon, five children and I met in a large kindergarten room. We were all oversized for the miniature table and chairs, but nobody seemed to mind. I remembered the two boys from the morning, when they had entertained my four-year-old while I talked to their classmates. Of the three girls I was especially familiar with Yao Chen-tao, whom I had met and talked with during my first visit. She was a sprightly first-grader then; now she was due to start junior high school in September. She*

* My first interview with Yao Chen-tao and her older sister Yao Chen-lin is found in Chapter Five. See below, pp. 247–54.

seemed quieter, and though her simple sweetness was unchanged, something else was present: another mood, I think. Her brows were thicker and darker, and she was more serious.

I asked each of the children to fill out an information sheet for me. It took them a while to complete. There was some discussion and occasional arguments, primarily between the boys and the girls, about how to write certain characters.

Chen Hai-qiang is eleven. His hair is cut very short, which accentuates his protruding ears and drooping cheeks. An untactful boy, he easily offends others with his strong opinions and quick temper. He talks loud and fast and likes to interrupt. The girls clearly dislike him. He has a way of inciting their anger. Yet this morning when I entrusted him with my four-year-old son, he was a warm and patient "older brother." His father is a factory worker and his mother a store clerk. He has two sisters, both in their twenties.

Ren Ji-he is nine and has just finished second grade. He has an angular handsome face with twinkling eyes and a puckish smile. Like Chen Hai-qiang, he is excitable and tends to get carried away, especially when he talks about his father. Indeed, he is quite simply the wildest child I encountered in China. He does not want to be restrained and tells me so. At home (he is an only child) his mother spoils him, he tells me, and he is kindly toward her; his father tries to discipline him, and he resents him. She is a factory worker and he an engineer.

In America, children like to play "pretend." [*I give some examples.*] *Do you play this game here?*

Chen Hai-qiang (CHQ): We play that. But we like to pretend to be soldiers in the Liberation Army fighting against the bad guys. The problem is that everybody wants to be in the Liberation Army, and nobody wants to be one of the bad guys.

Ren Ji-he (RJH): And then nobody plays.

Jiang Wei is a plumpish girl by Chinese standards, with a round face and short hair pulled back tightly in a tiny pony tail. She is ten. Chen Hai-qiang, who is in her grade at school, likes to tease her (there seems to be a long-standing feud between them), but she snaps right back in her nasal, high-pitched voice. She is not shy, yet when a question is directed to her or when she is revealing something personal, she seems self-conscious: she tucks her skirt between her legs and sways gently. Her father is a doctor and her mother a schoolteacher. Like Ren Ji-he, she is an only child.

Jiang Wei (JW) and CHQ (together, quickly): Sometimes we *pin*. We show our hands at the same time, palm up or palm down. The person who is different from the rest is "it."

CHQ: The one who loses, he is . . .

JW: He leaves! He doesn't want to play.

CHQ: Wrong! Only you girls are like that. We boys, if we lose, we lose. We are "true men" [*da-zhang-fu*]. We can take it. The person who is "it" closes his eyes, and the rest of us run and hide. The "it" has to leave his home base to find us. When he is away, the rest of us have to hurry up and run back and touch base. This is called "The telegram has arrived!" If the person who is "it" sees us and gets back to base first, he wins, and we play another game. We play this until we are tired out, and then we go home.

JW: Anyway, everybody wants to be a good guy, and nobody wants to be a bad guy. Sometimes we argue for so long that at the end nobody wants to play that game, and we play a different game.

Yao Chen-tao (YCT): The girls like to play "house"—a mother has several children and goes out shopping. And we say so-and-so is the mother and the rest are the children. But nobody wants to be the father. And so sometimes we say, "The father is dead." [She whispers this last sentence and giggles.]

CHQ: You girls have wicked hearts. We boys never join them in that kind of game.

JW: If he [pointing to Chen Hai-qiang] is the father, no girl wants to be the mother. [The girls laugh.] Sometimes we play jump rope with a long strand of rubber bands.

CHQ: And we throw bean bags.* Both the boys and the girls play bean bags.

* This game resembles American jacks.

JW: And we also kick shuttlecocks [*jian-zi*], usually in the fall.

Do you have arguments with your friends?

RJH: I don't have any good friends. They like to call me "a big fat pig." [*He has a round face but is neither big nor fat.*]

JW: Some kids call me "Jiang Jie-shi" [Chiang Kai-shek] just because my last name is "Jiang" [Chiang].

CHQ: Of course we argue, but after a while we are all right again. The more we don't play together, the more we want to be friends again.

RJH: We try to control ourselves until we can't stand it anymore, and the only thing to do is to be friends again.

Do boys and girls play together?

CHQ: That depends . . . if our teachers give us some push. *They* have to take some initiative to unite us since now men and women are equal. They have to encourage us to get together.

JW: But when boys and girls play together, usually the boys are on one side and the girls are on another.

RJH: We also play soccer. When we get back to the classroom, we are drenched with sweat. I'd love to get inside a refrigerator and cool off.

Have you ever played so hard that you forgot the time and went home late?

RJH: Yes. My baba, he got so mad and he spanked me. I don't run away. Last time when he tried to slap me, I ducked and his hand hit right on the bedpost. It hurt him instead. I am not afraid of him. When he spanks me, I try to get away from him. I hide under the chair.

CHQ: Sometimes I run into a room and lock the door. The only problem is that when dinner-time comes, you have to come out and eat.

RJH: I wait until my father is gone, and then I come out. My mother loves me the best. She never scolds me or spanks me. When my baba is gone, she calls me out to eat. When my baba comes back, she tells me to go and hide again. . . . We also play tag. Last time when we played tag, I fell and had a big cut near my eyebrow. See! [He shows me.]

CHQ: Although we get hurt, we still want to play.

RJH: I also like to draw. But I don't draw well, and so I also hate to draw. I like to draw ships carrying animals. I like animals.

Do you like to catch insects?

All (quickly): Yes!

CHQ: We do, but the problem is: it's hard to catch them.

What kind of insects can you find here?

CHQ: Butterflies, crickets, grasshoppers, praying mantis, cicadas . . .

RJH: After we catch them, we take them home and make them into specimens. We first soak them in alcohol so that they won't rot. If they drink the alcohol, their stomach won't rot either. And then we mount them on a board. They are stuck onto the board with pins.

What about frogs and toads?

JW: In school we are told that frogs are beneficial animals and that we shouldn't catch them.

RJH: We also catch stray cats. . . . [Trails off.] I hate to do homework. I like to play soccer and play cards. But if I don't do my homework, they smack me.

CHQ: We have to do our homework because we have to learn and we have to build the foundation for the four modernizations. We have to establish far-reaching goals. . . . [His repetition of these slogans is mechanical and clearly not meant seriously.]

RJH: Oh, please don't say these things! [He covers his ears.] I hate these slogans! My father says them all day long: "We have to lay the foundation for the four modernizations. We have to study every day and make progress. If we don't, we won't have any future." I am so tired of it!

Tell me about your mischiefs.

RJH: Once I pulled a roll of film out of the camera right after my baba finished taking the pictures. He went after me and I ran again.

Teng Sheng is a quiet and soft-spoken girl with refined manners. She is eleven and is ready to go to the fifth grade. She has a fifteen-year-old brother, her mother is a language teacher in a local middle school, and her father is a chemical engineer.

Teng Sheng (TS): Last time I was playing cards with my baba. We were playing twenty-one. He bet with me. He said that if we were playing five games, he would win all five. It turned out that I won five games. And we agreed beforehand that for every game that you lose, the other person can rub her finger against your nose ten times. I did that to him fifty times. [Laughs.]

What do you like to do more with your parents? Less with them?

RJH: I like to play cards with my baba. I hate it when he smokes. I get teary eyes standing next to him. I like to go out with my mama—anywhere. But I don't like to hear her scream and yell. It's so loud and noisy. . . . And my baba, he loves to talk about printing presses. Every day is "printing press, printing press." [He gets excited and waves his arms.] I am so tired of it! There is no end. It seems . . . [loudly] he wants to turn the whole house into a printing press!

YCT: I like to play chess with my baba, but I don't like him to have serious talks with me. He is so wordy and preachy. I like to do everything with my mama. I especially like to go out with her.

TS: I like to go to the bookstore with my baba to buy books, but I don't like to discuss books and authors with him. He gets them all mixed up. He likes to do math with me, ever since I was very small, but I don't like math that much.

I like discussing literature with my mother. She is a language teacher in a middle school. Sometimes she brings home essays she thinks are good and she lets me read them. She also asks me to memorize certain passages from them and also a few Tang and Song poems. I memorized a *ci* [lyric-meter poem], "Congratulating the Bridegroom," when I was seven and also Li Po's "Viewing the Waterfall at Mount Lu." My mama also buys me books of poetry annotated for children and also books that help me with my English.

CHQ: I like to play chess with my father. I also don't like to see him smoke. It wastes money and is harmful to his body. I like to go out with my mama, but I don't like her to talk so much. She can be so tedious.

JW: I like to go to the park with my baba, climbing hills, swimming, and rowing. I don't like him to scold me, like: "How come you are not doing as well as before in your studies?" "Your exam scores are getting lower," and so on. I like to go to the Xin-hua Bookstore with my mother. She always buys me language and math books. I don't like to go to the fabric store with her. She always picks the materials she likes, not what we like. . . .

Do your parents help you with your homework?

JW: Whenever I write a composition, my mother always gives me a start. After I write my first draft, she checks it over and makes some comments, pointing out my mistakes. Then I go back and write it again. Every time I write a composition, I have to do it three times.

TS: There are two compositions I wrote that I was quite proud of. One time we were eating watermelon. My mama asked me to write an essay that has something to do with watermelon. I wrote this essay and it's called "The Watermelon Farmer." It's about this person who plants watermelon seeds—his expectations when he was planting and cultivating them and his feelings when he was taking the melons to the market. Another essay that I wrote was about my favorite toy. And my favorite toy is a lamb carved out of jade.

If you could be an animal, what would you be?

CHQ: I would like to become a huge *peng* bird [a roc], taking a journey of ten thousand *li*. In *The Journey to the West* [*Hsi-you-ji*], there was a bad guy, and only the Buddha was more powerful than he. He also transformed himself into a big *peng* bird. Sun-wu-kong [the main character in this novel, who is a monkey] can go one hundred and eight thousand *li* in one somersault, but the other guy [the *peng* bird] can go one hundred and nine thousand *li* in one somersault, even further than Sun-wu-kong.

RJH: I want to be a wild horse, one that can run swiftly on the grassy plains. I want to see the world.

The children in this session are particularly lively and carefree. At times they seem a little out of control. The self-appointed prompters, Jiang Wei and Chen Hai-qiang, are not always appreciated. (When Chen Hai-qiang tells Ren Ji-he that he should say he wants to be a cat, Ren Ji-he completely ignores him.) Ren Ji-he tends to go off on tangents, talking about himself and revealing private scenes from his family life. Yao Chen-tao and Teng Sheng are quiet girls—detached but unassuming—and they are a little surprised by the boys' responses and seem somewhat uncomfortable with their "wild" behavior. To add to the chaos, my own children frequently turn up with questions and requests.

How would you like to change yourself?

TS: I would like to read books, to become a more knowledgeable person.

YCT: I want to change myself into a country girl. That's because country girls are carefree and unrestrained. . . .

RJH: I hate to be restrained by anyone. I like to be free. That's why when I fill my bowl with rice, I go to a corner to eat. I don't like to eat with *them,* and so in that way nobody can watch over me.

JW: I like to sleep on my side. My mama tells me to sleep facing up. That way I won't get prickly heat.

RJH: In this kind of hot weather [as we talked it was about 100°F.], my baba still wants me to put a blanket on. I tell him I am hot, but he says I have to cover myself or otherwise he will spank me.

JW: My baba also spanks me. This afternoon I was taking a nap, but he insisted I was reading the paper, and so he spanked me.

What would you like to be when you grow up?

YCT: I want to be a movie actress, a doctor, a researcher in some area.

RJH: I want to be a rider, riding a wild horse.

TS: I want to be a translator or a doctor—

CHQ [interrupting rudely]: So many people in her family, for generations, were doctors. Her mother also wanted to become a doctor, but she couldn't—

TS (snapping back): She changed her field.

CHQ: I want to become a photographer or a painter. I like doing Chinese paintings. I like to draw landscape, people, objects, everything. I do splashed-ink painting. My paintings were exhibited in Shanghai twice. There was someone from my class who even went to Japan to exhibit his painting.

JW: When I grow up, I want to become a teacher or an actress. My mother knows that I want to be a teacher but nothing about the actress part.

RJH: My baba doesn't know a thing. I wouldn't tell him anything. He says: You better want to go to college or otherwise I'll drag you to the toilet and make you stay there.

CHQ: What kind of thinking is that! How can everybody go to college? How can there be so many college students?

RJH: My jiujiu is a graduate student. My baba told me: "You better be like him or I'll throw you out of this house." But I want to be a horseman. . . . I don't want anybody to tell me what to do.

* * *

I am back at the Zhongxin Elementary School. A month has passed since my last visit. The good Mr. Li has arranged for another group of children to talk to me. The three girls and two boys in this group are wondrous—gay and jocular but never out of control. Occasionally they may talk at the same time, but basic decorum is observed, and the situation never becomes chaotic as it did with the previous interview. The fact that the school is in session is an important factor: Children exercise more self-discipline when they realize that they are back at school. Their personalities also seem to clash less. They may disagree with one another, but they are not argumentative or rude.

Throughout this conversation the topic often changes suddenly because one of the children recalls an incident in her life that she wants to share. This is an afternoon of remembering; the spaces are filled with voices and laughter.

Hua Wei is a ten-year-old boy. He is not loquacious but once he starts to talk, he can pack ten sentences in one breath. Each sentence usually begins with "And then" whether it follows from the preceding sentence or not. His father works in a textile factory and his mother teaches in a middle school. He has a sister who grew up with their maternal grandmother—"to keep her company," he said—and came back home only in the past year.

Gao Min, a spirited and playful eleven-year-old boy, is a wonderful storyteller, and it is easy to like him because he is so totally honest about himself. He tells me that he is a "bad sport" and a "chicken" at heart, and I find him irresistible. He is fond of many persons including himself, which is another source of his natural charm. His grandmother took care of him when he was younger, and she used to spin tales of her own, he tells me, so he grew up with stories of ghosts and spirits and fantastic birds. Gao Min is in the sixth grade. His parents are both engineers working in a chemical engineering research laboratory. He speaks affectionately of his brother, who is a year older.

We are talking about pets.

Hua Wei (HW): I like to have turtles as pets. I used to have a turtle as a pet. I had it for several months, but my mama told me it's too dirty to have it in the house. And so I took it to school. I also tried to raise goldfish—five times! The one I kept the longest was a year and a half. But finally they all died. . . . The turtle I told you about, it's in my mama's school now. The shell has six corners and the color is kind of dark. It doesn't bite. I put it in water. They say that if you put it in a warm place it will die. I used to feed the turtle a little cooked rice in the morning. The turtle ate it.

Many children I talked to had pet birds that they or their parents had caught. Do you have a pet bird, or did you ever have one?

HW: No, never. My baba and mama say that it's too dirty to have a bird at home. Besides, I couldn't concentrate when I am at school—I'd be thinking about my bird. They say I have a fish and that's enough. I like little animals. I also like to go to the zoo. There are pandas, tigers, and bears at the Shanghai Zoo. I like to go to the bird cages and look at the birds. . . . I also like to catch insects—crickets and dragonflies. Usually I let them go after I finish playing with them. I put them back on the grass. When I grow up, I want to be a biologist.

GM: I like kittens. Someone who works with my baba has an old cat. Once this cat had three kittens and he gave one to us. When the kitten first got to our place, she wasn't weaned yet. We had to feed her milk. Then gradually she grew up. We had her for about two years. We liked to put her on our laps and sit in the sun. We used to give her a ball of yarn, and she liked to play with it. . . . We always had a litter box outside, on the balcony, but once we locked the door to the balcony, and she couldn't get out. She couldn't help it. She had to go to the bathroom inside our apartment. My baba was very mad about this. He said, "This cat goes to the bathroom everywhere and stinks up the whole place. I have to throw it out." I begged him not to do it. But one night, when I was asleep, he took it and left it by the riverbank. I cried when I found out. One day I saw the cat by the riverbank. I called her, but she didn't come to me. I think she'd become a stray. I was in the third grade or fourth grade then. She was a good cat. Sometimes she scratched a little, but she couldn't help it. My baba says that he's going to get another cat for me. I miss my cat. I wish we could get another cat from somewhere else.

I had a myna bird before. My uncle caught it and gave it to us. But we didn't know how to take care of her and she starved to death. [Laughs softly.] This was about two years ago. My uncle told us: "Why don't you take it? Our place is too crowded and too noisy. We live too close to the train station. She won't survive in our home." He gave the bird to us because it is quieter at our place. We taught the bird to talk. She could say a couple of words. When guests came, she'd say, "*Ni-hao, ni-hao* [How are you? How are you?]." But one day I forgot to put food in her cage. When I got home, she didn't have any more energy. I put some rice in front of her, but she was too weak to peck the rice. She died the next day.

HW: My aunt once brought over a sparrow. My uncle had caught it with a hat. They put it in an incense box. This is the kind of incense that you use as mosquito repellent. I tied a string around the sparrow's leg and then I fastened it to a pole. We put a handful of rice next to the bird. At night I don't know what happened. She died.

GM: My baba, he works in a chemical engineering research institute. The institute plants a lot of wheat, and sparrows like to gather there. There is also a greenhouse nearby. The people that work there made a special kind of net to catch the sparrows so that they won't get to the wheat. When the sparrows are caught, there is no way that they can get out. They also have someone there to watch over the net. If a sparrow gets trapped, he takes it out right away. They catch sparrows all the time. Once they caught a small sparrow, a very tiny one. My baba took a piece of board from his lab and made a cage out of it. He then put the bird inside the cage. I think that piece of board was contaminated. Not long after, the bird died. Once he brought home a magpie. Then we didn't know that the cage was contaminated, and so we put the magpie in it. The magpie also died. My father brings sparrows home all the time. We braise sparrows in a stew. [Laughs.] They are delicious.

Hua Wei at this point jumps into our conversation. He talks very fast, practically without a break.

HW: I'd like to have a cat, too, but my baba says that cats go to the bathroom too much. Once I went to my older sister's place. That's in the Zhujiang Bay section [of Shanghai]. Most of the houses there are two stories. Almost every family has a cat. My jiejie's classmate has a cat and she gave birth to four kittens. But they fed them snail tails (*lo-si-pi-gu*), and the kittens all died of diarrhea. The second day [I think he means "the second time"] the old cat had four more kittens. After a month they gave away two and sold one, and there was only one left. They gave two kittens to their neighbors to catch mice.

What are snail tails?

Several children are all talking at the same time:

GM: The snails live in the water, in the sea. We stir-fry them, and then we eat them. When we eat them, we don't eat the whole thing—

A girl (interjecting): We leave a little tail behind and that's the snail tail. It's like the snail's guts.

HW: These people used snail tails as cat food. And then after the kittens ate them, they all died. Only the old mother cat didn't die. That's because they fed her fish bones and leftover rice that night.

Also one day we saw two spotted cats outside. And then we caught them, but no one wanted them. And then we put them in a cage. The next morning my mother brought food to them. But when she opened the gate, the cats started to run. I think they were scared and hungry. And then we caught one. We put her back in the cage, and we fastened the gate with a wire. But that night she still managed to get out, and she ran away. One day on my way home from school, I saw a man carrying a net bag with a cat in it. The cat looked very much like ours.

What do you like to do in your spare time?

GM: I like to play chess. Usually when I am home from school and I've finished all my homework, I like to play chess with my gege. My brother is twelve.

Who usually wins?

GM: Usually he wins. [Laughs.] Sometimes I pull a surprise and I win. But I have only done that a few times. When I lose, I get mad, very mad, and I turn over the chessboard. [Laughs.] But the next time when he asks me to play chess with him, I say, yes, again. And when I lose, I turn over the chessboard again. [Laughs.]

When you get angry, how long does that last?

GM: About half an hour. Usually I sit there and cry. When my brother pays no attention to me, then I stop. The first couple of times when I cried, he showed some concern. He said, "All right, all right, I'll let you win this time." Then I thought crying really worked. But after a while it didn't work anymore. Now he pays no attention when I cry.

I notice Gao Min's perfect pu-tong-hua *and ask him what dialect he speaks at home.*

GM: *Pu-tong-hua*. Ever since elementary school, we have been speaking *pu-tong-hua*. Now we are not used to speaking the Shanghai dialect. My baba and mama also talk to us in the *pu-tong-hua*.

Zhang Yue is twelve and is in the sixth grade. Both her parents work for a voltage regulator factory, her father as an engineer, her mother handling records and documents. She is an only child.

Zhang Yue (ZY): My baba talks to me in the *pu-tong-hua.* My mama talks to me in the Shanghai dialect.

Do you still know how to speak the Shanghai dialect?

GM: I know a little. When I go to the store, all the sales clerks speak only the Shanghai dialect, and so I have to do the same.

Are your parents natives of Shanghai?

GM: My mama was originally from Sichuan. My baba's native place is in Northern Jiangsu Province. After she finished college in Sichuan, my mama was assigned to work in Shanghai. Ever since she started working there, she began to speak more *pu-tong-hua.* She knows that *pu-tong-hua* is more popular. Now she speaks the Sichuan dialect only when someone from her province comes to visit. I can understand a little bit of it. When someone talks too fast, I can't get it.

Zhang Xiao-yun, the youngest in this group, is nine and is very much her own person. She talks in a high-pitched voice, and her pu-tong-hua *has a strong Shanghai flavor. She is a fourth-grader and an only child at home. Her father teaches in Shanghai's Jiao-tong University. Her mother is a factory worker.*

Zhang Xiao-yun (ZXY): My baba was originally from Southern Jiangsu Province. My mama is a native of Sichuan. My mama, now that she lives in Shanghai, she speaks the Shanghai dialect. But sometimes she also speaks the *pu-tong-hua.*

HW: My mama is also a native of Sichuan, but she speaks the Shanghai dialect. My baba is from Shanghai.

Tu Mei-hua is an eleven-year-old girl in the fifth grade. Her birthplace is Xinjiang, a vast, autonomous region in northwestern China once known as Chinese Turkestan. Tu has no brothers or sisters. She lived with her paternal grandparents in a different section of Shanghai until she was seven. Her mother works in the cafeteria of a cotton mill. Her father is a dispatcher in a factory that manufactures bean products.

Tu Mei-hua (TMH): I was born in Xinjiang. We lived there only for a few years. Then we moved here. When we were living in Xinjiang, I was very young. I don't remember anything about it. My parents told me some things . . . actually not much about it. They say that when I was little I was not thin like now. Now I don't eat a lot. When I was little, I ate a lot. I drank milk every day, like drinking tea. They say I was very fat then, but now I am too skinny.

Do you remember some of the naughty things that you have done?

TMH: This was when I was very little. Once I was playing in bed with my baba. We were playing tug-of-war with the bedsheet. By accident I fell on the floor. My hand hurt badly. My baba wanted to bring me to a doctor, to have him take a look. I didn't want to go. So he said he was going to take me to a photo studio, to have my pictures taken. I liked that and so I said, "All right." Anyway I did go to the doctor and my hand was O.K.

GM: When I was little, my parents were busy with their work, and they had to go into town to work. My nainai took care of me then, but she had to cook for us, too, and so she couldn't watch over me all day long. Most of the time I was left in the cradle by myself. I discovered that if I kicked the cradle with my right foot, it would swing toward the right; if I kicked it with my left foot, it would swing toward the left. Later I was so used to rocking myself that I didn't need to be rocked. It was like playing. . . . I was about one then, when I was still at my "cradle age."

My mama says that when I was little, my hair stood up like this. [He shows me, grabbing and pulling it up.] I was very ugly. [Laughs.] My older brother was better-looking than me. He looked like a girl. But now, my mama tells me, "You are a little better-looking." [Laughs.]

Nowadays I don't do anything naughty. My mama says that I am older now and I shouldn't do naughty things anymore. I think she is right. . . . When I was in third grade, there were a lot of sand piles over there. [He points.] We used to dig holes, open tunnels, and build fortresses. Then one day all the sand piles were gone. Trucks took them away to build houses. Then we just didn't play over there anymore.

HW: When I was a baby, I slept in a cradle, and that cradle had bamboo wheels on it. When my mama was not home, my nainai looked after me.

But sometimes she had to cook. Since nobody was there to rock me, I kicked the side of the cradle to rock myself. But the cradle was like a car—it could move. Once the cradle slid away and bumped against the wall. That hurt my feet and I cried. Then my nainai came over to see what was going on.

Just recently a classmate came home with me and we broke something by accident. We were playing with a little ball. When we got to my house, we put our bookbags along two opposite walls, and we said that they were the goals. And then we started kicking the ball. We pushed each other, trying to get the ball. And then by accident we bumped against the china closet. The closet rocked a little bit, and then a rice bowl fell down and broke. We picked up the pieces and tossed them out. When my mama got back, she didn't count the bowls. [Fast and excited.] But later when we had to use the bowls for dinner, she found out that one was missing. And I said, "A-ya, how come one bowl is missing?" [Laughs.] She said, "I don't know what happened." And then they just sort of forgot about the whole thing.

Even now they don't know about it?

HW: No. [Softly.]

ZXY: When I was small, I stood on top of the bed one day. . . . We had a piggy bank. It had a lot of coins inside. It was in the shape of a big-nosed elephant. I thought it was a real elephant. I held it in my hand and I started shaking it. But then I dropped it on the floor and it broke into little pieces. I tumbled down, too, and I cried. My mama told me, "At least it's better than what happened to your jiejie [possibly an older girl cousin]. When she went to Suzhou with your waipo, she fell into the canal. It was a good thing that your waipo grabbed her hair and pulled her up. [Everyone laughs.]

GM: That's right! Once my classmate did a naughty thing. Near our place there is some farmland. On the leaves sometimes you can find these big green caterpillars [either luna moth or sphinx moth larvae]. This classmate took one of these big green caterpillars to a river nearby. He put the caterpillar on a large leaf and said to it: "I sentence you to die!" [Laughs.] Then he threw the leaf with the caterpillar on it into the river. [Laughs.] We also catch these large caterpillars and slowly torture them to death. If the caterpillar wants to go forward, we turn it on its back. If it still wants to go forward, we pull out the red horn from its tail.

[Intensely.] At first we didn't know what that red horn was. We thought it was a vital organ. But the caterpillar didn't die. It was hard to kill it! And the caterpillar . . . was having a tough time. Finally it was desperate, and it started to roll. Then we tried to poke it with a stick. But it still didn't die, even when the white liquid started coming out. Finally we smashed it with stones and sticks—

ZY interrupts: *Big green caterpillars*—anyway they are harmful insects.

GM: I have held big green caterpillars in my hands before. But until fourth grade I didn't dare to touch them. When I was in the fourth grade . . . my baba one day told me, "You are a big person now. Then why are you still afraid of a big green worm? Do you really think you look like a fourth-grader?" And so I said, "All right, all right, let me try to catch one tomorrow." The next day when I came home from school, I especially made a detour. I went by the river, and I saw a big green caterpillar. At first I didn't dare to touch it. Finally I got enough courage and when I was just about to touch it, it started to move. I was scared, and I hurried up and drew back my hand. Then I told myself: You are a fourth-grader now. How can you still be afraid of a green caterpillar? Then I clenched my teeth and I took the worm and put it on a leaf and carried it home to show my baba. "Hee, hee, hee," my baba said, "now that's better!"

ZY: We only torture the bad insects. We show no mercy. . . .

GM: We never touch the good ones. The bad insects, they eat our vegetables. Especially when they are larvae, they eat a lot. There is also a kind of worm that lives inside of soybeans. They are also green. Also there are rice bugs [weevils]. . . .

ZY: I hate rice bugs. Once I cut a worm in half with a string. [Laughs.]

GM: We also cut earthworms in half. Earthworms don't die when you cut them in half. They can regenerate, and so we end up with two. [Laughs.]

TMH: There are three of us. . . . We are all from the same class. We are all girls and so we are not that brave. We are very close. Once one of us said that no one was at her home and we should all go to her home to do our homework. We did that. And when we finished, we started playing. But somehow we all got scared. There are two rooms and three of us. [Gao Min laughs.] Then we started talking about how scared we were. I told them not to talk about it because it was really getting spooky. Then all of a sudden we all started screaming. It's really funny now that I think about it.

GM: Once we went to an air-raid shelter to help move some Ping-Pong tables. Before we used these shelters for air-raid drills. Now it's peacetime, and so we don't use them anymore, and we store Ping-Pong tables there. . . . Since we wanted to play Ping-Pong, we had to move them out. When we got down there, there were many rooms. They were all so dark! Except for the place near the entrance, it was all pitch-black. They were like the cave dwellings, dark and huge. [Dramatic and excited.] We boys wanted to scare the girls, and so when we got in, we gave a loud scream: "Ah! Let's get out of here. Monsters are coming!" Everyone scrambled out, and they got dust all over them. Our gym teacher told the girls, "What are you scared of? They're just pretending." So we went back again. When we were taking out the tables, they all got jammed together, and so the kids in the back couldn't get out. They started screaming: "A-ya! Help! Let's get out of here!" People out there heard the noise, and they went down to see what was going on. They shone their flashlights, and it was just a mess. Our teacher said, "Don't worry, don't worry. Let's slowly move out." That's how we got the tables out. Some of the girls said, "A-ya, that scared me to death. I don't dare to go down there again." That was when I was in the fourth grade. Now we don't go down to the shelter so much. Even now I would be scared to go in.

Once it was raining outside. It was a rainstorm. There was thunder and lightning, and they were going "ke-la, ke-la," making a lot of noise. My nainai went out to see a doctor. I was alone at home. I was only around seven. We have three rooms and I was home all by myself. What was I to do? The thunder was going "ke-la, ke-la." Lightning was flashing. Finally I dragged a quilt from the bed, covered myself with it, and stood there until my grandmother came home. First she knocked on the door. I didn't answer because I was under the quilt and couldn't hear anything. She finally opened it with her own key. At first she thought no one was at home. Then she saw the quilt. She uncovered it and found me inside. I told her that we have three rooms and I was by myself; of course I was scared. Because I had my shirt and pants on and was covered by a quilt, I got all sweaty. I had a cold later, because of what happened.

Do you play any sports?

GM: Our class has a soccer team. Before we always played another class from the fifth grade—class five-two. Now it's class six-two since we are in the sixth grade this year. We always compete against each other. They say they are better than us. We say we are better than them. Well, actually we *are* just a little better. [Laughs.] But sometimes when it comes to scrambling for the ball, they are pretty aggressive. [Louder and more intense.] We are better at controlling the ball, and they are better at scrambling for the ball. I am a fullback on my team.

Are the best players very popular at school?

GM: If a player is good, he gets to play an important position the next time. In the spring and fall, we get to play a lot of soccer. We are always drenched with sweat. In the summer we get "Ping-Pong fever." As soon as classes are over, we run out and try to grab a Ping-Pong table.

After doing your homework, do you have any free time?

GM: I do. Usually after I finish my homework, I help my baba, mama, or nainai to do some chores. Sometimes I go out and play. Now the teachers assign a lot less homework than before. After homework, we have some time before my baba and mama come home. In school we always have an hour of study hall. I do part of my homework then, and when I get home I finish the rest. It takes about half an hour. I don't really like to go out and play. I like to stay home and play chess with my brother.

Why don't you like to go out and play?

GM: It's too dusty outside. Besides, most of my classmates have moved away. There are only a few of us around and it's no fun.

Have you always lived in an apartment building? Do you like living there?

GM: I have never lived in a house with a yard. I like living in a building. If there is a flood, we don't have to worry. [Laughs.]

At this point Zhang Xiao-yun joins the conversation once again. Being a young child, she does not stay with one subject. She talks about whatever comes to her mind.

ZXY: Originally we lived in someone's study.[?] Then we bought a house. . . . When I was small, I liked to sing and dance. My father bought me a little toy piano. At first I didn't know how to play it. I just banged on it. That was when I was three. When I was about four or five, my baba taught me to play the piano with just one finger. Now I use five fingers. My father knows how to play the phoenix lute [*feng-huang-qin*]. A phoenix lute is long. You use a piece of circuit board, and you scrape the strings [attached to it].* Now I still play my little piano. . . . In my old school we had a platoon leader and her name was Wang Mei-juan. She was very mean and very bad. Once she stole something from the rice store. Then they reported her to our school. She also tried to put chalk powder in other kids' mouths. Our teacher told her not to behave like that. That was when I was in the second grade.

[To Zhang Yue] You are an only child. Do you sometimes get lonely? Do you wish that you had a brother or a sister?

ZY: I get lonely sometimes, but I don't want to have a brother or a sister. At my waipo's place, there are lots of kids. I have four uncles. Two of them already have kids. If there're any more, it'll be too noisy.

GM: I like little kids. They are cute, like kittens.

ZY: My waipo's neighbor, on the next floor, has a six-month-old baby. She is so cute, with two fat cheeks.

TMH: My neighbor has a little girl. She is around two. She is very fat. I like to touch her. She is so soft.

GM: I have a didi [younger brother]. Actually, he's my uncle's son. He comes to our home all the time. I like to hold him whenever he is around. He is about one. I take him everywhere. Our bed is a spring bed. He likes to sit on it because it's so comfortable. He likes to bounce on it. He goes "deng," "deng," up and down on our bed. Sometimes he likes to kick me. I ask him: "What in the world are you kicking me for?" He doesn't listen to me, and he gives me a few more kicks. He is adorable. I like him very much.

ZXY: I don't like small children very much. I have two friends upstairs. They are both in the second grade. When my baba and mama both go

* The phoenix lute is probably a homemade instrument.

to work, I am alone at home. When I am finished with my homework, I go and play with them. Sometimes I can't find them, and so I just stay home by myself.

HW: On our third floor, there is this three-year-old kid. He always comes to our home and makes a lot of noise. He wants this and he wants that. Whenever he comes over, I can't even do my homework. I don't like children very much.

GM: I like babies. But when they are a little older, they make too much noise—

TMH interjects: They are not cute anymore.

GM: Babies are plump and chubby. When they are not walking yet, they are cute. But when they are about three, they can be pretty noisy. There is a boy who lives downstairs from us. Every day he takes his two broken cars and he pulls them with two strings and comes to our place. He says, "Gege, Gege, look at my cars!" I tell him: "Your cars are broken." He says, "Whoom, whoom. . . . I can drive them by myself." He comes to bother me every day. When I am doing my homework, he likes to butt his head against my back. I can't even write. I tell him: "You better go home. Hurry up, go, go!" [Laughs.] There is no one at home to take care of him. That's why he comes to our place all the time. His nainai hasn't been home recently. She has some other business to tend to. His parents sometimes ask their neighbor to keep an eye on him. So he comes to our home to play. I don't like him too much because he is too loud.

How is the relationship among neighbors?

TMH: We all have very good relationships with our neighbors. We visit each other all the time. When something happens, neighbors always help each other out. Once I forgot my key. I couldn't get in and so I couldn't eat my lunch. My neighbor made me lunch.

GM: We all have good relationships with our neighbors, very harmonious, always helping each other out. And the children always play together.

When you are sick, who takes care of you at home?

ZY: I stay with my waipo.

GM: I have an older brother. When he comes home, he keeps me company. When he is in school, I have no choice. I stay in bed by myself. Sometimes my nainai is home. She tells me a story.

TMH: My father works the night shift, and so he takes care of me.

HW: I stay home and read in bed. I read and read, and before long I am fast asleep.

ZXY: If my temperature is not too high, I stay home by myself. My baba and mama always make me lunch before they leave. If I have a high fever, my baba takes half a day off. Ever since I was six, I have been staying home alone whenever I am sick.

What about in the summer? Who takes care of you during vacation?

ZXY: My father, he is a teacher. He is on vacation in the summer. But he is new in this school, and so he has to go there all the time, even in the summer. I often stay home by myself. Sometimes I play with my two neighbors. When I am alone, I read. My mother borrows novels for me from her factory. Sometimes I play my little piano. I can take care of myself, and I do my summer homework on my own.

TMH: There are kids in my building, but most of them have gone to visit their grandparents. So I don't have anyone to play with, and it's boring. I do my homework, and I like to work on my stamp collection. I look at my stamps, and I like to sing. This summer I got in this music ensemble. Since my baba is home during the day, I sometimes play chess with him, and I don't feel so lonely.

HW: Up until this summer my jiejie was still living with my waipo, but now she is back because here is actually closer to her middle school. . . . I have a lot of friends living nearby. I always go to their home and play.

Your older sister did not live at home?

HW: She used to live in the Zhujiang Bay district. That's also in Shanghai. She used to stay with my waipo. That's because at my waipo's place there are only two older people, and they are lonely, and so they took my sister there. Now since her register is over there, she is considered a resident of Zhujiang Bay, and when she took the high school entrance exam, she could not get into a middle school like Caoyang Middle School Number Two, because it does not belong to her district. She could only try for Caoyang Middle School Number One, and she got in. But to go to her school from Zhujiang Bay is farther than from here. And so she has decided to come home. Now she is staying with us.

TMH: I lived with my yeye and nainai until I was seven or eight. I came back home when I was ready to go to school. They live on Changshou Avenue. That's also in Shanghai. I go there all the time. I still have friends there. When I was living with my yeye and nainai, my parents did not come to see me on Sundays. When I got to be a little older, my yeye taught me to write letters. I even sent pictures of myself along with my letters to my parents. My baba especially saved them, and I still have these pictures now. I saw my parents whenever they came to visit. They came whenever they had time. I like living with my baba and mama. It was kind of lonely living with older people, but I had a lot of friends there, mostly girls, some a little older than me. We still have fun together, even now.

Gao Min and Zhang Yue tell me that they also grew up with their grandmothers. I ask them, What kind of things did you do with your grandparents?

GM: When I was younger, my nainai always told me stories—fairy tales and folk tales. Stories like Jing-wei the sun god. She said that Jing-wei or his offspring are still alive today. She also told me many riddles. A lot of the times I couldn't solve them. Now I read a lot. My parents buy books for me, like the *Biography of Yue Fei.** I read that book so many times. Now it's all worn out. I have also borrowed *The Water Margin* from the library. . . . Now that I am older, my nainai rarely tells me stories.

TMH: A lot of times when my parents tell me stories, I am very interested as I am listening. But afterward I forget what these stories are about. [Laughs.]

* A popular novel based on the story of the Song general Yue Fei (1103–41). See note on p. 230.

HW: Before I went to kindergarten, there was an old woman [*a-po*] taking care of me because my mama and baba both had to go to work. I was very naughty and the a-po couldn't keep me still. Finally she told me stories. One day she told me the story of a "wolf grandma" [*lang-waipo*]. My mama came to pick me up from her place that afternoon. That night I had a dream. It was so scary that when my mama got up in the middle of the night to make sure I had my blanket on, she found me covered with sweat. Ever since then I am more easily scared of things. I am always afraid of the dark. Once my baba and mama went out to see a movie, and I had to stay home all by myself. I was so scared. I got in my bed and under my blanket. Ever now and then I opened my eyes to see what was going on. I even crawled under my bed to see if there was anyone under there.

Do you still remember the story of the "wolf grandma"?

HW: Yes. I am still scared when I think about it. The story is about a "grandma" who ate several children. . . .

All five at once start to tell me the story.

GM: A wolf swallowed a grandma in one gulp and dressed in her clothes. Then she went to her grandchildren's house. They asked the wolf: "Why do your clothes smell so bad?" She answered, "I didn't have time to wash them. I was herding sheep." The children all said, "Herding sheep? We didn't know you changed your profession." [Laughs.] They also asked the wolf, "Why is your tail so big?" The wolf told them that it was a rope made of hemp. Then the first son and second son discovered it was a wolf. But the third son—he was also plump—he was the only one who didn't know about it. That was because he was under her spell a little. You see, ordinarily he liked their grandmother the best, and the wolf was paying special attention to him because he was very plump. And so the youngest grandson didn't suspect at all. Finally she ate him up, but then she couldn't find the first and second sons anywhere in the house. She went out and found them sitting in a tree. The wolf asked them: "Why don't you come down?" They said, "We won't. We know you are an old wolf." The wolf then said, "Very well, now that you know I am a wolf I am going to take my clothes off." Then she took the grandma's clothes off and showed herself as a wolf. The children told her: "If you want to eat us, we can pull you up." The wolf then went to find a straw rope. She tied it around herself and handed the other end to the children. The children pulled the wolf up and then quickly let it go on purpose. "Dong!" The wolf fell to the ground. They said to her, "Go and find a stronger rope and then make a loop and tie it around your neck." The wolf did this. She tied the rope around her neck, and the children pulled the rope with all their might. You can't really say that the wolf was strangled to death right away. They tied the rope on a branch, and then they climbed down. Slowly, after a while, the wolf stopped breathing.

HW: My story is different. There were three daughters. The oldest daughter told their mother: "Don't take the small path because there is a wolf there." The second daughter also told their mother, "Don't take the small path through the woods because there is a wolf there." But the youngest daughter said to her, "Go and take the smallest path. It is the nearest path. Hurry up and go to Grandma's house and bring me back some pears!" And then the mother took the nearest road and met a wolf on the way. And then the wolf called from behind. He said, "Why don't you stop and we can rest for a little bit." But the mother told him, "No, I am bringing some pears to my daughters." The wolf said, "I'm hungry. Why don't you give me some pears to eat?" He ate up all the pears and even the old mother. He put on her clothes and went to her house. The oldest daughter asked him, "Why are your eyes so red?" The wolf answered, "Because some sand got into my eyes and I was rubbing them." Then they asked, "Why do you have such a big tail?" The wolf replied, "This is a rope that your grandma gave me. I forgot to take it off." Then the youngest daughter said, "You guys talk too much. See, I'm not asking any questions." The wolf then said, "The fattest one can sleep next to me." The youngest daughter said, "I am the fattest." The first two daughters said, "We are skinny." So the wolf slept with the youngest child, and in the middle of the night, he ate her up. The other two daughters wanted to get out of the house. The wolf asked them, "Where are you going?" The oldest daughter answered, "The clothes are still on the clothesline. I am afraid the wind will blow them away." The second daughter said, "The kindling is not stacked. I am afraid the wind will blow it away." So they ran out and climbed up a tree. The wolf ran after them and forced them to come down. The children said, "We know you are a wolf." The wolf then took off his clothes and showed his true form. Then came Brother Magpie. The magpie dropped an iron rope down and carried them up in the air. The wolf told the magpie, "Don't listen to their lies. Give me a rope." The magpie gave him a straw rope.

The children then asked the magpie for a burning stick. They lit up the straw rope, and the wolf fell to the ground and died.

The story sounds like "Little Red Riding Hood."

GM: Not exactly. There is another story—the story of the seven sheep that were eaten by the wolf. The wolf disguised himself as the mother sheep. The little sheep said, "How come you have long hair on your paws?"

At this point all five join in to tell the story.

GM: The wolf burned off his hair and washed his paws clean. The little sheep then asked, "How come your body is brown?" The wolf hurried to the flour mill. He said to the owner, "I want you to give me some flour and rub it all over my body." The owner didn't listen to him. The wolf said, "If you don't give me some flour, I am going to eat you up." The owner had no choice but to rub flour all over the wolf. Now he really looked like a sheep. Then the sheep children said to the wolf, "Something is not right. How come your voice is so hoarse?" The wolf got a piece of dough and swallowed it. Now his voice was soft and gentle. . . .

ZY (in a soft and gentle voice): Kids, I am home! [Everyone laughs.]

GM: The little sheep then said to the wolf, "Let me look at your paws." They were white. Then they said, "Let me look at your body." It was also white. Finally they let him in. The old wolf, Aw! In one gulp swallowed all seven sheep alive. They were still alive in the wolf's stomach when their mama came back. The mama sheep cried out, "A-ya! all my kids are gone." Then she saw a wolf asleep under a tree. His stomach was still moving up and down, and so she knew that her children were still alive. She took a pair of scissors and went "ka-ca, ka-ca," and cut open the wolf's stomach. All her children jumped out. She then put several stones into the wolf's stomach and sewed it up. When the wolf woke up, he noticed that his stomach made a "hua-la, hua-la" sound. He said to himself, "Oh, it must be the little sheep's feet, 'gour-de, gour-de,' hitting against each other." Then he said, "A-ya, I am so thirsty, so thirsty!" He went to the well to get a drink. As he was leaning forward, and his head was getting closer to the water, "Dong!" He fell into the well and was drowned.

ZY: I like to read . . . what's that you call it . . . *Folktales of the World. . . .*

Hua Wei interrupts. He has thought of a story he wants to tell. Without any introduction he begins:

HW: Once there was a merchant. He was very wealthy. He had made all his wealth with his own effort. He bought a camel, and he put all his gold and silver on this camel. Then a poor man came. He was very greedy and very lazy. He said to this rich man, "Why don't you give me some money?" The rich man gave him half his money. Then he thought to himself, "If I can get all his money, I would be a millionaire." He asked the merchant again, "Why don't you give me the rest of the money? That way you don't have to carry it with you." The rich man agreed. He said, "All right. I'll give you all my money." Then the poor man heard that the rich man had something precious—a treasure. He asked the rich man to give him that, too. The rich man did. It was a bottle that you can sprinkle water out of. Then the poor man had sand in his eyes. He thought the water from the bottle would help to wash it off. He put a drop in his right eye. It felt all right, and so he put a drop in his left eye, too. He became blind in both eyes.*

GM: I like to read *The Arabian Nights.* That's my favorite.

Do your parents encourage you to read?

ZXY: Yes. Also teachers encourage us to read books outside of school.

GM: My mother says that reading books helps me to broaden my knowledge.

Do you like to sing or dance?

GM: I don't like to sing. My voice sounds terrible. . . .

ZY interrupts: His voice is too hoarse.

GM: But in kindergarten I used to be on the dance team. [Chuckles.] Ever since I got to first grade, I haven't done any more dancing.

* Note the irony of the story. The rich merchant is the good guy, hardworking and generous. The poor man is the bad guy, lazy and greedy.

HW: In school I used to dance, but my baba told me: "You better not dance anymore. Otherwise you are going to wear out your shoes."

What are some of the things you have done that you are proudest of?

GM: Actually I didn't do this, my brother did. When he got in Shih-da Middle School (which is one of the best schools in the country), he brought prestige to me, too.

TMH: I was very happy when I got into the music ensemble.

HW: In third grade I had the highest score in our final exam. That time our final was very hard. I was the only one who got higher than ninety in our language exam.

GM: I was number four in our midterm exam. I was very happy because the first three were all cadres—hee, hee, hee . . . and I am not.

Who can become a cadre?

GM: Like her [pointing to Zhang Yue]. She is a committee member in her platoon.

ZY: She [pointing to Tu Mei-hua] is a platoon leader. . . .

TMH: No, committee member. Platoon leader, it's not my turn yet. . . . Cadres are those who work hard. Those who are well rounded and have high abilities. The teachers don't pick them. They are elected by the students.

HW: You choose whomever you like. . . .

GM: No, no, no. Whoever fits the job. You don't choose him just because you like him. [Laughs and points to the girls.] She is a squadron leader. She is also a squadron leader. She is a committee member of her platoon. And I am a nothing.

HW: I also am an ordinary citizen [*yi-ban-xiao-min*].

Do you want to become a cadre?

GM: Ever since first grade I've wanted to become a cadre. But I'm still not one.

* * *

I am in the reception room at the Institute of Scientific and Technical Information in Chongqing, where I met Fang Kan and Wang Lian. This new building, only partially complete, will house the institute's staff. Outside there is a basketball court, where high school boys and drivers from this work unit are playing a vigorous game in the intense heat.

The children at this interview, two girls and a boy, are junior high school students. They all live in the residential community on the hill. Each has one or both parents affiliated with the institute. In this particular session, all are eager participants. They all express their thoughts in the pu-tong-hua, *even though they are more accustomed to speaking in the Sichuan dialect. During our chat a woman from the maintenance staff comes into the room several times to refill our cups with hot tea. The Chinese and the Japanese believe in the magical power of tea: it refreshes the body and mind and encourages good conversation. On this hot August day, I, too, have become a believer.*

Wen Yen-yun is almost fourteen and has just finished her second year in junior high. Her face is framed by neatly cropped hair, her eyes glisten with intelligence and dogged determination, and her voice, strong and impassioned, at times can become brash and defiant. She is an only child, singularly concerned about her "autonomy." She loves reading novels and essays and examining butterflies at close range; "the Russian Leonardo," Mikhail Lomonosov, is her hero.

Zhu Qi-hong is fourteen and still wears her hair in two long braids. I imagine she may have looked like this ten years ago: not only her braids but her smile and her glance remain childlike. She dreams of being far away from her parents someday and finds the remote northwestern region of China alluring. When she was very young, she lived with her paternal grandparents in Zhejiang Province but came home to Chongqing when she was four. She has an older brother who is fifteen. Her father does research on nuclear physics, and her mother is a second-grade teacher.

What places, outside of Chongqing, have you visited before?

Wen Yen-yun (WYY): I was born in Shenyang [in Liaoning Province]. I have been to Beijing, but I didn't stay there very long. I went with my mother. She was on a business trip. I have also been to Chengdu [the other large city in Sichuan] and two other places in Yunnan Province. My mother was originally from Yunnan.

Did you find any differences in terms of the people's temperament and the local customs?

WYY: People from Chongqing are straightforward and unconstrained. They are frank and outspoken. My mother tells me that people from Chengdu don't tell others how they really feel. My parents' families were originally in Yunnan. I stayed there once for about a month. People there celebrate New Year differently from us. They always make their own things, like the popped rice candy. We always buy everything, but they are different. Most of the people there know how to make these things. And these popped rice candies taste better than the ones that you buy in the store. I spent two New Years in Yunnan. Also in these places they have small "cultural centers." And on New Year's days, they have dragon lantern parades. We always have four days of holiday for the New Year. The things that we eat on New Year's Eve. . . . We eat sweet rice dumplings [*tang-yuan*]. No, we don't make meat dumplings [*jiao-zi*] that night like the Northerners do. Also the children in Yunnan, they get money on New Year's day, but we in Chongqing usually don't get anything.

Is it because your parents confiscate the money that you receive on New Year?

Zhu Qi-hong (ZQH): My parents always confiscate mine.

WYY: My parents let me keep a few dollars, but they take the rest. But the only time I received anything was the time that I was in my mother's hometown in Yunnan. I don't have any relatives in Chongqing. Anyway, they hardly give out any money here.

What about pocket money?

WYY: I get about three or four yuan a month.*

ZQH: I don't get any. If I need anything, my parents always try to buy it for me, but I don't have any money of my own.

Deng Yue-sung is twelve and has just finished his first year of junior high. He has an older sister who is fourteen. His father is a chemist and his mother a physician. He is a good calligrapher, enjoys reciting poems (preferably in the Sichuan dialect), and is well versed in Chinese history. But his first love is still science—UFOs and flying saucers—and he also likes the martial arts. The youngest in this session, he readily joins in the conversation and is completely at ease with the two girls.

Deng Yue-sung (DYS): Each month I get about a yuan. Sometimes I return it to my parents if I didn't spend it. If I need something, as long as it is for legitimate reasons, they'll get it for me.

WYY: I like to spend my money on books. My mother doesn't have the habit of buying books. She only subscribes to magazines for me. So often I'll spend a whole afternoon browsing in a bookstore.

DYS: I like to read a lot. I enjoy reading classical novels more than modern novels. I have no problem understanding them. I also like history.

What are your thoughts about your past culture and tradition?

WYY: I don't like Confucius and Mencius at all. I personally feel they are pretentious and preachy. They are so self-righteous. We always have to write compositions about something that they have said. It's so boring!

DYS: But I think Confucius . . . he had his own views. These views have meaning for us even today. Let's say what he said [pauses] . . . about those things . . . anyway, what he said has positive values. I think his ideas are correct.

WYY: I like classical poems and songs better. I don't learn them by heart, but I like to read them. My favorite poets are Meng Hao-ran and

* In 1984, one yuan = forty-three cents U.S. at the official exchange rate.

Bai Ju-yi. I also like the lyric-meter [*ci*] poems of Li Qing-zhao and Xin Qi-ji.*

DYS: I also like Cao Cao and Cao Zhi.†

WYY: And Tao Yuan-ming,‡ his landscape poetry. I like his style.

ZQH: We study these poems mostly at school. Without the teachers' explanation, they are too hard to understand. Our parents are too busy with their work. They don't have time to teach us.

WYY and DYS together: That's true!

DYS: Usually after the teacher explains a poem and if I like it, I'll memorize it. I always recite it in Sichuan dialect.

* Meng Hao-ran (689–740), a major poet of the early High Tang period. Known for his landscape poetry, he drew his inspiration from the awesome mountains surrounding his native place, Xiangyang in Hubei Province, and from his travels in the eastern and central Yangtze regions.

Bai Ju-yi (772–846), a major Tang poet and one of the most prolific. His work is characterized both by great lyrical qualities and by social awareness. Bai was sensitive to the plight of the common people, whose lives and sufferings form his main themes.

Li Qing-zhao (1084?–1151?), one of China's foremost women poets. She lived during a time of great social and political turmoil—the interregnum between Northern and Southern Song—and her personal losses were many. Yet Li Qing-zhao's poems were never sentimental or self-indulgent; they sing of life and its astonishing powers. In one verse she says:

> No dallying in bed for one who grieves,
> when clear dew descends with the dawn,
> and the wu-t'ung tree is about to bud.
> There are so many diversions in spring.
> The sun is rising: the fog withdraws;
> see: it will be a fine day after all.

Xin Qi-ji (1140–1207), a major poet of the Southern Song dynasty, was a master of the lyric-meters. His compositions are characterized by patriotic themes and heroic sentiments.

† Cao Cao (155–220) was the most powerful general during the last decades of the Han dynasty, a period of deep political division. When he failed to reunite the empire, he consolidated his hold in northern China and set up his own kingdom—the kingdom of Wei. The story of this period is retold in the classic novel the *Romance of the Three Kingdoms.* Cao Cao was also an accomplished poet and prose writer.

Cao Zhi (187–226), son of Cao Cao and younger brother of Cao Pi, who was the first emperor of the Wei dynasty. Unlike his father and brother, Cao Zhi never had much political power, but he was the greater poet.

‡Tao Yuan-ming (365–427), was a poet of the Six Dynasties. Though he lived a life marked by poverty and disappointment, he was able to find serenity amidst need and anxiety:

> I built my hut in a place where people live,
> and yet there's no clatter of carriage or horse.
> You ask me how that could be?
> With a mind remote, the region too grows distant.

When I ask him if he would like to recite one for us, he answers briskly, "Sure." Then rhythmically he chants Cao Cao's "Duan-ge-xing" ("Short Song Composed During a Banquet")—a treat for all of us.

DYS: I started memorizing poems when I was about three or four. At that time the adults taught me some. Now that I am older, I recognize a lot more characters, and I try to understand by myself what these poems mean. And when I have difficulties, I usually go to the teacher. Parents are very busy. Unless we ask a specific question, most of the time they don't . . .

Do you wish that your parents spent less time at work and had more time with you at home?

WYY: Not at all, *not one bit!* Now my mother, sometimes she works at home. It seems . . . anyway, I don't want to ask them questions, even if they have time. [Slowly.] That's because when they try to explain something, they are wordy and long-winded. They don't make themselves clear and we are all confused. But if we ask our teachers or classmates, they give us a quick answer and that's it. With our parents, often afterwards, we even get a lecture: "Next time, you have to listen well. . . ." [Imitates their voices.] When they are home, the atmosphere is—

ZQH interjects: We don't feel comfortable.

WYY: I am not comfortable at home. I don't have any freedom. If they go to work, when they come home, they are very concerned about our health and what we eat. If they don't go to work, they'll be watching me even more closely.

DYS: When they are not home, I have the freedom to arrange my time, when to study and when to rest. I feel that being somewhere else, like my waipo's house, is better than being at home. Other people look after us but let us develop freely. My parents say that whenever my sister and I go to our uncle's house, we are like birds flying out of their cage. My uncle lives near here. He is in his twenties and is not married. He works in a hotel.

Do your parents share your interests?

DYS: We share some, but because we have a big age gap . . . It's not the same with my jiujiu, my mother's younger brother, and my erbo, my father's younger brother. They are all in their twenties, and we have a lot in common. For example, last time when I went with my jiujiu and erbo to climb a mountain, my baba also came along. He was the one who said, "Don't go on this path! Don't go on that!" He went home first. And when he was gone, we explored everywhere—in the cane and high grass. I had a great time! Sometimes I was in front. Sometimes I was behind. My feet were scratched and bruised, but I feel I had a lot of endurance. It was really worth it. Anyway, whenever we go out . . . [trails off]. I can't quite describe it.

ZQH: I like to go out with my own friends.

WYY: On Sundays, we often go out as a family. But on outings I prefer to be with my friends or classmates. If I go swimming, my parents say, "You have to have a friend with you" . . . [imitating their voices] . . . "Make sure you have everything." Also I like to go to the bookstore, but they don't let me do that that often. I can only go about once a week; and I have to wait until they are in a good mood to ask for it. As long as I've done my homework, I wish they'd leave me alone, and let me have my own thoughts and ideas.

We talk about the difference between children's views and adults' views. A child may find climbing boulders fun and adventurous, but his parents may see it as potentially dangerous.

WYY: Like when I was in elementary school, there were two paths to get to school, one, a regular road, and the other, a path passing through a hill—the Eastern Hill. There are many caves on the hill, and we tried to scare ourselves, saying that there were evil spirits living in these caves. And the more we talked about it, the more we wanted to take a look. . . . We like to do things like that. When I was small, they were digging a tunnel to put in a gas pipe. Right around the Information Center, they dug a big hole. One night—it was pitch dark—a couple of kids—these were my friends—and I said, "Let's go over there and take a look." The hole was very deep. One of my friends was the leader. She said that she'd go in first. She did and shortly after, we heard a loud scream. That was her. She climbed out and said that there was a pair of green eyes in there staring at her. I didn't believe her, but nobody else dared go in there again. And so I went in there myself. There was a person in there. He jumped and I screamed. I turned around and ran out. My head bumped against the pipe. It hurt, but I didn't care. I was so scared. When I got home, I didn't dare to tell my parents. It's funny now that I think about it. [Laughs.]

From the time when you started school until now, have there been any changes in your relationship with your parents?

ZQH: When we were very young, we did whatever our parents told us to do. Now we have our own ideas, and we like to do things according to our way. If parents tell us what to do, we are not too happy about it. We wish that they would stay at a distance.

What about changes in your relationship with your teachers?

WYY: From first to fourth grade, there was nothing unusual about my relationship with my teachers. But in fifth grade, we had a new teacher. She was in charge of our class. We had a very special relationship with her. She was very concerned about us and was very kind. After school we often went to her home, to play or to borrow books. After class we liked to go to her office, to talk to her. I had a classmate who was the mischievous kind. This teacher was very concerned about her because she knew that this girl spent too much time with her boyfriend. But this girl still liked her a lot. Once she told her parents that when she starts working, she'll give her first month's salary to her.

She was a language teacher. The whole class became interested in literature because of her. I think, compared to my fifth-grade teacher, my middle school teachers are too inflexible.

ZQH: I think middle school teachers . . . in primary school, teachers mainly tell us to listen to grownups and to study well. But in middle school, the teachers place more emphasis on helping us to see right from wrong—to understand what the meaning of life is and what is a correct way of life. Some of my classmates think that what the teachers are telling us is too far removed from what we know and what we understand. For example, the teachers say that not passing the college entrance exam will have great consequences for our future. Some students realize this but others don't.

DYS: From first grade to third, the teachers more or less guided us by the hand. When we got to fourth and fifth grade, they tried to enlighten us.

I think that especially in the fourth and fifth grade, the teachers should be younger. We have more things in common with a younger teacher. In fifth grade I had Teacher Huang, a math teacher. Her way of teaching could draw responses from us. She showed us many different ways of solving one problem. It made us think. In middle school, the teacher in charge of our class also lets us develop independently, but she always leaves right after class. We don't have much contact with her. And there's one thing I don't like about her: whenever we do something wrong, she always makes us do extra cleaning—that's her way of punishing us.

WYY: The teacher I like very much—well, I remember at that time not only were we all very close to her but our whole class was very harmonious. If anyone had a new toy, she shared it with everyone else. If anyone had something good to eat, she let everyone taste it. And our teacher used to tease us all the time. Now in middle school if a teacher sees us buying popsicles, her face drops, and she gives us a stern look.

ZQH: I still like my middle school teachers better. Like my physics teacher—he's very strict, but he is good. He wants us to concentrate during class. Anyone who gets restless and doesn't listen well is punished. Those who don't do well on tests always get a lecture. He commends the good students and encourages competition in class.

Do you find homework to be useful?

ZQH: Basically yes. But when we were preparing for the high school entrance, our teachers assigned so much homework and we had so many tests that we got very little sleep. We all complained. It seemed like we were cramming to the last minute. Sometimes in one evening, we had math and physics homework and then on top of that we had to write a composition. Even three or four hours were not enough to finish everything. So we went to bed about eleven or twelve every night. First thing in the morning we had to hand in our homework because the teachers didn't want us to discuss our solutions or copy from each other. Some of us think it's not a good idea to have so much homework. We prefer our teachers spending some time in class explaining the material and then letting us have the rest of the time for asking questions and discussing problems together.

This summer we have just finished taking our high school entrance exam, and we're not supposed to have any summer homework, but our language teacher still asks us to practice our calligraphy. I think it's useless. We are much older now, and our way of writing is already set. It really doesn't matter now.

DYS: I feel that teachers should not assign too much homework, so that we'll have more time to figure out the problems ourselves. Some of the homework is easy, but some is very hard. Usually I ask my sister. I like to ask her because we learn things pretty much the same way. If I ask my parents, they explain everything from the very beginning. It takes them fifteen to twenty minutes just to answer a simple question.

ZQH: But then about forty percent of the students love to fool around. If you don't give them enough homework, they become lazy. The teachers mainly have these students in mind when they assign homework. To get anywhere you really have to work, to make an effort.

DYS: Students in junior high are not like students in a high school. They still love to play. We all can't wait to finish our homework and play. Actually we prefer to play first before starting homework.

WYY: Two years ago I had a classmate who was very smart. In fact he was number one in the whole school. But this year he failed a grade. That's all because he didn't study. In fifth grade one of our teachers was a man teacher who was very strict. This student got a beating almost every class. He had to be watched closely; otherwise, he wouldn't concentrate. Actually it was no use telling him to pay attention. The teachers had to whip him. Even his parents asked the teachers to discipline him. And he did very well when he was under strict discipline. But once he got to junior high it was different. The teachers couldn't watch him that closely anymore. There are different teachers for different subjects. I remember once we had a test in geography and he handed in a blank paper. During class he draws and does other things. He doesn't really care.

Do teachers physically punish students?

WYY: Very rarely. Like this man teacher I was talking about—actually he was very kind. He was very nice to good students, especially to the girls. He was stricter with the boys. He could be very tough on those who liked to goof off.

ZQH: In primary school, teachers flog only those students who did something terrible, those students who are a bad influence on everybody else.

My mother is a primary school teacher. She thinks it's good that primary schools have stricter discipline. She says that middle school teachers are too easygoing. I don't agree. I feel . . . students in middle school are older, and it's embarrassing to punish them physically. But I have this English teacher—she is patient and teaches pretty well, but some of the students think English is boring. They have no interest. Our teacher puts in a lot of effort. Sometimes she even skips lunch to help these students, but they still seem indifferent. . . . To learn anything well, you have to have the interest first.

DYS: Some of my middle school teachers are not so gentle. The teacher in charge of our class, he whips us on the palms of our hands if we don't do well on our English dictation.

WYY: But I don't like teachers who are too gentle, too lenient. They can't handle the bad students. I once had a teacher who was firm but gentle. He was very kind to most of the kids, but if you tried to get smart with him, he could be very mean. Then we have another teacher—our teacher last year—who was always accommodating the bad students. Let's say you have a fight with someone. If he finds out, he'll ask you: "Did you have a fight with so-and-so?" If you say, "Yes," he'll tell you you are very honest and he won't punish you. As a result our class is in total chaos. Our class used to be one of the best in our school, but not so anymore; now I think we are one of the worst. If there is a test coming up, let's say tomorrow, usually more than twenty students will skip class in the afternoon. That's what happens, and it makes other students—the ones who go to class—very unhappy. They just hope for a stricter teacher.

The subject returns to the family.

Do you get along with your brothers and sisters?

ZQH: I don't. Not with my brother. I grew up in my native place [in Zhejiang]. When we were very young, we spent very little time together. My older brother, when he was little, was used to being alone, without any brothers or sisters. And so when I came back home, he was very unhappy. When he and my father went to Zhejiang to pick me up, that very first day, right after we met, we had a fight. Now sometimes we get along well. Sometimes we don't even talk to each other.

DYS: My older sister and I grew up together, and we have always had a good relationship. We have a lot of fun together, but then we also fight. But as we get older, we are much more patient with each other, though sometimes we still have arguments because of our different points of view. But we also like to exercise together every morning. Because she doesn't have good health, I have become her "coach" in a way.

I like sports. Boys like to play soccer and do other sports together. I like soccer very much, but no, I don't want to become an athlete when I grow up. I want to be a scientist. I'd like to do things like building a flying saucer.

WYY: I change my mind all the time about what I want to become. Sometimes I'd like to be a zoologist. Sometimes I'd like to be a writer because I like literature very much. But my mother wants me to become an engineer or some kind of a specialist. And so I don't tell them what I want to be. I like to collect butterflies, to press them in my books. I like to take their scales off and see what they look like under the scales. But if my parents see me doing this, they say I'm not doing "proper work." If I see a strange plant that I've never seen before, I like to press it in a book, and sometimes, I take my specimens out and examine them.

I especially admire the Russian scientist Lomonosov. He had many talents. He made great achievements both in the area of literary writing and in physics. Some people said that he alone was a university. He was the son of a peasant, and at that time it was very difficult for someone like him to accomplish anything great. He went through a lot of hardships. He founded a university in Moscow, in the seventeen hundreds, when Russia was still under the Tsar.

Do you have books about animals and nature?

WYY: It's not easy for us to find books about nature. The books in the bookstore are mainly for small kids but not for us. We learn something about plants and animals in school, though. We all like books, but we don't have enough. Sometimes we go to the library. . . .

DYS: But the library doesn't have much either—at least not the kind of books that kids at our age like to read.

ZQH: I like physics. I hope in the future to be like my father, to do research in physics. I want to become someone like Madame Curie, someone who is strong. Many grownups tell me that I should become a doctor, but I don't want to be a doctor. If I am interested in physics, I want to be a physicist. I'm not doing that well in physics now, so I have to work harder to achieve my goal. Of course, my father is very supportive of me. But my mother is quite unhappy about this because she wants me to become a primary school teacher. I told her I didn't want to become a teacher. I want to go to college like my father.

What changes would you like to see in yourself?

DYS: I wish I could withstand hardship better. I lack endurance. Being under my parents' care, I am like a flower growing in a greenhouse.

Changes in your parents?

DYS: I wish that my father would let go a bit. If he doesn't watch us so closely, we will have more freedom to develop ourselves. A lot of times I feel he is like a Bodhisattva chanting a sutra. He is overly anxious about our studies. I wish that my mother would not worry so much about us . . . that in our everyday life she would let us take care of ourselves. That way, when we grow up, we'd be better able to live independently.

WYY: My father is very good to me. He thinks I should choose the path I walk on for myself. But my mother is not like that. I like to read literature, but she says: "This is not going to be on your exams. Study something more useful!" If my father catches me reading, he just sighs, not saying a word. Still, it makes me feel bad, and so I try not to read in front of them. At home I don't openly do the things that I like to do. I don't want to hurt their feelings.

ZQH: My father is very good to me, very concerned about me. My mother is a schoolteacher, and she has an occupational disease. [Laughs.] From morning till night, she talks without end. At school she teaches first- and second-graders. At home she treats us like first- and second-graders, looking after everything, every detail of our lives. Each day she repeats the same thing over and over again. I wish she'd devote more time to her career. That way she'd leave us alone.

Changes in your environment?

DYS: I wish that we had better sports equipment and facilities. Our soccer field is too small—it's about the size of this room. Many students like to exercise more. . . . Also we should plant more trees in our area. We have a lot of pollution, and we should be more concerned about problems of pollution.

WYY: My circumstances are quite good. My family situation is fine, but when I was born, my mother gave me this name *yen* [wild goose], hoping that one day I would be like a wild goose soaring to the clouds [*yun*]. She didn't want me to be confined in a small environment, to have a narrow view. Now that I'm older, I, too, want to achieve something, but then I am also an only child. . . . Deep down I feel torn between. . . . I like to be close to my parents, but at the same time I have my own hopes and plans for my future. I am sure I can be independent someday. I was at a day care center at two and I went to kindergarten at three. At that time I was only home on Sundays.

ZQH: In the future I'd like to be far away from my parents. I like to go to places. From what I have seen in the movies, someday I would like to go to the Northwest, maybe Xinjiang.

WYY: I have a cousin who volunteered to go to the mountain area right after he had finished Qinghua University. As soon as my mother found out, she gave him a long lecture. I don't think that's right. I argued with her many times about it.

If you could be an animal, which would you like to be?

ZQH: I'd like to be a huge wild goose [*da-yen*]. I'd like to change the character *hong* [meaning red] in my name to *hong* [meaning wild goose].

WYY: I like swans better. When a swan is small, she is an ugly duckling, but when she is full grown, she is graceful and beautiful. She can fly in the sky, walk on land, and swim in the water—she is not confined to any one place.

DYS: I want to be an animal that can live for a long time, even longer than the tortoise. I want to see the development of mankind.

* * *

In 1984, I went to Beijing twice. During my second visit, the reception room at the Institute of Scientific and Technical Information of China, as in Chongqing, became a meeting place for children and me. My host, Mr. Lin, had magical means: within a day he assembled several groups of primary and middle school students. His wife even packed me lunch so that I could spend all my time with them.

The reception room we are in is large, and since there are only four of us, it seems natural to cluster around the corner of a table to talk. The three boys I'm talking with—two in primary school and a third in junior high—know each other well. Either or both of their parents work for the Institute.

Mu Tong, twelve, and about to enter the sixth grade, is short with a round face and very round eyes. He is always grinning slightly though he does not realize it. The grin, which is also a frown, gives him a quick distinction: he is both comical and serious. As his name Tong [child], suggests, he has the unaffected and playful stuff of an eternal child. At home, where he is the youngest of three, he is loved and pampered by his parents and two sisters, much older than he.

Zhang Jun is a little older than Mu Tong and inches taller. His face is also graver and his manners more reserved. He speaks in a low and soft voice, and throughout our interview he holds on to Lan Hang's hand as if he were an older brother. His father is in the foreign service and is rarely home. His mother is a retired factory worker.

Lan Hang, fifteen, is going to begin his third year in junior high. His father works for the Information Center as an architect and his mother as an assistant researcher. He is tall and lean with a narrow face and pointed chin. He talks slowly and deliberately and likes to end his sentences with a chuckle. His responses are full of surprises, but they leave the listener wondering whether he is half-teasing. He likes to talk and is very inquisitive, yet there is a shield about him that makes it difficult to penetrate to the real person. I will probably never know how much of his story is true and how much an invention.

Mu Tong (MT): We knew each other even before we moved here. We moved here from [the residential area attached to] the Chemical Engineering Institute last year, last November. We haven't changed schools yet. I ride our work unit's bus to school every day. It takes about an hour to get there. There are about four or five of us doing the same thing.

Zhang Jun (ZJ): I take the public bus with another boy. I can't take the unit's bus or I'll be late for school.

When school starts this autumn, we'll still be going to the same school over on the other side. When we take our entrance exam the year after, we'll try to get into a middle school in this area.

MT: Anyway, there is no good [primary] school here. [Quickly.] Even if there were, we couldn't move our register here.

ZJ: The middle schools over here are not that good either.

Lan Hang (LH): When I moved here, I was transferred to a school here. That was very difficult. My mother had to think of *ways* to get me here. [Laughs.]

Why was the transfer difficult?

LH: The schools here only accept students who have connections [*guan-xi*]. [Laughs.] Ordinary students are not admitted. I was transferred about three or four months after I moved here.

Why is it difficult for ordinary students to be transferred?

LH: I am young. I don't understand things like that. It's something that concerns adults. [Laughs.]

Did you have problems adjusting to your new environment?

LH: No. It's easy to adjust. There is only one other person around my age who moved here with me. He didn't change his school, though. . . . Making new friends? That's not hard. It takes less than a week to know everybody. It's easier to make friends in the same class, but with kids from other classes. . . . I don't know kids from my neighborhood that well.

MT: We don't have any problems because we are going to the same school and our friends are still over there.

Do you spend a lot of time on your homework each day?

ZJ: We are very busy right before exams.

MT: When exams are coming, I don't even go home—I have to stay at my old neighborhood with my mother. After we moved here, my mama still had many colleagues over at the old place. Some of them we know very well. And so just before exams we live with them. We are very tense then. At night I usually have so much homework that it's impossible to finish it all. This is during the "big four exams"—the two midterms and two finals. We would go over there the week before and come back after the exams were over. We are tested on math and language. The exams are not hard, though.

ZJ: The math is easy. The language is more difficult.

What is your language test like?

LH: There is a part on our basic knowledge of language, and then there is always a composition. The composition usually counts fifty points. We have all kinds of topics to write, like "My Friend."

What kind of composition did you have to write for your entrance exam?

LH: We had to write about "change."

How did you write it? It sounds a little difficult.

LH: We are all well prepared beforehand. [Slowly.] This kind of topic, . . . like describing a person, we all write it this way, . . . like writing about your playmate, someone you know, . . . as long as it is about a person, we all write it this way: we say that this person originally was not very good, and then something happened to him, and he became better. [Laughs.] It's always like this—"eight-legged."* [Laughs.] This is also the way I write: A person, after learning from others, becomes better. That is the safest way to write.

If you don't have to write it this way, how would you write it?

* From the mid-Ming, this was the standard and stylistic form in which the essays of the civil-service examinations were to be written. Until the mid-Qing, examiners were interested more in the structure of an essay than in its content. Mass-produced handbooks on how to write eight-legged essays were available to prospective candidates. The term now refers to any writings that follow prescribed forms.

LH: [Silence.] I need time to think about it.

Do you always write compositions the way your teachers would approve?

LH: I almost always follow the approved way of writing. If it's an informal piece, a short piece, I write it more the way I want. But if it is a formal piece, I follow the "correct path." This was what I did in primary school. In middle school, there were some changes. I don't follow the "correct path" so closely. I am more daring. Now I write more or less the way I feel.

What about writing your views of a book that you don't think much of?

LH: Sure, I have to do that sometimes. Everyone has his own views. Some feel it is good and others feel differently. But I don't ever write about the faults of a book. I try to look for its strength and write about that. . . . Usually when a teacher asks us to write a book report, it's because most people feel the book is worth reading. If I think it's no good, it is my own opinion. If I criticize it, it won't meet the teacher's "requirement."

If I say that a book is no good, it doesn't mean that it has fundamental problems. It's just that I find it uninteresting. If the teacher asks us to read it, it must be that he thinks that it's worthwhile or that most people regard it as good. And so in that way my own views might very well be wrong.

Is the teacher always right?

LH: He is right most of the time. Some of the things I disagree with him about . . . maybe I'm wrong.

What about your parents?

LH: I have minor disagreements with them, trivial things in daily life. My parents, they aren't strict. They are very concerned about me. In fact that's why I disagree with them. Sometimes they are too concerned about me. I ask them to let me be more independent.

I don't disagree with my teachers. No, of course not. I don't dare to. [Laughs softly.] But still, I think they're right most of the time. The teacher I had last year is a good teacher. That's because he is a Party member. [Zhang Jun chuckles.] He is also the teacher in charge of our class. Because he is a Party member, he is a good teacher. [Laughs softly.]

Do you mean it?

LH: Yes, of course.

Why do you respect him?

LH: It's hard for me to give a concrete example. But from small things, his everyday behavior, we can say that he is our role model. And in our hearts, we feel that he is almost always right. It has something to do with how we feel emotionally. I simply respect Party members.

ZJ: The teacher we have now is pretty good. The one before, he was quite tough. He assigned us too much homework. No matter how hard we tried, we couldn't finish. Now our teacher helps us to review, and he doesn't assign too much homework. In the sixth grade we have different teachers for different subjects, but before that we had the same teacher doing everything. Other than math and language, we also have geography, science, political affairs, art, and physical education. We have these classes twice a week.

What do you do in the summer?

MT: When we were still living in the old place, we usually played Ping-Pong in school. But the schools over here don't have any sports equipment. At home we don't have much to do. Sometimes we go over there to play. During school days, on Tuesdays and Saturdays, we have only half a day of class, and so we stay and play. Now in the summer when we get very bored, we go over there. There are also no children to play with. Since most of us just moved here, this place is quite deserted.

ZJ: Most of the time, I just stay home and read books. The middle school has a basketball court, but we can't get in because schools are closed during the summer. I like to play soccer, but we can't find a place to play it.

What books do you like to read?

ZJ: War stories and stories about revolutionaries. I also read the abridged version of *The Water Margin* and the *Romance of the Three Kingdoms*.

LH: I have heard those stories on the radio. I know generally what these stories are about, and so I don't see any point reading the books.

MT: I don't like to read books. Sometimes when there are a couple of kids around, I play card games with them.

What do you like to do with your family?

MT: At home I am very easy, very loose. When grownups come back, I like to tell them jokes to make them laugh. Sometimes there's no one at home and there isn't much to do and I feel very lonely. When everybody gets back and I am very relaxed . . . then I tell jokes to make them laugh. I make up jokes myself. I imitate other people, how they act. I also impersonate people I see on television. I watch a lot of television.

Do your parents ever spank you?

ZJ: Yes, but not because I misbehave. It's usually when I get into a fight with somebody and I break something. Actually we don't really get into fights. It's just fooling around. Last time I was fooling around with him. [Points to Mu Tong.]

MT: He tried to grab my hat. . . .

ZJ: Then I tried to hit him with a stone, a little pebble. I missed and it hit another person passing by. It happened to hit his head, and he was bleeding. I told my mama about it later and she spanked me.

LH: I don't remember the exact incidents, but I have done similar things before. I was fooling around with classmates, hitting them with schoolbags, and I didn't know that pencils were sticking out of the bag. Then someone got hurt accidentally.

Tell me about something you did that you feel very proud of.

MT: Once when I was little, I went to the Northeast. My family was originally from Jilin Province [in the Northeast]. I was in the first or second grade then, and I didn't know any better. I was staying with my uncle. Everybody there was spoiling me, and they didn't want to see me getting upset for any reason. Anyway, I saw a transistor radio. I was playing it, turning the knobs back and forth, and thinking that it was fun. After a while people wanted to listen to the broadcast. They wanted it back and I wouldn't give it back. I knew that nobody wanted to upset me. But when they kept asking me to give it back, I threw the radio out of the window and started crying. Then my mother came in . . . no one knew what to do. I was the guest and I came from far away. . . . At the end my mama did something unprecedented. [Laughs.] She bought me a transistor radio. But that was in the Northeast, and I was only about five or six. And I did as I pleased. Yeah, that's the way it was.

Do you get along with your sisters?

MT: We get along pretty well. They are much older than me, but we still fight—mainly it's with my second sister. But after a while, we make up. Our relationship is pretty good. We always think of each other. And when she is in a good mood, she lets me have my way. But when she's grouchy, that's different. That's when we fight. My second sister is a senior in high school. She is going to take the college entrance exam next year.

ZJ: My older sister is already working. She didn't get into college after high school, and so she started working. She just got married recently. She doesn't live with us anymore.

Do you get along with your brother?

LH: We get along pretty well, but we fight, too. Our fights are very nasty. We are boys, and we both are very mischievous. . . .

Zhang Jun mumbles: Leghorn chicken. [They both laugh.]

LH: My brother always calls me names. He gives me nicknames. He calls me Leghorn chicken because my name [Lan Hang] sounds like *lai-heng* [Leghorn chicken]. [Everybody laughs.]

Mu Tong interjects: I play with his brother all the time.

LH: Sometimes we both want the same thing. Usually I have to let him have it because I am older. That's what my parents ask of me, and I have to do it. Sometimes I get too impulsive. I grab and run. I know when it comes to grabbing, my brother is no match for me. [Everybody laughs.] But after a while, we're fine. We don't ever fight for food. Just mostly things we play with.

Do you often have talks with your parents?

MT: In the summer when we sit outside in the evenings to get some cool air. But usually we don't have much time with our parents. Parents are very busy. Most of the time when they get home, it's already very late. After dinner, they are ready for bed.

Is there any special thing you like to do with your father?

MT: When he is in a good mood. . . . Well, I rarely do anything with him. But once we saw this program on television about children making their own kites and flying them in Tian-an-men Square. That night my baba made a big kite for me. He made a very good one. He used rice paper. The kite even flew.

How about with your mother?

MT: My mama is very good to me. Whenever I am out shopping with her, she always buys me something I like to eat.

ZJ: I live with my mother. My father is abroad, in France. He has been there for four years. He has to stay there for another two years. He came back two years ago for a month. That was when he was on vacation. I write him once a month. I miss him very much. There is nobody to take his place there, and so he can't come back.

If you could change your parents, how would you change them?

MT: [Silence.] My father is sometimes very stubborn. I wish he were not so stubborn. My mother . . . has a loud voice. [Laughs softly.] I wish she could lower her voice.

ZJ: Parents can't be changed. I wish my father would come back soon.

LH: You can't change my father. Even miracles won't work. Did you ever hear of a son who is able to change his father? I think it's the way my baba treats me. Sometimes he doesn't let me voice my opinions. He thinks I don't know anything. When I get older, I'll have the right to speak out. Now whenever he gets angry, I just shut up. . . . I wish my mother were not so concerned with me, that she would give me some independence. [Pauses.] Maybe the reason I feel this way is because I am grown and I think I know everything. I am too confident about myself.

In what ways would you like to change yourself?

LH: I want to correct my faults. Sometimes I'm not patient enough. I'm not quick or alert. [Everybody laughs.] Whenever something happens, I panic. I have to learn to be calmer. Sometimes I talk too much, like a little while ago. [Laughs.] I don't need my parents to tell me that I talk too much. I know it myself. One of my classmates read my palm before. He said that not only won't I have a lot of money in the future, but I'll lose most of it. I think he's right. I tend to get carried away. I like to talk in a bombastic way. In other words, I say a lot of nonsense. [Laughs.] Most of the time I am half-joking about what I say.

What about a little while ago?

LH: I was serious about what I said to you. Also, sometimes I am not open. I'm not at ease with myself. . . . It's too hard for me to go into it. We don't have enough time.

What about your environment? What changes would you like to see there?

LH: I want to raise my status at school. In my former school, I was way up there. I was much more . . . how should I put it . . . at least among the boys, I had some position. I was one of the so-called characters in school. I was what you might call, a minor official . . . well, at least to my troops. I was a group leader. But now in this school, I have to assume "public duty." It seems that all the positions in class had already been taken before I came. Now that I am here . . . I can't seem to break into the establishment. Isn't this the same with the overseas Chinese in America?

Perhaps. I think you are right. If you could have three wishes, what would they be?

MT: My wishes are . . . I change my mind all the time. Sometimes I want to do this, and sometimes I want to do that. Once I liked soccer, and I wanted to be a soccer player. But now I like radio. I joined the radio team at school. But then when I am at home all by myself, I imagine I can invent things. I imagine these things, but I can't really build them. [He cannot quite describe what he wants to invent.]

LH: I like to fantasize. I fantasize about everything. My ambition is to become a high official. [Laughs.] You probably think it's funny, but I really mean it. I want to become a high official. Nowadays, it's easy to become an official. Of course, some of the officials are not very competent.

Who do you think can become high officials?

LH: That's hard to say. First you have to study well. Then you have to have ambitions.

Do you have high ambitions in politics?

LH: Umm . . . you compliment me too much. [Grins.] . . . I fantasize about everything. . . . Sometimes I fantasize that I have conversations with foreigners. I want to know about world affairs, about U.S. politics, for example. I am interested in their presidential election. I always read the *Reference News*. This paper mostly has translations of articles from foreign newspapers. I don't like to read other papers, just this one. I like to read articles that praise China. They make me feel good. I don't know whether their observations are correct or not because there are many things in China I don't understand. They say China has made a lot of progress. I think this is correct. I am glad that foreigners can see China in this way. There are also English and Japanese news reports that praise China, but they also criticize China. They point out problems like environmental pollution and they say that our way of doing things is inefficient. I don't feel these are important issues. I want to know in the United States whether the pro-Taiwan force is stronger or the pro-PRC force is stronger.

I don't think you'll be interested in knowing the politicians' point of view. They have their reasons for supporting Taiwan or the PRC. As for the people, it's hard to know how they really feel about this issue. Actually they are less interested in supporting a particular government but more in reading and learning about China and the Chinese people.

Are you interested in political thought?

LH: I have never studied political theories in any systematic way. I pick up something and I read a couple of pages. Mostly what I read is Marxism. When it comes to understanding theoretical things, I am still young and immature. If I read about other points of view, they might confuse my thought. Marxism is the orthodox doctrine. You won't make any mistakes by reading books on Marxism. I am still young. As I get older and as my ability to comprehend increases, of course, I would like to know more. For now I am satisfied to know just a little bit about what others have said.

At this point, Lan Hang asks many questions about Western thinkers. He wants to know, for example, whether scholars in the West categorize their philosophies in terms of subjective idealism, objective idealism, mechanical materialism, and dialectic materialism. He is curious and yet cautious. When he senses that our conversation is getting off tangent, he reminds himself—and me: "Anyway, I don't really understand it. Let's not talk about it. I am still a child."

Lan Hang uses a great deal of ideological language. Among all the children I interviewed in 1984, he is the only one who tells me that his hero is Mao Ze-dong. Yet beneath this protective layer is an unpredictable boy with an uncommon sense of humor.

Our topic switches to animals and pets.

MT: Once I caught a gecko. It's hard for this type of animal to die. Even if you don't feed them at all, they can live for three to four weeks. This one I had even laid eggs. The eggs didn't hatch. We usually didn't feed her, but sometimes I gave her insects or a handful of rice.

If you could be an animal, which would you be?

MT: A monkey. A monkey is quick and smart.

LH: I want to be a fox. A fox is crafty and cunning. [Laughs.] I don't think being cunning is bad. [Everyone laughs.] Why? That's easy to answer. Everybody knows that being cunning is better than being stupid.

* * *

Our second day in Hangzhou, August 6, 1984. This morning before we were up, Mr. Yuan, our contact and guide here, had already been to the residential area attached to his work unit, talking to the children there. During breakfast he announced that there would be three children joining us in our outing today. He had invited them of his own accord, and we were delighted when we heard of this surprise.

Our trip that day began with a boat ride across the West Lake to the Zhong-shan Park. The first part of our conversation was taped on the boat.

Tian Jun seems older than his actual age of twelve years. He is worldly and confident. Perhaps this is why Bao Xiang-min calls him Boss Tian. He talks and acts like a "big brother." He is fond of Bao Xiang-min—the two often have their arms around each other—though he also condescends toward him. His mother sells meat in a butcher shop; his father is the deputy secretary of the Party committee in Hangzhou's Science and Technology Exchange Center.

Bao Xiang-min is ten and a half and is getting ready to go to the fifth grade. He has a sister who is fifteen. His mother works in the library of the Information Center, and his father is a section chief in the same work unit. He is very close to Tian Jun. He looks up to him but holds his own. He does not like his friend to challenge him—what he says and what he is able to recall—and when that occurs, he snaps back with a "what-makes-you-so-sure" kind of response. He is still a child: he acts without thought. Though he does not have Tian Jun's worldliness, he is just as confident and vocal. Everyone calls him by his nickname, "Little Min," which also means "common citizen." Little Min is short and thin with a small head. When he wears his white cap, his eyes disappear under the visor.

Zhu Bin is twelve and is about to enter eighth grade. She is slender and delicate, dressed in a pink blouse and a yellow floral-print skirt. Her hair is tied in two pigtails. She wears a white cap most of the time; a blue, transparent visor shades her light complexion.

Zhu Bin climbs trees and plays war, and seems very close to the two boys. During our conversation, she laughs and giggles a lot but has very little to say. She is reserved and cool when speaking to me. When all the children are out exploring, she keeps an eye on my two, even though she remains distant. Her parents are both engineers in the Science and Technical Information Center. Her mother, however, holds a higher position than her father. She also has an older sister who is eighteen and is already working.

Tian Jun (TJ) [to Bao Xiang-min]: Little Min, I caught some swallowtails yesterday and pinned them on a piece of board. Guess what I found this morning. Their heads were missing. I think the cockroaches came out last night and chewed their heads off. Their wings are still intact, though. It's just the heads that are gone.

Bao Xiang-min and Zhu Bin start to giggle. Tian Jun turns around and says to me:

When we pin the butterflies on the board, they're usually still alive. I have so many, but they're all headless now. We also catch cicadas, grasshoppers, and crickets. We feed the grasshoppers to the chickens. The grasshoppers are all over the place. In a couple of hours we can catch about twenty of them.

Do you have any special techniques when you catch butterflies?

TJ: You wait until they have landed on the flowers. Then you have to be very quick. . . .

Bao Xiang-min (BXM): You know you can row boats here, but I've never done it before. My baba has never rowed a boat with me before.

TJ: I have, several times. But that was before. Now my baba is very busy with his work. He doesn't do things like that with me anymore.

When we arrive at Zhong-shan Park, our three guests are already on familiar terms with my children. The five climb boulders and trees together and drink water from the same canteen. At one point they are preoccupied with the minnows darting around the edge of the lake, all five on their knees trying to scoop up the fish in their cupped hands. The problem is, what to do with the fish then? Tian Jun quickly takes Bao

Xiang-min's cap and uses it as a container. The water sieves out, and immediately the children search for a different solution. They go through a garbage can and find a paper cup. The paper cup doesn't last long, and with some reluctance they abandon the minnows.

While in the park, we come upon a garden bed of tall, multicolored zinnias, attracting numerous swallowtail butterflies, fluttering about as we pass by. I ask Tian Jun to demonstrate the skills of a butterfly catcher. He is quick and nimble, and in minutes is holding a large, exquisite swallowtail in his hand. My four-year-old son quickly warns him that he might injure the butterfly's wings. "Please let it go now," he begs. "The wings are already broken," Tian Jun tells me quietly, aside. He is right: one wing is clearly torn, and the butterfly cannot fly. While everyone is focusing intensely on the injured creature, now on the pavement, Bao Xiang-min quickly steps on it, smearing it onto the pavement with his sandal. This action catches us all by surprise, and for twenty minutes my son Yar mourns openly and uncontrollably for the dead butterfly. The two boys in the meantime feel awful and awkward, but they do not understand Yar's behavior. "Why was he so upset over a butterfly?" they ask me later.

After our morning adventure in the park, we return to our hotel for lunch. This is followed by a long chat in our room.

When we are all seated, and the children see that I have my tape recorder turned on, for the first time they begin to feel a little uneasy. Bao Xiang-min gets up and squeezes into Tian Jun's little chair, practically sitting on his lap. They point to each other and say, "You go first!" and start to giggle.

BXM: My mama is going to be transferred soon. Where? I don't know. . . .

Tian Jun calls me Little Min [Xiao-min].

TJ: And he calls me Boss Tian [Tian-lao-ban]. [Both laugh loudly.]

BXM: I was born in Beijing and lived there until I was five. Then I moved to Hangzhou. I don't remember exactly who took care of me when I was little. I think it was my waipo.

What do you do in the summer?

BXM: I get up in the morning about six and do some homework for about ten minutes or so. [Zhu Bin, the girl in the group, laughs.] Then I eat my breakfast and do about thirty more minutes of homework. Then I play in the yard with him [pointing to Tien Jun] until about ten o'clock. After that, I come home and cool myself in front of the fan, rest a little bit more and have lunch around eleven-thirty. After lunch I eat a piece of watermelon, and then I take my nap. If I don't feel like sleeping, I get up at one. If I do fall asleep, I get up around two-thirty. During the summer, my sister and I are home. Sometimes my waipo is here visiting us. When she is here, she cooks lunch for us. Otherwise my sister has to cook lunch. My baba and mama are home for lunch. After my nap, after my nap . . . I don't do much. I mope around and I play a little. . . . Sometimes I also play with Little Fang. She's a girl, about two years younger than me. We like to play war. We all like to play war. [He points to Zhu Bin.] She likes to play war too. [Both Tian Jun and Zhu Bin burst out laughing.]

How do you play war?

Zhu Bin (ZB): We do some shouting and screaming.

TJ: We also carry wooden guns that we make ourselves. We saw a piece of wood and shape it into a gun—well, as long as it looks a little bit like a gun. . . . We also like to play hide-and-go-seek, tag, and we like to catch cicadas. We try to catch those that have just finished molting. We take them home and play with them until they are dead. We also like to catch birds.

BXM: Once we brought home a wounded bird. Someone had shot it with a BB gun. We brought it home and took care of it, and it lived. Then for some odd reason it started banging against the side of the cage. After a while, it died.

TJ: I think it was too lonely. It was a siskin. Siskins eat the fruits of the camphor trees. There are a lot of them around. Their feathers are gray and white with a little bit of yellow. Their beaks are black. . . . It's very hard to catch birds ourselves. Even when they are hit with slingshots, they just won't fall down.

Are you allowed to have cats and dogs as pets?

TJ: In the past. But not anymore, not since a couple of years ago.

BXM: Uncle Xiao-wang—that's the driver who lives in our yard—he used to have a dog, and we played with that dog all the time. We can have cats, but there is no cat in our yard. We used to have one, but someone took it away.

TJ: There are other stray cats, not in our yard, but around our neighborhood. The stray cats, they like to fight and bite each other. You can hear them at night. They also steal fish. No one keeps them as pets. They are all strays. They come from the mountain.

(*To Bao Xiao-min:*) *Do you ever fight or argue with Tian Jun?*

BXM: No, never. Sometimes we fool around and we wrestle on the grass, but that's just for fun. . . . Tian Jun and I have been good friends ever since I moved here about five years ago.

Do you play with other boys in your yard?

BXM: Before there were a lot of boys, but now there are just the two of us left. They have all moved away. Now basically there are only the girls in our yard.

They start to name the boys who have moved away. They are all nicknames, and I overhear the name "refried dough stick" [lao-you-tiao]*—a nickname for someone who is crafty and stingy.*

Who is lao-you-tiao*? Why is he called* lao-you-tiao*?*

BXM: I don't know. It's because Tien Jun calls him *lao-you-tiao* and so I call him *lao-you-tiao*.

BXM: Before, when we went out in the evening, there was this huge gang of kids, about twenty kids. . . .

TJ: No! Only about ten or fifteen.

BXM: Twenty-some! [Then they start counting the names again, and Tian Jun is right; there were less than fifteen.] We went to a terrace across from our yard.

TJ: We did a lot of fighting, but most of that was just fooling around. There was never any real fighting.

BXM: If it was real fighting, someone might get killed.

TJ: Sometimes I go with a couple of my friends to climb mountains. Our parents let us go there. I was allowed to do that ever since I moved here, and that was about five or six years ago when I was seven.

BXM: Ever since I was little, I was allowed to go out and ride the bus by myself. I've ridden the bus by myself since I was in first grade. . . .

TJ: First grade! Your sister rode the bus with you then—

BXM: Bullshit! What do you know! That was in kindergarten. I rode the bus by myself when I was in first grade.

Do you have many relatives?

BXM: Too many. My waipo has nine brothers, and we call them Oldest Jiugong [granduncle], Second Jiugong, Third Jiugong, Fourth Jiugong and so on. Their sons are my uncles, and so you can imagine how many uncles I have. They don't all come to visit, but some do, about once or twice a year. My jiujiu from Shanghai comes most often. He has two children, but I don't play with them because one is working already and the other is in senior high.

TJ: I have a lot of relatives too. Most of them live in Hangzhou. They are all my mother's younger brothers and sisters. My mama has five younger sisters and one younger brother. They come to our house very often—basically every night. They have children, but the children are all younger than me. And then there is also my waipo and waigong.

How do you celebrate New Year?

TJ: We eat a little better. There are fireworks and we play with firecrackers. The family and relatives get together for New Year's dinner.

What about ya-sui *money on New Year's day?*

BXM: Sometimes my baba gives me twenty cents, sometimes a dollar. [Zhu Bin laughs.] Like this year he gave me twenty cents—

TJ: He didn't behave. . . .

BXM: I did so behave! And that's why he gave me twenty cents. I didn't ask him why he only gave me twenty cents. But that's fine with me, twenty cents or whatever, it's all the same with me. No, I didn't get any *ya-sui* money from my relatives.

TJ: Sixty cents, seventy cents. . . . Actually I am worse off than Xiaomin. I should have sixty dollars but didn't see a penny of it. My baba used it all. Usually the parents keep all the *ya-sui* money . . .

BXM: It's the same with me. Even that twenty cents—I let my mother use it. But there was once, my waipo gave me five dollars. My baba and mama didn't take that away from me. I still have it in my drawer. Now I have saved more than ten dollars in my drawer.

TJ: Every year I get that much, but I don't get to keep a penny. On New Year's day we also pay New Year's calls on relatives. . . .

BXM: We don't.

What do you like to do with your parents?

BXM: I like to play chess with my baba. Other than that I don't do anything else with him. Whenever he has a little time, he goes upstairs to work—to study. His office is upstairs, just above where we live. At night, he doesn't get back until after ten, and that's when I am in bed already. Most of the time I am with my mama. I like to go shopping with my mama, but I don't like to go to the fabric shop with her. I don't like fabrics, and I have to wait for a long time. She is so choosy—this doesn't seem right and that doesn't seem right. It takes her a long time to decide on something.

TJ: I like to play chess, go swimming, and play Ping-Pong with my baba, But he doesn't have any time these days. He leaves early in the morning and gets home around six-thirty. After dinner, he goes out to cool off. He goes to bed after that. I have very little time with him. My mama, I have abacus contests with her. We see who is faster on the abacus. Sometimes I win. Sometimes she does. We just started doing this a couple of days ago. I also like to help her cook—wash the vegetables and cook the rice. I don't play chess with her because she doesn't play chess, and there is nothing I can do about that. My baba plays chess, but he doesn't have time. My mama has lots of time, but she doesn't play chess.

ZB: My mama is usually not home.

BXM: She is always traveling on business trips just like my baba.

Zhu Bin's mother is a department head in the Science and Technology Exchange Center and Bao Xiang-min's father is a section chief in the same work unit.

ZB: She travels about twice a month. If it's a short trip, it's about three to four days. If it's a long trip, it's more than a week. Last time she was in Italy for about half a month. When she is not traveling, she leaves early in the morning and comes home after ten, after I am in bed. . . . When I was little, my waipo took care of me. My baba is home every night about six-thirty. We all have dinner together, but my mama has to go back to the office right after dinner.

If you could change your parents, how would you change them?

TJ: I like my baba the way he is, except maybe he could become better tempered. He is too mean, too strict. He doesn't let me do too much reading. He bundles up my books and does not let me read when I have tests. In the summer he doesn't let me read either—he says, to protect my vision. But I like to read, biographies, history, historical novels; anything to do with history, I like. Sometimes when I'm all finished with my exams, my baba will let me read two books. He also doesn't let me watch too much television. . . . I wish my mama wouldn't do too many chores. Whenever I tell her that, she just ignores me. I help her with the chores, though.

If you could be an animal, what would you be?

TJ: A Manchurian tiger, because it's fierce and it's also a national treasure.

BXM: I would like to be a panda because it's a national treasure.

ZB: Why not a monkey? [Zhu Bin's suggestion was perfect.]

BXM: No, that's no good. Why not? Because it's no good, therefore, it's no good.

5

To Make Images and a Substance for Their Dreams and Imagined Order

When my husband lectured at Zhejiang University in Hangzhou in 1984, he told his hosts about my work, hoping that they would introduce me to children. They immediately thought of the computer camp sponsored by the university. The participants were high school students from the Hua-dong region, all selected on the basis of their academic performance.

The camp director, Mr. Guo, met me at the gate, and we walked a short distance to the girl's dormitory, where seven girls were waiting for us in a room crowded with beds, benches, and a long wooden table. We began our conversation immediately and were soon joined by four boys. The boys did not have classes that afternoon, and Mr. Guo had gone to their rooms to fetch them. This was the first time they had stepped into a girl's dormitory, one commented, and it was their first conversation with the girls in the program. They went to classes and labs at different times and after class spent most of their time studying. Even within their own group, they rarely talked about anything except their studies. In a way they were all strangers to one another.

The format of this particular session was different from others I had conducted in China. It was primarily a group discussion of issues and ideas. Although much of our conversation touched upon personal lives, the intent was to bring to light the participants' various viewpoints; it did not focus on the individual experiences of growing up.

The session lasted the whole afternoon. Three girls and two boys came back with me to my hotel and dined with my family and me, and we continued our conversation well into the night.

Zhu Yuan is an avid talker. Her voice—passionate and hurried—is heard on nearly every subject. For this reason I come to know her better than anyone else in the room. She is also the oldest one in the group—nineteen. One of the two camp counselors there, she is a sophomore in Zhejiang University. Her home is in Linan, a town not far from Hangzhou. She tells me: "After my parents graduated from college, they both went to the North to work. I was born in Linan. My mama came back to Linan to have me and then went back North. I grew up with my nainai. When I was ten, they moved back and I went to live with them." Her father is an engineer in a hydraulic plant. Her mother is an accountant in a paper mill. She has one older brother. Her paternal grandparents and maternal grandmother are still living. "My yeye and nainai live about ten steps from us. Linan is a small town with few residents. Most people live in the country nearby. My waipo's home is in the country among the peasants."

Li Ying is the other student counselor. She is quieter than Zhu Yuan and more conscious of her image. She tells us that she is fond of classical music and prefers Hamlet *and* Anna Karenina *to modern literature, yet it is difficult to engage her on those subjects; she does not seem emotionally convinced, herself, of her likes and dislikes. She is only eighteen but already a junior in Zhejiang University. Her home is in Hangzhou, where both her parents work at the university, her father teaching Chinese literature, her mother in the administration office. Li Ying has a fifteen-year-old brother. She lived in a small town when she was a child: "I was with my mother then. My father was in Hangzhou. We moved here when I was seven."*

Mei Jing is sixteen but might be twelve. Her hair is slightly curled, tied in two pigtails, and her attire is girlish—a simple blue cotton dress zipped up the back. She is straightforward and vocal, and likes to hasten through her sentences. At home—she is from Nanchang, the capital of Jiangxi—she is an only child. Her father, an engineer, and her mother, a middle school teacher, were sent to the countryside for reeducation during the Cultural Revolution. She was with them throughout that time, and when she was eight, she returned home to Nanchang with them and has been living there ever since.

Do you have differences with your parents?

The response from everyone is a spontaneous "yes."

Zhu Yuan (ZY): But at the end we usually give in. We comply with their wishes. Before taking my college entrance exam, I had to put down my top choices, and I recall I wanted to go to a school in the North, but my parents didn't let me. At the time I was very stubborn. I cried and I made a lot of fuss. But at the end I yielded. It was harder to bear their tears. After I got here I understood their reasons for wanting me to be here. They were not just concerned about the geographic location but also about my field of study and the convenience. I gave in to their wishes, but my brother didn't. He thinks that boys should be more independent, and he wanted to be far away from home. He went to a college in the North, and he was very happy there. He felt life was a little harder there, but he enjoyed living with the Northerners. After college he was assigned to Shanghai. But now he doesn't care—anywhere is fine. Take me, now I feel it's all right for me to be at a school close to home. I am more at ease here.

Li Ying (LY): It's not quite true that we always listen to our parents. The other day, for instance, I had a big argument with my mother about a women's issue. We argued and argued. Finally she got angry and I told her that I refused to go on arguing. At the end, I think, each of us still insisted on her position. Neither of us yielded an inch. My mother kept on trying to convince me to see things her way. She wants to make sure that my way of thinking fits within the framework that she defines. Parents always want to see their way of thinking and our way of thinking come together. A lot of times, because we respect them, we don't get hung up on our differences, and that stops us from continuing an argument. But deep down inside, in our hearts, we haven't changed our point of view.

Mei Jing (MJ): A couple of times when I was upset at my parents, I wanted to go to my friend's house and spend the night there, but I could never carry it through. Halfway there, I'd start thinking to myself, They're probably out there looking for me; they must feel awful about the whole thing now. Then I'd begin to feel guilty, and I'd just quietly sneak back.

ZY: I do a lot of things like that. Most of the time what I did was inconsistent with how I felt. That's because I think about my family; . . .

if I do something against my parents' wishes, I won't be able to face up to them. So with a lot of things, I either change my mind or I'm indecisive. Before, even with trivial things, I'd write home and ask my parents. Now I am a little better. I am more independent.

Are girls more soft-hearted? Is it easier for them to give in to their parents' wishes?

LY: Very soft-hearted, like when parents start to cry. Especially when mothers start to cry. Whenever my mama starts to cry, I give in to her on anything. . . .

At this point the boys come in. They move chairs into the already crowded room and sit down.

Tian Ren-zhi is easily excited, whether over a social issue or the color of rice paddies. He is direct and honest, quick to provoke disagreement or laughter. Though his beliefs at times may seem backward or even "feudal," he neither bends nor softens his words when under attack. Labels do not make him timid. He tenaciously defends his prejudices while gallantly admitting that they are prejudices.

Tian Ren-zhi is seventeen and has just completed his first year in senior high. He is from a small village, Yunlin, in Danyang County, Jiangsu: "I have always lived in Danyang. My father is the principal of Yunlin Middle School. He teaches physics there. My mother works in the field. My family has always been in the country. . . . My grandfather, my grandmother—we all live together. We have a large family. It's a small house, but we all live together in the same house." He attended a middle school in the city of Yangzhou, about sixty kilometers south of Danyang, because it was better than any local ones. He has a brother and a sister: "I fight with my brother all the time. All the time. And I always argue with my sister."

Zheng Pu is a sixteen-year-old with pimply skin and spiky hair. His eyes are small, barely visible when he smiles. They give the effect of his existing on a threshold between the waking and the dreaming state. He wears dark-framed glasses. He is kind and witty, and he is still moved by the stories of the old revolutionaries. He is not dogmatic, just romantic.

Zheng Pu comes from Shandong Province, in northeastern China. His home is in Qixiang District, which just recently became part of the city of Yentai: "My yeye was originally from Yentai. I have been going to school in Yentai since junior high." There are five in his family: "My father teaches in Yentai Middle School Number One, which is also my school. In fact my father is my language teacher. He often criticizes me. My mother works in the People's Hospital in Yentai. She is the head nurse in the Department of Obstetrics. My older brother is at Shanghai Huadong Teacher's College. This time when I came to Hangzhou, I went to Shanghai to visit him. My brother is four years older than me. We are very close. In fact I just received a letter from him. [Smiles.] My sister just took the college entrance exam this year. We don't know yet how well she did. We are all very close in our family, very harmonious."

Chang Pei-xun is a clean-cut and serious boy who rarely smiles or laughs. Although he does not actively participate in the discussion, he remains interested and watchful, and even a little threatening. If we hold back at all, he would be our reason why, though we do not know why this is so. Perhaps it is his self-righteous pose. He is from Fujian Province. His parents work for the Bureau of Commerce; his father is a cadre. His nainai and jiujiu live with him and his parents.

After the boys introduce themselves, I direct the next question to them: How do you resolve your differences with your parents?

Tian Ren-zhi (TRZ): This problem is very complicated. [Laughs softly.] My father's views and mine are usually not the same. When I was younger, I felt that most of what he said was right, so I listened to him and tried to change my world view. But after a while, let's say now, I have my own views, and I don't necessarily listen to him. Sometimes I have conflicts with him. In fact, I have conflicts with him most of the time. [Laughs.] Sometimes he loses his temper, and so we put a lid on the dispute. After I have some time to think about it, sometimes I feel I was wrong, but then there are other times I feel I was right. Either I bring it up again or I keep it to myself and do things the way I think is right.

What about with your mother?

TRZ: Most of the time, when she starts to cry, I soften my stand. I give in. The other day I had an argument with her. At first she tried to convince me, but I didn't listen. Then she became *that way*—she seemed to be very unhappy—and I backed down; I didn't insist on my point. I don't think it's necessarily true that boys are less sensitive than girls to their mothers' tears.

Zheng Pu (ZP): Sometimes I argue with my mother. I am quick-tempered and it's easy for me to have a confrontation with her. She doesn't argue as well as I do. [Everyone laughs.] And so she sits in a corner, blaming me and endlessly grumbling. By then I know for sure that she's angry, and so I shut up. Either I go to another room and close the door or I go out for a walk.

What is the nature of your conflicts with your parents?

LY: Most of the time it's over small problems. But I'll say this: I have a sort of different relationship with my parents. Now that I am in college, I know a little bit more, and the kinds of things we discuss have a lot to do with social issues. Sometimes we have different points of view, different ways of looking at a problem. The argument I was talking about before, the one I had with my mama, was about a women's issue: my mama thinks that after a woman is married, she should go out and work. She feels that women who choose to stay home are no good. Absolutely no good, she insists. But that's not necessarily true. Some women decide to stay home because there is a conflict between family life and career, and they choose to give more attention to their families. It doesn't mean that they are just like the Japanese women. They are not just staying home. But my mother feels differently. She has no respect for women who do not work outside their homes. I don't think she is necessarily right.

Nowadays in China, are there women who choose to stay home?

LY: There are, but very few.

MJ: My mama is a middle school teacher: she is rarely home and hardly ever does any housework. She usually leaves for work early in the morning and comes back late in the evening. She likes to stay in school and talk to the students and their parents. She hardly does any work at home. But my baba does a lot more housework. Most of the time it's my baba and me. We do all of the housework.

ZY: My mama does a lot more. My baba is an engineer. He usually works on his designs well into the night. My mama is the one who is always making all the sacrifices. But then she is willing to do it because she thinks taking good care of her family and her home is a woman's virtue. [Everyone laughs.] But that's exactly what she said!

TRZ: Most people feel this way, though.

LY: Even though my mama feels very strongly that women should be out there working, she does the same thing: at home she does all the housework.

ZY: My mama now even tells me that in the future if I marry a capable man with a promising career, it's me, the woman, who should make all the sacrifices. Only when the man doesn't amount to anything, then it's up to me to make something out of myself.

Do you boys feel that the mother should do most of the housework even though she holds a full-time job outside of her home?

TRZ: I think it should be that way. . . . [The girls are shaking their heads.]

MJ: Boys always feel that way.

TRZ: Usually we feel that men have more potential professionally. This is the general consensus, and I feel the same way.

The girls all object to this statement. They begin to talk at the same time.

MJ: I've never heard of such a thing!

TRZ: But this is a common phenomenon, a common belief. [His voice is getting louder.]

Granted that this is the traditional viewpoint, do you yourself ever question its validity?

TRZ: There must be a basis for this traditional view. If both husband and wife want to be successful professionally, who is going to do the chores at home? The chores cannot be ignored.

ZY: What about working together? What if the woman is more capable?

TRZ: I am sure that this is rarely the case.

Tian Ren-zhi can be blunt. The girls and I know he is a male chauvinist, yet somehow we can tolerate his "Dark Age" views. I think it is because he is so totally true to himself.

Chang Pei-xun (CPX): At home there are heavier chores and lighter chores. I think the women should do lighter chores; the fathers and sons should be responsible for the heavier ones. The more tedious work should be left to the women.

ZP: I think the mother and father should be concerned about each other. My mother is the head nurse in the delivery room. She is usually very tired. Every night she comes home very late. Things like cooking—my father often does them. He teaches in the middle school. He has many responsibilities and a large class to take care of, and sometimes he comes home late. And if my mother comes home first, she does some of the chores that my father would normally do. I feel as long as the parents care about each other, there will be harmony at home.

Do you find your relationships to your mother and your father to be different?

LY: Mothers are usually more caring. Fathers don't worry that much.

Chen Dong-yen, an only child from Nanjing, lived in Suzhou, her father's original home, until she was six. Her father is a teacher, her mother a research scientist, both at the Nanjing Polytechnical Institute.

Although she is dressed in a brightly colored and patterned blouse and skirt, she looks grave—years older than her actual age of sixteen—perhaps it has something to do with the half-frame glasses she wears. She has taken on the appearance of an erudite, yet when she speaks she is full of energy and speed, and she has a habit of punctuating her sentences with an "uh-he."

Jin Tan comes from Shanghai, and she has never lived anywhere else. Her mother is an ophthalmologist and her father a political commissar in the People's Liberation Army. She grew up with her mother: "My father came to live with us when I was ten."

Chen Dong-yen (CDY): When I was little, I liked my mother better. Now that I am older, I can't say that I like my father better, but I do feel that I am becoming closer to him. I always feel that as girls get older they have better relationships with their fathers.

ZY: I feel the same way. Until I was five, I was closer to my mama. Later I find that with my baba you can talk about anything under the sun, but my mama just does work around the house, and there is not much of a conversation I can have with her. With my baba it's different. When he takes the evening paper in his hand, you can sit next to him and have a wonderful chat with him. My mama is easily satisfied. She'll do anything to put my baba in the limelight. In fact, she doesn't let him do any work around the house. She tells him: "If you want to do scientific research, then do it right. Act like a scientist!" It's true! Nowadays I like my father better.

MJ: Most girls do like their fathers better. Like me, when I was younger, my mother was more concerned about me, but then she became more involved with her work. Although my father leaves early and comes back late and doesn't have lunch with us—for lunch there are only the two of us, my mama and me—still I am closer to my father. He gives me guidance, but he also lets me have the freedom to think and analyze things myself. My mama, she insists I do things in accordance with her line of thinking and her way. My baba more or less allows me to think independently, and when there's a problem, he lets me decide how to resolve it. That's why I am closer to my father.

Jin Tan (JT): What others are saying about their fathers—that you can talk to them about anything under the sun—makes it sound as if their fathers are more knowledgeable than their mothers and so when they are older there are more things to share with them. But my mama reads not only technical books in her own field but also books that we all like to read, and so we talk a lot, and I enjoy talking to her. My father has always been in the military. When I was young, he was never home, and we had a lot more time with Mama. And Mama has always been more concerned with our everyday life. She loves us very much, and I have a very close relationship with her. I want to stay with her forever.

Very rarely do Chinese children reveal their affection for their parents as directly as Jin Tan does. Her relationship to her mother seems special.

When I ask whether I am correct to assume that as they grow older they are closer to the parent with whom they can share their thoughts and ideas, most agree, and add that their parents' education and intellectual ability are important factors.

CDY: In my family it is a little different. I would say that professionally my mama is more successful than my baba. My mama cares a lot about home and is doing very well in her work unit. My baba is also doing very well, . . . he has gone abroad and everything. But if a person's salary is in any way a reflection of his performance—we Chinese always talk about higher and lower ranks; the rank really refers to the person's salary—well, my mama's salary is higher than my baba's. Anyway, when it comes to disagreements at home, a lot of the time, I am on my mama's side. I am an only child, and my baba says that in our family the ratio is two-to-one, and he is always the "one."

My mama is very busy with work, but she loves to grow plants and flowers. Our terrace is filled with flower pots. Usually she comes home late, and we are waiting for her to eat dinner. Baba usually cooks it, and it is ready on the table and we are eager for her to get home. But when she gets back, she doesn't sit down and eat. She immediately goes to the terrace to check her plants. My baba often gets a little irritated and says, "Let's eat first and then you can look at your flowers." He also warns her: "Next time if your flowers come first, I'll throw all of them away!" [Laughs.] But then I'll be on my mama's side and say, "When you come home, it's all right to check the flowers. Otherwise, it'll get dark and you won't be able to see anything." And whenever I defend my mama, she tells my father, "My daughter and I, we make a majority, two to one. Why don't you stop complaining?" So that's the way it is in our home.

When I was little, I was quite afraid of my father. He was serious and rarely smiled. I always thought Mama was wonderful. But now that I'm older, he has a lot to say to me, and I can talk to him. He even jokes around. Now I feel we get along much better. Maybe it has something to do with growing up.

MJ: When a person is young, she wants love and warmth. In her mother's arms, she can get that. But when she grows up, she needs a lot less of that. She feels that she needs to develop her mind. It's acquiring knowledge that is more important. And the father is happy to help her in that way.

CPX: When we were younger, we felt a greater need for our mothers. Before we are capable of independent thinking, we are more dependent on others. That's when we were younger. At that point, our mothers could help us more. We relied on them and we were closer to them. Baba, when we were younger, gave us a lot less in comparison. But when we are older, it seems this way: Mother cares more about the day-to-day details, about our physical well-being; Father gives us more in terms of the development of our intellect and character. So the older we get, the closer we are to our father, especially if he is democratic. Mother does not offer us much in that way.

When I ask what kind of relationship they would like to have with their children when they become parents, everyone laughs. I sense that they are a little embarrassed.

LY: We want to be able to communicate thoughts and ideas with our children. We want to become friends with them.

ZY: I think parents should read the books their children read. If you want to become a good parent, you have to be aware of what your children read. Only then can you communicate with them. Otherwise there's no common interest. There is nothing to talk about.

In your view which group is the closest to your parents—relatives, friends, or neighbors?

ZY: Mostly friends, especially their friends from college and middle schools.

TRZ: I think it's relatives.

MJ: Brothers and sisters, especially if they were close when they were children.

ZY: In the country, it's neighbors. I lived in the country before, and I know. When someone cooks something special, she carries it around, from this family to that family, letting everybody taste it. If a person is sick, and no one is home, that's all right—neighbors will take him to the hospital. When someone needs money, everybody chips in. My waipo lives in the countryside near my hometown. When she first moved there, she had no place to stay. The peasants asked her to live with them, and later they helped her to find a place.

TRZ: My home is in the country. We have no neighbors living nearby. We are pretty much alone. But I know with others if they live close to one another, they get along very well.

What about in the cities?

ZY: I know with my relatives in Hangzhou, people living in the same neighborhood hardly know each other.

TRZ: That's true. I know someone who didn't even recognize his neighbors next door. Now in China, if you don't live in an apartment building, but in the older housing—on a courtyard with three or four houses facing each other, neighbors are close. But if you live in a big building with individual units, when you close your own door, you don't see anybody.

ZY: If you see the houses in the country, they are set up on what we call a lane. When you walk along a lane, there are many houses crowded together on each side, and everyone has his door open. A lot of times, your house and my house are only separated by a wooden wall. And when it's like that, everybody is close.

What about the lack of privacy?

LY: I like the city better because everyone minds his own business. I don't like to live in the country—everybody knows everybody else's affairs.

ZY: I lived in the country for two years, then we moved to a town nearby. Because my parents have to do a lot of reading at night, they don't like to live in a place where there's a hodgepodge of people, and so we moved out, though my waipo is still there. In the country, if you want to do any learning, any serious studying, forget it! [Laughs.] People make a lot of noise day and night, even after bedtime. The lifestyle is very simple. [Laughs.] It's a primitive kind of living. [Laughs.]

TRZ protests: You can't say it that way!

ZY: But people live harmoniously and peacefully and they are very close.

TRZ: Where I come from, if something happens to you and you tell someone about it, pretty soon there's a whole group of people gathered around. Sometimes you spend the whole morning talking about it. This is especially true among women. When they get together, it's impossible to break them up. [Laughs.] They talk and talk endlessly. They talk about this and that, family, lots of trivial things.

LY: Country women like to talk about trivial things.

ZY: Older people also like to chat. In fact a lot of what they say is very funny. Maybe at the time you don't realize it, but afterward when you think about it, it's very funny.

TRZ: When older people talk, usually there's a group of kids standing around listening. Children like to listen to their stories and gossip.

LY: This is also true in cities. Especially in town centers, where the houses are close together, people love to get together and talk. But in our section of town, it's different. It's mostly intellectuals living there, and people mind their own business. My grandmother lives in the town center, and she knows everything that goes on around her.

Do China's changing economic policies have an effect on this community spirit?

TRZ: The system has created a lot of changes. Before, we had joint production. Everybody worked together, and we did everything together. There's really nothing you can't say to each other. After all, you sweat together. But now people tend to go their separate ways. Certain things they just wouldn't say in the open.

ZY: Also, with the smaller family units nowadays, the concept of family is becoming less and less important. The bond is weaker. It's the same in the country. Now that the peasants have adopted the responsibility system, the extended-family bond is weaker.*

TRZ: That's not necessarily true.

When was the responsibility system put into effect?

TRZ: It depends. In Jiangsu, we didn't see it until two years ago.

ZP: Our place, Yentai, was the *last one* in China to adopt the responsibility system. [Laughs.]

* The responsibility system is an economic policy, introduced in 1979, which reversed the idea of collective farming. Under this policy, land is cultivated by individual peasant families and not jointly in production teams. When a family has fulfilled its annual quota, its members are free to consume or sell all the rest of the harvest from their allotted fields.

Why is that?

ZP: That's because of our local leader. Where I came from, for a long time they continued to refer to the Cultural Revolution as "the Great Cultural Revolution" and how great it was. That was about the only thing our leader talked about. [Everyone laughs.] Until last year, when we had our big assembly honoring the model workers, he was still playing records from the Cultural Revolution days. We were still listening to songs praising the spirit of the Cultural Revolution. [Laughs.] Finally they changed our leader, and the responsibility system was adopted last year.

TRZ: It's very similar in our province. Sometimes the policies that are carried out are wrong. Several leaders from our province thought that the circumstances in Jiangsu were very different from elsewhere and that there was no need to get into the responsibility system. But they were wrong, and they were removed from their positions. It wasn't until two years ago that the responsibility system was adopted.

A lot of times it depends on the province. Each has its own policy and administration. Usually the poorer provinces are the first ones to try out a new system, a new policy. If they are successful, then it's extended to other provinces.

The subject now shifts to friendship.

What, do you think, is the basis for friendship?

LY: When two persons are very similar—their interests are alike and also their personalities.

Do you change friends often?

LY: You keep on making friends. You have different friends in different environments. But friends always remain friends. Old friends are still friends.

How do you resolve conflicts?

LY: The best way is not to mention the problem again. It takes only a couple of hours to resolve it.

Does competition affect friendship?

LY: That depends. Some people feel that competition comes first. If you are better than me, then it's difficult for us to be friends. But others think friendship comes first. It's easier for them to make friends.

CPX: Generally speaking, in our environment, there is little chance of avoiding competition altogether. But I don't think competition is so fierce that it would affect friendship in a serious way. It has little effect among students. But as Wen Yuan-kai said, there are two types of jealousy. There is the Western type—if you are good, then I will be just as good. It's all right to make friends in this circumstance since you wouldn't jeopardize our mutual regard just because of competition. But then there is also the Oriental type of jealousy—if you are good and I am not as good, then you can't be good either. With this kind of person, there is no point becoming friends. Luckily there are not so many of them around.

ZY: Some of the things Wen Yuan-kai said are right on target. I think what he said [about the Oriental type of jealousy] is more applicable to adults. Among students—

CPX: Among students, you see some of that, but it's not too common. Maybe in one or two specific incidents, you see this kind of behavior coming to the surface.

Why do you feel it's more applicable to adults?

ZP: The Cultural Revolution created this type of situation. This is what I've understood from my parents. Before, people were simpler and purer, but after that experience, we became more complicated.

Do you often talk to your parents about the Cultural Revolution?

TRZ: I do. That's why the other day I had an argument with my father. His school was involved in gathering information about the Cultural Revolution. Specifically they were looking into the three cliques that existed during that time. For example, there was one group of people who believed in "strength through conflicts."

The principals from nearby schools visited one another and compared notes—my father is the principal from his school—and they all came to this conclusion: that we must totally and thoroughly denounce the Cultural Revolution. But I feel there were some good things in the

Cultural Revolution. You can't deny them and you can't wipe them out. In this regard my father was different from me.

What do you consider as the good things?

TRZ: In the beginning what they did was right. At that time, there really were Rightists among us. Undesirable elements. They should be attacked. With some people, what they did, . . . well, they didn't initiate the purification effort themselves. They were influenced by people on top who were no good. Chairman Mao's people. [Everyone laughs.] The blame is not completely theirs. After all they were influenced. A full-scale denouncement of everyone, including these people, is a little too much. It lacks understanding and compassion. . . . Now the situation is like this: if any of these people are still around, they have to be forced from their positions. Several principals from our area fell just because they did something wrong years ago. Some of them were actually learned men, but they were forced out.

Do you feel that those on top should take all the blame or the people should share part of the responsibility?

Many of the children start to talk at the same time. They take different stands:

ZY: The Cultural Revolution did have the populace as its basis. People were loyal to the Chairman and fervently supported him. The revolution was able to get its start because of their support. If the people at the bottom were clear-headed, the revolution could not have started. So I think the people should be partly blamed for what happened.

JT: But their fanaticism also had its historical reasons. Because of a certain kind of background. . . .

ZY: I agree, but after the fervor cooled down, people should sober up. . . .

JT: But by that time, they couldn't. . . .

LY: I think the people at the top should be responsible, because before the Cultural Revolution personality cult had already been prevalent. So when the Cultural Revolution started, the people believed that no matter what the top leaders did, they must be right, and so they did what they were told.

TRZ: I don't think it's completely that way. There were those who took advantage of the situation. They used the opportunity to do certain things that were normally considered wrong. These things were not necessarily what the higher-ups wanted them to do, like the time when there was a lot of fighting, primarily between two factions. Many went against their conscience and beat up those from the opposite camp. Some even committed thefts. Now these people should have been responsible for their own actions. They just wanted to satisfy their own selfish desires.

ZY: Usually the wrongdoings did not involve the masses. It was those lower-ranking cadres. Let's take the brigade leaders. They made false claims about the size of the grain harvest. Surely the top leaders didn't want you to lie about production. They just wanted your production level to be raised. When the brigade leaders made up their own figures, this did not represent the spirit of our leaders. They made false reports and benefitted from these lies. Of course, it was the top leaders' fault that they didn't conduct any investigations to verify these reports. But the guilty ones were those who purposely lied. The people in general were basically good. They just went on with their work. So the ones I am referring to are the middle-level ones, the opportunists who wanted to advance. You can't put all the blame on the central government.

Do you discuss these things among yourselves?

TRZ: No, because where I come from, this is what happens: if you talk too much about issues like this and if you happen to make a mistake and it gets passed around, people will form an opinion against you; they will think that you have ideological problems. Now that's quite serious and so you have to be very careful.

LY: Usually I talk about these things with my close friends.

MJ: Friends you know very well.

TRZ: Most people can't do this because by talking you are taking certain risks.

CPX: I don't think it's as serious as that.

ZP: It's different where I come from. In our class, there are about seven or eight of us, boys. After school we talk about all kinds of things, politics, international affairs, and so on. We are not necessarily close friends, just classmates, and we have lots of chances to talk. Sometimes our history teacher joins in our discussion. He used to be a Red Guard. At one time he was very "red." [Laughs.] He was the Deputy Director of the Shandong Province Revolutionary Committee. Now he has *stepped down* to become our teacher. [Everyone laughs.] To tell you the truth, many of our views are probably wrong. And the Party secretary from our school likes to pay us visits. Several times he invited us to have talks with him, but that didn't stop us. We still have our discussions.

Take the Cultural Revolution. I don't think it was completely wrong. When Chairman Mao initiated it, his original intent was to address China's future. He didn't want to see China regress. I believe the problem lies in how it was carried out on the lower level. Take Yentai, for instance. At the time what they did there was absolutely crazy. Several old revolutionaries were badly beaten up. It was those cadres. . . . Actually it was not the cadres who did the actual beating, but they instigated it. They urged the lower-level opportunists to do the actual beating. And those opportunists climbed fast. Some of them are still around. So a lot of people in Yentai even now are not very happy.

You have to look at any matter from both sides. And if you do that, you wouldn't conclude that the Cultural Revolution should be totally negated. I think the leaders on top, particularly Chairman Mao, should not be given a large portion of the blame. At the time they probably didn't understand the actual situation. Those on the lower level deceived them with false reports—

TRZ interjects: And the Cultural Revolution was expanded until it finally went out of control.

ZP: But to judge the whole thing as wrong, and to say the leaders were wrong to initiate it. . . . I still believe the original intent was correct and good but there was a lack of understanding of the actual situation. After it was launched, the leaders were not in touch with reality.

TRZ: And there were some who took advantage of the situation and helped to expand it.

MJ: It was mainly those small cliques, like the Gang of Four. There was no way for Chairman Mao to obtain all the correct information. And so these people reported to him: "In our country, situations everywhere look good." Having gotten this kind of report, the Chairman thought that he was doing a good job, and he said, "Let's continue with it."

ZP: Looking at history, I have come to this conclusion. Maybe it's wrong, but no matter whether it's before or after the Liberation, in any case throughout history, the loyal ministers were usually the ones who at the end are brought to ruin. Most of the time, the inferior men caused their downfall—like the case of Qin Kui and Yue Fei.* Here in China in 1962, we had a "party rectification" movement. Some people were killed by mistake. They were usually the ones who dared to speak their minds.

The other day I was reading the *Culture News*. I got very angry. There was a person called Pan Hai-men from Shanghai. Before the Liberation, he was involved in the underground. He was very good at it, a real genius. But right after the revolution, he was attacked. He suffered for many years. Even just before his death no one did anything to redress his case. There were also Chen Yi, He Long, Peng De-huai. I have read the quotations from Peng De-huai.† Peng De-huai was a rare person to come by. If he had any views or opinions, he wasn't afraid to make them known. He didn't care who you were.

Do you feel that Chairman Mao was responsible for what happened to Peng De-huai?

TRZ: Of course he should be held responsible—

ZY: He had to bear a large part of the responsibility—

* For the Chinese, Yue Fei was the archetypal hero—upright, brave, patriotic, and tragically frustrated—and Qin Kui the archetypal villain—crafty, cowardly, and a slanderer; one was the Confucian noble man and the other the inferior man. They lived during the Southern Song, when the Chinese ceded everything north of the Huai River and Qinling Mountains to the Jurchens. Yue Fei at an early age committed himself to a military career and to the cause of restoration. Being a disciplined soldier and a clever strategist, he did well on the battlefield, but his career was cut short when his ruler decided to listen to the advice of his chief counselor, Qin Kui, who advocated peace. Yue Fei was arrested and later murdered in prison. See note on p. 173.

† Peng De-huai was the defense minister during the Great Leap Forward (1957–59) when Mao tried to organize China's countryside into twenty-four thousand self-sufficient communes. By 1959 it was clear that Mao's ambitious plan had failed, but that did not stop him from having Peng, a critic of his policies, purged and banished to a hard-labor camp.

TRZ: Yes, but as for the Cultural Revolution, his original intent was good.

ZY: But there were other reasons for initiating the Cultural Revolution—

ZP: I feel we should forgive Chairman Mao. His knowledge of the outside world was too limited. [Laughs softly.] People like Deng Xiao-ping have studied abroad and have a better understanding of other countries. But our Chairman after the Liberation went outside of China only twice, and both times he was in Russia. [Laughs.] In Russia the idea of personality cult, Stalin's idea of personality cult, must have had a strong influence on him.

Do you talk to your parents or grandparents about their life experiences?

TRZ: My parents tell me that they have always been cautious in everything they do. When something happens, like when a political movement is launched, they don't become overexcited. And when the movement is over, they are untouched. They are not targets of attack. They are the middle-of-the-roaders. There's something good about that because they are morally upright to begin with. It's not like those opportunists, who climb high, but through improper means. These people should be attacked, should be brought down. We should denounce this part of the Cultural Revolution. But then there are those who are actually morally upright. They made some little mistakes along the way. Now they shouldn't be. . . .

Do you share your parents' view about being prudent?

MJ: Each person should have her own mind. She should not be swayed by others. She should not give up her beliefs just because it is safer or more beneficial to do so under certain circumstances. She should know what is correct and what is morally right and she should do things accordingly. Like in my mama's school, there was this teacher who was running for a position in school. But the school officials didn't have a good opinion of her, and so they decided that she should not be elected, but they didn't make clear that this was what they wanted. This put all the other teachers in a very difficult situation. The officials wanted to prevent the woman from getting that job but the question was how to do it. They didn't want it to look too obvious. Every day the head teacher told others privately not to vote for her. At the end most teachers didn't, but there were three who did. I asked my mama how she voted, and she said she voted against her. I told her: "If you think this teacher is good, you should have voted for her. You shouldn't worry about what others say to you." She admitted that she hadn't handled it right.

How would you compare your education at home and at school?

ZY: My parents always tell me to have more patience and endurance, but I can't do it. It's hard.

MJ: I think our education at school seems more open, but then you can't do or say anything that is too extreme.

ZY: Especially our opinions about political matters.

MJ: My parents always tell me to be more careful about what I say in school. The school never tells us expressly to watch what we are saying, but we all know not to be too careless.

ZP: Our school is like this: sure, you can say whatever you want to say, but then they will give you "small shoes to wear." [Everyone laughs.]

TRZ: It's the same in our school. There are kids who have worn these shoes before. A good friend of mine has worn them twice.

What do you mean, "small shoes to wear"?

ZP: They try to clamp you down.

TRZ: Restrain you from doing anything.

LY: It's like forcing you to wear a pair of shoes too small for your feet. You feel very uncomfortable in them.

ZP: If anything happens, they'll interrogate you first.

TRZ: Last year someone from our school got into trouble. He said that people have too much freedom these days. He said that not only to me but to our political science teacher. And somehow words got passed to the top. He got in a lot of trouble.

What about academic work at school?

LY: I find, with math, that most of the time we learn it by rote.

ZY: Math problems, most of the time, do not open up your intelligence. It's the notion of "practice makes you more proficient." The whole idea is to keep on doing as many of these problems as you can. Those kids who do fewer problems and prefer to do other things are more likely to make mistakes. There are pages and pages of work, huge quantities. My aunt's children—they are both in primary—know how to do the math, but the problem is they don't do it fast enough. There's just not enough time.

Kids are given more and more tests all the time, and on tests they don't use what they've learned to find the answer. So the kind of life they live is quite rigid. They face entrance exams for junior high and high schools, and they are pressured to get into a "key school." On every level there is an elevator, and you have to get on. It's very hard on them. The minute you get home, you have to start on your homework.

TRZ: That's so true. My younger sister has just taken her entrance exam. Before that, every day she had to get up very early in the morning, and at night she was still there, studying, writing, copying.

What about word problems? Is there a great deal of emphasis on them?

LY: A lot of the primary-school children are quite scared of word problems. The boys are pretty good with them but not the girls.

TRZ: Even with the word problems, they can also be rigid. There are also set formulas. On tests, it's trying to fit the problem into a pattern that you've memorized, not applying the concepts that you've understood to problem-solving. . . . The Chinese—actually the intellectuals—most of them are good with calculation but not with practical application. I know of this one kid. He didn't have good grades. And then through some personal means he was able to go to the United States. In America, he is the first in his school. He's not good with calculation but he is good with problem-solving.

LY: There are some kids whose grades are sort of mediocre, but they are very smart. They can do a lot of things. Usually when they start working, then their abilities become more apparent.

There are studies that show this. Many who did average work in college made important achievements later when they started working. And those whose school grades were up there at the top are not doing so well at work.

What do you do for fun?

MJ: In school we can join in group sports or get involved with performing arts. With friends, we go biking and swimming together. . . .

TRZ: I think, with friends, we spend more time studying and reading together. [Everyone agrees.]

LY: Except for vacations, there is virtually no time for anything else other than studying. It's very tense during school term. We hardly play at all. We do have some group activities, though. And during weekends we have a little time to relax—we go see a movie or go on an outing.

What about during summer vacation?

ZY: A lot of television. We sit in front of the television all day.

WY: We know the programs are no good, but once we sit down in front of a television, we're glued to it. It's like a habit.

What books do you like to read?

CPX: I don't like fiction that much, especially long novels. I'll read short stories—stories that have a certain influence on me. Usually they are the ones that have gotten some kind of award. I know these will definitely affect me. I have no interest in reading popular fiction.

TRZ: When I was younger, I read anything, especially short stories. I wasn't choosy. I thought that anything that is in print should have some value. Now I like to read books that will open my mind and enhance my ability to think, books that deal with ideas and moral cultivation. We are all at a stage when we are forming our own views. We all need this kind of book—like *Twelve Essays on Self-Cultivation for Young People* and *General Discussion on Civility and Respect*. Almost everybody has this kind of book. There are very few translated works. The only one that I've read is an essay by Bacon.

When I was younger, I read classical novels—*The Water Margin,* the *Romance of the Three Kingdoms, The Dream of the Red Chamber,* all of them. Now I sometimes go back and reread parts of *The Dream of the Red Chamber.* When I was a child I couldn't quite appreciate it, but now I really enjoy it. In fact, I've reread most of the classical novels more than once.

ZP: I like to read memoirs of old revolutionaries. [Everyone laughs.] Also history, historical novels, books about current events.

ZY: When I was in high school, I was very busy with schoolwork. I didn't read many novels. Now that I'm in college, I have more time and I read anything. I especially like biographies, lives of scientists and eminent people: Madame Curie, Edison, Einstein. . . . Sometimes when I'm tired of studying, I flip through some pages, and that stimulates me.

LY: I like Western literature, translated works, Russian novels, *Anna Karenina. . . .*

MJ: They're too long. It's impossible for a high school student to read them. It takes too much time.

CDY: I like poetry, the poems of Byron and Shelley. I also like modern Chinese poetry. I sort of lost interest in Tang and Song poetry, because we are required to recite them at school.

Are you familiar with the Analects *and* Mencius, *and what is your assessment of these two thinkers, Confucius and Mencius?*

LY: We read selections in our textbooks.

TRZ: Nowadays we don't criticize them any more—

ZY: But we don't worship them either—

TRZ: We don't worship them, but we openly acknowledge their contributions.

ZY: We now feel they were very close to being sages. [Laughs.]

Do you get confused? Seven or eight years ago they were harshly criticized, but now they are considered as near-sages.

ZY: I think we're more or less used to it. [Everyone laughs.] After all that's the way it goes with any person—you can say he is good or you can say he is bad. We are all used to it.

ZP: The criticisms during the Cultural Revolution were completely unfounded. Human beings—and their ideas—are limited by their time. Confucius lived so long ago. His thinking definitely had its limitations, but much of his thought has been transmitted down to the present. Now that says a lot. He was from the Spring and Autumn period [772–481 B.C.], and for him to have that kind of philosophy then was not easy.

ZY: To judge Confucius' ideas according to Communist ideology—you just can't do that. [Laughs.] You can't impose our standards on him.

TRZ: At that time there was no such thing as Communism. [Everyone laughs.]

What kind of relationship do you have with China's past—her history and culture?

LY: I think there is a gap—

Why?

LY: I can't quite explain it. I just feel it, intuitively.

JT: I disagree. The thought of Confucius and Mencius has pervaded Chinese history. During classical times, China was under imperial rule, and Confucianism was the ideology of the ruling class. If the Confucian way of thinking had not existed, Chinese history might have followed a very different course. But that was not the case, and so even today the influence from the past is still with us.

ZP: I think there is quite a large gap [between our past and present]. It seems as if a knife has cut off all that came after 1949 from the rest of the thousands of years of Chinese history. One basic difference is that now, of the one billion Chinese, nobody is hungry. This is a rare thing. For thousands of years China was unable to solve this problem. But after the Liberation, we solved it. And also our progress in science. For a long time before the Liberation, it was at a halt. But after the Liberation, China really made some headway. I think this is the kind of thing that we should thank Chairman Mao for. Compared with world standards, we are behind, but since 1949, we have moved ahead in science and technology.

Is progress the result of the Liberation?

ZP: Liberation is the basic cause, but then there are other factors. Let's take Taiwan. Taiwan has also made progress in science and technology. We have to admit that.

What do you mean by "Liberation is the basic cause"?

ZP: Because of the Liberation, the living standard for the common people has been raised. Mechanization has increased production. But in the past ten years or so, we have also made mistakes—mistakes in administering policies. That's because we didn't have enough experience. All the socialist countries in the world have been on the wrong track before—the Soviet Union and also the Eastern European countries. We all don't have enough experience. Now no one can point out a model for socialism, *no one*. Since the founding of our country, we have made many mistakes. And so our scientific development has met with obstacles. Without these mistakes we should have progressed even faster.

Without the Liberation, there still would have been development in science and technology—this I admit. But I think scientific development should be carried out for the sake of improving people's livelihood. If the Guomindang [KMT] were here, I don't think they would try to improve the people's lives. And so scientific development would lose its meaning. In science and technology we are behind, but our way of life has been improved.

Who are some of the persons you admire?

MJ: Cao Xue-qin. I like his work *The Dream of the Red Chamber.** He

* *The Dream of the Red Chamber,* written in the eighteenth century, is regarded by most modern critics as the greatest of all Chinese novels. Deeply autobiographical, it is the kind of literature that concerns itself primarily with the inner lives of hidden people.

was able to take such a large clan and describe each character so vividly. You don't have to see the person and yet you know what he or she is like. Also we find many poems in his novel. That isn't easy. He was a real genius.

ZP: I'm not too interested in literature, but I like those people in history who were spirited and spontaneous. Maybe it's because I am from Shangdong. For instance, I like Xin Qi-ji.* I also like the characters from *The Water Margin*. They were all from Shandong. I like their magnanimous and spontaneous character.

TRZ: I like intelligent and talented men. I read the *Romance of the Three Kingdoms* several times. I especially like Zhou Yu.† But I don't think the book was very well written. The way Zhou Yu was portrayed, it was not . . . it was too biased toward Liu Bei. Though it didn't treat Zhou Yu too favorably, he is still the character I admire the most. I think he was a better person.

Xu Gang is a boy from Nanchang, Jiangxi, who grew up in Shanghai with his waipo. His parents "are both editors." He tells me: "At home we have all kinds of literary magazines. Maybe that's why I'm not at all interested in literature. I like science—physics, chemistry, astronomy, UFOs, things like that." He has a younger sister.

Xu Gang (XG): Ostolovski. I have read his book *How Steel Is Refined* several times.

I have never heard of him before.

CPX: He was a Russian writer, very well known in China.

ZY: He was of the Communist persuasion. [Laughs.]

XG: His writing gives us a push, the effort to strive . . . especially in the last chapter, when he talks about the meaning of life, there is so much enthusiasm there.

CPX: I feel that as I grow older, my heroes keep changing. When I was little, whenever I saw a movie, its main character became my hero. In my

* Xin Qi-ji was a native of Li-cheng, Shandong. See note on p. 182.

† Zhou Yu was the chief counselor to Sun Quan, the ruler of Eastern Wu. See pp. 55–7.

eyes he was the greatest. But it only lasted a short time. It wasn't permanent. Also as I got older, certain characters from the classical novels became my heroes. Then starting in junior and senior high, the people I came to admire the most were the great scientists, those who made important contributions to mankind, especially physicists, like Einstein, Edison. . . .

A girl in the background adds, "Madame Curie."

TRZ: I have read Madame Curie's biography. I don't think she was so great. [Laughs.] When they [pointing to the girls] try to give examples, they always end up with her.

MJ: Women always look up to great women. [Laughs.]

ZY: That's not necessarily true. I have many heroes, but the one I admire the most is still Premier Zhou [En-lai]. I think he was a perfect person. I also like heroic and unrestrained persons, like Napoleon. [Laughs.] I don't know why. I also respect scientists. When I am learning and studying, they are the ones I try to emulate. But we're talking about who has lived a meaningful life. Our premier was a great person—

CDY: Like what they were saying about Madame Curie, I also admire her a great deal. But most of all, I admire political leaders, like Napoleon and Hitler. I don't think Hitler was necessarily bad. He was clever and manipulative.

Are you familiar with the plight of the Jews under Hitler's regime?

MJ: We have read something about the Third Reich, but we are not very clear about it. We know that many Jews were killed in concentration camps. . . .

LY: The details of what happened, we don't know.

The topic of our discussion shifts to the potential conflict in the future between private fulfillment and public responsibility.

Let's say after college you are assigned to the Western region, for example Xinjiang, and you prefer to stay closer to your family in the South, what would you do then?

MJ: It's hard for us to think that far. It's scary. . . .

TRZ: It's hard to say. When it's not time yet, it's . . . we do think about it, though. If I could be reassigned, I'd definitely come back. If not, there's nothing you can do about it. But if I can, I want to return to my native place.

LY: When you're older, it's nice to come home. But when you're young, it's good to go out there and do something constructive.

MJ: I think every human being has an emotional tie to her native place.

TRZ: It's natural that we do, especially the Chinese. We all wish that when we have our own family, we'll go back to where we grew up.

How do you account for the strong tie?

LY: We were born there and raised there, and the tie is naturally strong. . . .

ZY: Also our parents and grandparents have always lived there, and our aunts and uncles are close by.

MJ: When I was very young—it was during the Cultural Revolution—my parents were sent to the country to a small town also in Jiangxi Province, for reeducation. I was there when I was one and didn't return home to Nanchang, capital of Jiangxi, until I was eight. Now when I think about that place, I long to go back, to see all those people I knew when I was little. I want to see how the place and people have changed, whether my childhood friends are still there.

TRZ: If you grow up in the country, you're also attached to the land. . . . The countryside, the fields are magnificent, absolutely magnificent! [Excited.] Here in Hangzhou when I look out of the window, it's like this. So what! So what's the big deal? It's a small place crowded with shops. People are here to buy things, but no one is looking at the scenery. Where I came from, when it's just the right time, all you see is fields upon fields of vegetables. [He moves his arms up and down like waves. Everyone laughs.] Sure, some places stink, and they are dirty, but when you go past the fields, you feel so good inside.

There is work in the fields and at home. We have to do everything. I do some work, but my mama doesn't let me do too much. She wants me to study. My mama is always so tired. She is tired because she wants to put us through school. She doesn't want us to do any work, but we can't just sit around and watch her work so hard, so we do what we can to help. We plant rice and wheat, but we also have to have another business on the side. So we grow mushrooms, lots of mushrooms. Growing mushrooms is also hard work. You have to pick them at the right time. At night you have to watch them to make sure that they don't pop. If they pop, they're no good. A lot of the time my mother plants rice during the day and watches the mushrooms at night. She hardly gets any sleep. But if my parents didn't grow mushrooms, we couldn't afford to go to school. So it's very hard on them. My father often helps. He's pretty good about it.

ZP: Those of us from the city feel the same way when we are out in the fields.

MJ: Where I grew up, there were lots of orange trees. In the fall, it's so beautiful, the green leaves and the golden oranges . . . especially at night when they turn on the lights to keep people from stealing the oranges.

ZY: Where I came from, it's all right to steal watermelons. We all go to the watermelon patches and eat watermelons there. If an old peasant sees us, we just call him Old Grandpa [Laoyeye] and everything is all right. [Laughs.] In fact he doesn't have to be old. It doesn't make any difference, no matter if he is old or young, we call him Yeye.

MJ: I am from Shanghai, and I don't have any contacts with nature. Even though we long for it, we have no chance to do so.

If you could be an animal, what would you be?

ZP: I've never thought of it. I like horses. They benefit mankind. So maybe I would like to be a horse.

TRZ: That's easy for me. I want to be a tiger. [Everyone laughs.] A tiger knows everything, and that's pretty good. . . . If it were me, that's what I will say, yes, most definitely. It doesn't mean that I am pompous and wild. And even if I am, there is nothing wrong with being pompous and wild. [Everyone laughs.]

MJ: I want to be a swan, a swan that can fly.

ZP: I want to be a gregarious animal, one that lives in a flock or colony. I think being independent. . . . If you want to be alone in a world and be creative without the help of others, it's impossible. Living in this world, we have to care for one another and help one another. Maybe [I want to be] an ant.

In fact I remember when I was little we liked to dig out two ant hills and then dig a separate hole and dump the two ant hills into the hole and mix them together. [Laughs.] That was fun.

We are in the outer room of my hotel suite. There are five students with me: three girls (Zhu Yuan, Li Ying, and Jin Tan) and two boys (Zheng Pu and Tian Ren-zhi). Mr. Guo, the camp director, joins in the first part of our discussion. He is around twenty-seven and has recently become a father. He is a graduate student of the Zhejiang University Engineering School and not long ago joined its faculty. The students are on familiar terms with him, teasing him about his awkward haircut.

My children come in and out of the room. My guests enjoy talking and playing with them. The situation is a little chaotic, but we are all very relaxed. We have just had dinner downstairs in the dining room. The food was not spectacular, the service even less so, but we are all in a jovial mood.

We are discussing the changing roles of men and women in Chinese society.

ZY: Nowadays men do a lot of housework. Some cook very well. . . .

Mr. Guo: How much a man is willing to help often depends on how much education he's had. In the country, I remember—this was when I was in grammar school—there was a clear distinction between men and women. This was in the mountainous region, around the time when the Cultural Revolution just started. Women could only eat things made of dark flour. Even if women were to eat buns made of white flour, there was always a dark layer on the outside. And there was no such thing as women sitting down at the same table as their husbands during meals.

ZY: Those poor women! What about your mother?

Mr. Guo: My mother was different. She had left the countryside and had gotten an education. It was the women from my father's family, those who chose to stay.

What about now? Do men and women in the country eat at the same table?

TRZ: Most of the time. Except when there is company, men sit there and women cook in the kitchen. They cook, bring out various dishes, and at the end wash the dishes. It's always like this during New Year and holidays. During these meals my mother is usually busy cooking.

JT: It's not that you are not allowed to sit down—

ZY: And it's not that you are so busy. It's a kind of unwritten custom—

TRZ: Men sit there and women bring out the food.

ZY: And men take it for granted.

LY: In the country the attitude is feudal, much more feudal.

Mr. Guo: They regard men as superior to women.

TRZ: My sister just finished elementary school. My mama told her: "You can continue in school, but you have to do all the chores at home, too." And she always scolds her: now it's "you didn't cook well"; then it's "you didn't do the dishes tonight." My sister is expected to do all these things.

Does your mother ask the same from you?

TRZ: No, never. I don't agree with her. I often wash the dishes. Sometimes my mother hits my sister when she thinks that my sister didn't cook well. Whenever I can, I tell her I did the cooking and in that way she leaves my sister alone. . . . This doesn't mean that I get along with my sister. We argue all the time.

ZY: Anyway, you are pretty open-minded.

TRZ: This kind of attitude still exists. In fact it is quite widespread.

Mr. Guo: Now in places where the peasants are better educated, the idea that men are superior to women is not carried to an extreme.

What about the relationship between mothers-in-law and daughters-in-law?

ZP: Before it was the mother-in-law mistreating the daughter-in-law. Now it's the daughter-in-law hitting the mother-in-law. [Laughs.]

TRZ: The problem is quite serious. Once there was a family living next door to us—they've moved now—and the mother was sick in bed. The daughter-in-law never looked after her. But whenever the mother got a little better, the daughter-in-law would ask her to do the wash. She'd go to the movies while her mother-in-law was home doing the wash.

ZY: Some even fight on the street, the daughter-in-law pulling the mother-in-law's hair.

Mr. Guo: I wouldn't say that's very common. The situation is not very serious. Whenever something like this happens, people like to spread it around.

ZY: That's because people pay more attention to moral values. . . .

Mr. Guo: This sort of conflict is something people hate immensely. It's something wrong morally and so people like to talk about it.

TRZ: Something happened in a distant town about a daughter-in-law mistreating a mother-in-law, and we even heard about it in our village. In our area at the textile mill, for example, they hire girls just graduated from junior high school. That's because young girls' hands are quick and flexible. After a while, their hands become stiff from spinning, and the factories don't want them anymore, so they hire a new group of young girls. For the boys, it's easier to get a better education.

LY: Also in raising children, most parents feel that boys should be more independent. When they are older it's all right for them to be far from home. With girls, it's different. Parents are more worried about their daughters—

ZY: And traditionally, it is considered a virtue for girls to yield to their parents' wishes.

ZP: In Shandong, the people's attitude has always been like this: daughters all eventually belong to someone else's family. You wonder why they feel this way. They have their reasons. They say that their daughters all end up with someone else's last name. [Laughs.] Now with the responsibility system being established in the country, the peasants have more reasons to feel that daughters don't amount to much: they can't do the heavy work in the fields.

In view of this, what effects does the single-child family policy have on society?

TRZ: There are two families in our village, one with a daughter and the other with a son. At the time it was not easy to find a wife, and so it was suggested that the son be married into the family with the daughter. This meant that the son would be living with the girl's family. He and his parents are not willing to do that. The situation is still at a standstill. He wants to have a wife but not at that price. If he is married into the girl's family, it seems that he is lowering his status. That is very clear.

ZY: Actually there are cases where this kind of arrangement works very well.

Mr. Guo: Still it's hard to reverse a traditional custom even though it can work out very well.

JT: Something like this should be worked out in a natural way. It is very different in Shanghai. There, because we have a housing problem, whoever [the bride's or the groom's family] has more space, he or she would go to that family. It makes no difference whether the man goes to the woman's family or the woman goes to the man's family.

TRZ: It's different in the country. It has a lot to do with status.

ZY: Originally we lived in our yeye and nainai's house. But when my waigong [maternal grandfather] died, my father thought that my waipo was too lonely, and so he asked her and her whole family to come over. That was no big deal.

LY: In the cities, it's different. A lot of parents look after their daughters. They always give the best food to their daughters.

TRZ: The bias toward boys is more widespread in the country. At our place there is one family with five daughters. They still want to have a son. Three daughters are married already, and so they are gone. Originally the parents wanted to keep one, but no one was willing to stay. And so there is nothing they can do about it.

LY: Now that we have the one-child family system, some families don't want their daughters.

ZY: Girl babies being drowned by their parents—this kind of thing does happen in the country.

TRZ: Now the peasants are richer. Our neighbors, for instance, first had a daughter and then they had a son. They paid the fifteen-hundred-yuan fine for the second child. It's the same as using fifteen hundred yuan to buy a son.

ZY: It's not that simple anymore. They've raised the fine. The peasants around our area are willing to pay as high as five thousand yuan to have a son.

ZP: Traditional thinking has a lot to do with it. Sons can work in the fields.

ZY: There is also the idea that there is a man in the house to "carry the grain." And when there is a son at home, the mother dares to argue and fight with the neighbors. Without sons, you'd better close your door and shut up.

TRZ: It has a lot to do with the way we live.

ZY: It has to do with the parents' education. Parents with a good education will not do anything barbaric or say anything vulgar. In the country, when parents scold their daughters, they say terrible things. . . . In the future we should really change.

LY: With culture and education becoming more widespread, it will be better in the country.

ZY: It is already much better than before. Now with the college entrance exams, everybody is studying. Everybody wants to go to college.

[*To Tian Ren-zhi*] *After you have finished college, suppose you are given an opportunity to go to Beijing, where the work and pay are better, would you still choose to stay near your village?*

TRZ: It would be difficult for me to decide. Sure, I'd prefer to work in a good environment, but then I should return to my native place even if the conditions are poorer. A person does not necessarily achieve in a large city, in a good environment. Just the opposite, in a small town he might accomplish something great. I know many examples. The other thing is that my parents and all my relatives are all there, at my native place. How wonderful it is to come home!

JY: We all have strong ties to our native land. . . .

TRZ: All Chinese are that way. . . . Our concept of family is very important.

ZY: I remember my first semester in college. At the end, even before exams were over, we were all ready. We had our blankets all bundled up and we were all packed to go home. The night before, we couldn't wait, and the next morning, at daybreak, we were already on our way. . . . At the end of the vacation, it's nice to stay home even just one more day. . . .

* * *

I first met Yao Chen-lin in 1979 in Shanghai's Zhongxin Elementary School, when June and I picked her out from a group of twenty children—an exceptionally beautiful child, tall and slender, with delicate features, dimpled cheeks, and an affecting smile. She was thirteen then. The school principal told us about her younger sister in first grade and suggested an interview with the two together. We were delighted.

Although there was little physical resemblance between the two girls, their sisterly bond was obvious. When we talked with the older one, Yao Chen-tao frequently interrupted us; she was inquisitive and spontaneous, and addressed most of her questions to her older sister—"How do you write this character?" "How does the cassette recorder work?" Yao Chen-lin answered all her questions with gentle patience.

The following was our first conversation, when both were still in grammar school. My questions were primarily addressed to Yao Chen-lin. Her sister, being only seven, had a shorter attention span, but she occasionally interjected a comment.

What is your day like?

In the morning, I usually get up at five. I have to get up and study English, to memorize vocabulary words. I have been learning English for two years now, ever since fourth grade. Around seven we get ready for school. We come home for lunch, around eleven-thirty, and we do some reading or listen to the radio. I also start cooking the rice. My baba comes back a little later, and he finishes cooking the rest of the lunch. He does not want me to do too many chores. He wants me to concentrate on my schoolwork. I do simple things like washing the dishes, washing my own clothes, and sweeping the floor—

Yao Chen-tao (YCT): I know how to sweep the floor, too.

Yao Chen-lin (YCL): After lunch, we return to school about twelve-thirty. We take a little nap in our classrooms until one-ten when classes start again. We usually have two classes in the afternoon, and at two-thirty we go home again. After we get home, we start on our homework right away. Now we are reviewing for the final exams and we are using every minute we have to study. But even when we're not preparing for exams, we do our homework first. I am also doing some more advanced math on my own—math that's taught in the middle school. I usually study for three hours each day, from three to six. My baba gets home around four. My mama comes home much later, around five-thirty. My baba cooks the dinner, and we all eat around six. After dinner, if we have more homework, we finish that. Otherwise, we watch some television.

Their father is a mathematics professor in a local technical college. Their mother is a skilled worker in a television and radio factory. Yao Chen-lin tells me, "My mother assembled the television we have at home herself. She bought all the parts and put them together."

Have you and your sister always lived here in this neighborhood?

Ever since kindergarten, for five years. But my sister, when she was very little, she lived in the countryside because nobody was at home to take care of her. I was then also very young, and I couldn't really help my parents, and so she had to stay with my great-grandparents in the country. Their home is also in Jiangsu Province [where Shanghai is situated], but we have to take a train to get there. She stayed with them until she was five—altogether about five years. She came back to Shanghai when she started kindergarten.

At this point we are interrupted by Yao Chen-tao, who says that she wants to write a letter to show us. She quickly changes her mind and says she wants to draw a picture instead. "But what shall I draw?" "Why don't you draw a Chinese and an American?" her older sister suggests. "Why don't you draw anything you like?" is my immediate response. When June asks her whether she needs a pen or pencil, her older sister decides for her: "You should use a pencil." Yao Chen-tao has one more question before settling down: "Should I copy from another drawing?" I tell her we'd prefer something that is her own creation.

Do you see your grandparents often?

Our paternal grandparents live here in this workers' village. Sometimes we go to their place to play. When my sister was a baby, they couldn't take care of her because they had our uncle's children to look after. A lot of kids I know grew up with their grandparents. Some stayed with neighbors when their parents were away at work.

My maternal grandparents are from Nanjing. We hardly get to see them at all. Nanjing is too far. It takes half a day on the train.

How often do you go to the countryside to visit your great-grandparents?

Quite often, during summer and winter vacations. We go there because the houses in the countryside are much bigger. They can build extensions. We also like to go there because there are a lot of kids to play with and a lot of animals on the farm—pigs and chickens.

You mentioned studying hard for your exams. Do you hope to go to college someday?

Of course. I even want to go to a university in your country someday. I like mathematics very much. One day I want to become a scientist.

Is this also your parents' hope for you?

My baba wants me to do well on my entrance exam so that I can get in Huadong Shida Number Two Middle School. This is one of the best schools in the country.* All parents want their children to go to college.

How do your parents encourage you?

They tell me to study diligently so that someday I can make some contribution to mankind and to our socialist country.

What if you don't do well on your schoolwork?

If I didn't do well, they'd encourage me. And if I misbehave, they scold me or spank me.

If you do very well in school, how do they react?

They usually don't say much. They don't tell us they are proud of us. And they never praise us in front of others because they don't want us to become too proud. But even though they never say anything, we know. When I disappoint them, they don't want to talk to me; they don't want to be bothered with me. But if I do well in school, though they don't praise me, they seem to have a lot of things to say to me.

If a child misbehaves or isn't motivated at school, what does a teacher do?

The teacher spends more time with him and she gives him encouragement. If that doesn't work, she has a conference with his parents and tells them the problem. She doesn't physically punish him. At the most, she criticizes him in class.

Are there many students like that in your class?

Not now. But a couple of years ago, when the Gang of Four was still running loose, there were a lot of them around. In the classrooms there was confusion and disturbances. When the teacher was teaching, many of the students would talk at the same time. They'd say, "If you have the

* A year later she did get into this school.

right to talk, we do, too." It seemed there were constant quarrels between teachers and students and among students themselves. The poison had seeped too deep. . . . Then going to classes was the same as not going at all. There was no order or discipline. Many students went to school just to play. Some of them even got into fights. The teachers had no control. When they scolded the ones who misbehaved, the students talked back, reminding them they were merely doing what the newspapers told them to do.

This was when I was in second and third grade. Those years were the worst. When I was in first grade, I didn't know anything. But when I got to second and third, I knew much more what was going on. It was when I was in the fourth grade that the Gang of Four was crushed and order was restored.

At that time parents were also under a lot of pressure. They were all confused and didn't know what to do. Where they worked, the factories and work units, the same kind of thing was happening. Parents didn't know what to do in their own situations, much less their children's.

I remember even though I wanted to learn, I couldn't. The classrooms were too noisy. My baba taught me at home—mainly math, but also language. He taught me whenever he had some time. My parents were very worried that I wasn't learning anything.

Who taught the children to create disturbances in school.

The newspapers and the radio broadcasts. Even little children listened to what they said. They told us to go against the tide. They told the teachers not to emphasize learning, not to praise those students who did well. Kids who studied well were considered as bad students. Hooligans from the middle schools taught the younger kids to fight and throw rocks. At the time we didn't understand anything. All we knew was that we could play during classes and quarrel with our teachers. But now all the kids are well behaved.

What made them change?

Our country's policy has changed, and Chairman Hua* encourages us to study diligently every day. Teachers and parents work together to improve the students' education.

* Hua Guo-feng, Chairman of the Communist Party from Mao's death in 1976 to 1980, when he was ousted by Deng Xiao-ping.

What about students who can't keep up with the schoolwork?

They repeat a year. But most of us work very hard. In each grade we are divided into four classes: one for the good students, one for the average students, one for the below-average students, and one for those who are going to repeat a year.

Yao Chen-tao has been busy drawing. Ignoring her older sister's suggestion, she has decided to use a ball-point pen. The finished work is a detailed picture of a girl with a spear and a younger boy, each with an explanation below. She reads the written descriptions aloud for us. First the girl: "I am a little Red Soldier. My name is Yao Chen-tao. In my family we also have a younger brother. His name is Yao Chen-jie. Come and see who is beside me!" Then the younger brother: "He is my younger brother. He is learning from me. He is doing his morning exercise. He is thinking: 'I want to build up my body even better.'" Next to the spear is written: "This is a red-tasseled spear." Of course, there is no Yao Chen-jie at home. He is an imaginary brother. (Five years later Yao Chen-lin tells me, somewhat grudgingly, that their father always wanted to have a son and that in a way, he brought her and her sister up as boys. I confirm this when I visit the Yao family with my children. Mr. Yao, seeing my son, remarks to me several times that I am fortunate to have a boy.)

My questions from this point on are primarily addressed to Yao Chen-tao.

Who taught you how to read and write at home?

My sister. She also taught me how to draw. I love to draw, but I don't really draw well.

Having answered my question, she becomes interested in the presents we have brought. She wants to know what each one is and how it works and tests everything out to make sure she has it right. (She told me in 1984 that in second grade her curiosity nearly got her into trouble: "One time I broke a plaster ball in school. When I first saw it, I thought it was a rubber ball. I picked it up and it was very heavy. I didn't quite understand it. It didn't have any air in it, instead it was heavy and was different from other balls. I tried to bounce it on the floor and it broke. This happened in the office, and the teachers at first thought I'd broken a thermos bottle. The ball belonged to an art teacher. Luckily the art teacher liked me very much, and so she didn't ask me to pay for it. But this kind of ball was hard to find. The teacher used it as a clay model for sketching.")

What do the stripes on your sleeves mean?

I am a committee member in my platoon. You can have three stripes or two or one. Two stripes mean you are either a platoon leader or a committee member. Three stripes mean you are a regiment leader.

YCL interjects: I have two stripes, but I'm a platoon leader.

What are the responsibilities of platoon leaders and committee members?

YCT: I am responsible for singing and dancing. Whenever we are doing dances, I have to come out and make sure that everybody is doing a good job. Another committee member is responsible for organization. A third one is responsible for learning. The main platoon leader . . . whenever someone is applying to become a platoon member in the Young Pioneers, he has to gather information about this student and see if he is qualified.

Who helps you with your homework?

My older sister. She is always very nice to me. She never quarrels with me or fights with me.

(*Five years later I ask her again about her relationship with her older sister. "Sometimes we argue over small things. A lot of times it's just fooling around. Let's say my baba and mama buy something for my sister and nothing for me, I'll get mad for a while, for about an hour. Most of the time I am very close to my older sister. She teaches me a lot of things and she is very patient."*)

What kind of games do you like to play with your mama and baba?

We don't play any games together. They have to work very hard. Sometimes at night before we go to bed, they tell us stories, fairy tales. They also give us problems to solve.

YCL interjects: They want us to use our heads.

Do you still remember living with your great-grandparents?

My great-grandfather still comes here quite often, but not my great-grandmother. And so I don't know her anymore. I mean, I do know her but just a little bit.

When I was in the country, I just played all the time. I liked to go with my friends and play by the river. I didn't go to school then, and I didn't do any homework. And because I wasn't in school, they didn't scold me even if I played all day. But now if I do that, I get a scolding from my baba and mama.

Do you prefer living in Shanghai or in the country?

In Shanghai. I like living with my baba and mama. Also the country is not as neat and clean. Shanghai is flat. In the countryside there are too many hills to climb.

* * *

When I saw Yao Chen-tao five years later, in the same reception room where we had taped our first conversation, I did not recognize her at first. She knew me because Mr. Li had told her I was coming, but she sat quietly with five other children listening to him and me reminiscing, and only when Mr. Li asked the children to introduce themselves did I realize who she was. Aside from being several inches taller, there was little change in her appearance, yet the sprightly girl who had delighted June and me five years before with her drawing of an imaginary brother seemed quieter this time—and more sensitive. Right away I asked about her older sister. "She is waiting to see you," she replied. "If it's all right with you, she's going to be here this afternoon. Also my father is home during the summer, and my mother has taken the afternoon off, and they have asked me to invite you to our house. They're eager to meet you." I was deeply touched. Thinking back on it, I wonder what was going through Yao Chen-tao's mind when she was sitting there with her schoolmates listening to me talk with Mr. Li. Her family had already made plans to see me, and yet she waited until I recognized her first to tell me.

Yao Chen-lin came to school with her sister in the afternoon. She was now a senior in high school, but her hair was still tied in two short pigtails, just the way she wore it before. She called me "Jin-a-yi" (Auntie Chin) and showed me the Polaroid picture we had taken together five years before. We were elated to see each other again.

We first talk about changes over the five years:

Five years ago when you were first here, I was just about to take the junior high entrance exam. At that time I had my mind set on getting into a good middle school, and I did! My school is considered a "key school" according to the national standard. There is only one in Shanghai. Last week in the *Culture News,* they reported that in this year's college entrance, our school holds the highest average in science and engineering, literature and history, and foreign languages.

I have been here since junior high. I had to take the high school entrance two years ago and I was placed here again. The competition was very fierce. I remember that five years ago, only three from my elementary school got in this school. We have one hundred and sixty in our class now, and they come from all over Shanghai. (There are ten districts in Shanghai metropolitan plus several suburban districts.) In our grade we are divided into four classes, with about forty students in each. My parents were very happy when I got into this school.

What field would you like to study in the future?

I am taking the college entrance next year, so I've been thinking about this recently. I'm interested in computer science, in automatic control. I like physics but I don't like to sit there and do problems. I think I like engineering better because I like to solve practical problems. My mother works in a radio and television factory that manufactures communication equipment. She assembles parts for television sets, and she also works with radar. Maybe that's why I like mechanics, and why I like to find out how things work. I like to work with my hands.

Do you do this at home?

No, we don't have the means to work like that at home. But in school we have elective classes and classes in our field of interest, and for my elective, I chose computer science, for my special interest class, radio communications.

What are some of the other elective classes in your school?

There are Japanese, mathematical theory, biology for premedical students. When we get to our junior year, we are divided into humanities and science majors. Those who will be studying literature, history, and foreign languages are in one class. Those who are good in the sciences are in the three other classes. Humanities majors have electives in Japanese and other history and literature courses. Since I'm a science major, I don't have much to do with the humanities courses. Other than the electives, there is math, physics, chemistry, language [Chinese], political affairs, history or geography, and foreign language [English]. The three years of math in junior high are mainly for laying foundations. It isn't very deep. But when we get to high school, the math is much more difficult. We learn trigonometry functions, sine and cosine, logs, and functions of several variables. In our junior year, we have analytical geometry and coordinate transformations. . . .

Are science and humanities of equal weight in the eyes of the teachers and students?

We feel that it's more advantageous to be in the sciences. In China there's a tendency to regard the sciences as superior to the humanities. But in our school, students in literature and history are also high achievers. I've already mentioned, in this year's college entrance our school had the highest average in all three categories: sciences, literature and history, and foreign languages. But still I feel students in the sciences are smarter than those in literature and history. Among ourselves that is the general consensus. But even though we consider history and literature majors to be lower, their standard is already very high compared to others.

How did you and your fellow classmates arrive at this level of achievement in your view? Do you think success has to do more with ability or effort?

Of course everyone needs some inborn ability to succeed, but we believe that even geniuses have to be industrious. They have to apply a lot of effort in order to succeed. For instance in our kind of school, the competition is fierce. If you don't study hard enough, your grades are bound to come down.

Does the competition affect your relationship with your classmates?

Let's say there's a math problem, and someone from my class solves it, but I am having a hard time with it. If I were to ask her, she most likely wouldn't help me. When this happens, you can only depend on yourself or you can ask the teacher. Most of the time we depend on ourselves. We don't ask anyone because nobody wants to discuss the problems together. Or sometimes we use reference books.

I think during this period when we are in school learning, it's very hard to build up a true friendship. Two kids start out as good friends, but as a result of the competition, their relationship can go sour. I feel, with the Chinese, that those who live in the country and work in the fields, those who go through a great deal of hardship to make a living, those people more often can build true and lasting friendships. When times are hard, they're all in it together, they all bear the burdens together, and then they also share the good times, enjoying the better days together. After many years there is a great deal of care and affection for one another. Their relationships somehow thread them together.

I have many friends, but they are not very close friends. I can call them friends, but they are not my intimate friends. I don't have a best friend. It's very hard to find a best friend.

Do you regret that?

No. That's because we rarely find our lives empty. We study all day long. We don't have time to think about those things. We are all so preoccupied with homework and exams, and so there is really nothing to regret about it. I've heard from our teachers who have been to Japan and America that kids over there don't have much to do. They play most of the time and don't spend much time studying. They say that they feel listless, bored, and spiritually they are empty.

I try to respond to some of her questions and misconceptions about American children—primarily their attitude toward learning. Our discussion eventually shifts to a broader topic: what does she consider as fulfillment in life?

I think that each person should depend on herself and not on her parents. When I study and learn, I acquire knowledge through my own effort. I depend on myself and I feel good about that. We've seen on television what it is like in America—the most comfortable conditions and the best facilities. We envy you and we are determined to study diligently. We want to build up our country. We want to help. But what I can't understand is why American children have the good fortune to be in a comfortable environment and yet they don't care to study.

In America, if a small child tells his parents that when he grows up he wants to be a cook or a construction worker, they will probably smile and show no signs of disapproval. What about in China?

Chinese parents feel that if a child is high-minded, he or she must want to become a scientist or some kind of specialist. But wanting to become a cook. . . . [Laughs.] Now that's a different story.

I think that in the process of growing up, a person may change his mind about what he wants to become. Maybe as a child, he's very interested in something, but when he grows up, he'll probably change his mind and think about what is more practical. Most of the kids from our school want to go to graduate school someday. They are more interested in areas like physics, chemistry, computer science. Most of the girls want to go into chemistry. They all admire Madame Curie. Most of the boys like to study physics or biophysics.

Among your classmates and your friends, who are your role models?

Famous scientists—those who discovered certain physical laws or invented something. In our classroom, on our walls, everywhere you find portraits of scientists: Einstein, Newton, Madame Curie. . . .

Since most of your classmates—boys and girls—have their goal set on doing some sort of scientific research in the future, does the notion that boys are better in math and the physical sciences and girls are better in the arts and humanities still exist?

Yes. But in a way this is true. For example, in the class with all the literature and history majors, about thirty are girls and only ten are boys. In the three classes with the science majors, there are more boys than girls, and the boys get better grades. In our school more boys are at the top third of the class. Mostly girls are at the middle third, and then again a lot of boys are at the bottom third, boys who would rather play than study.

In the past five years, do you see any changes in your relationship with your parents?

When I was little, I didn't know much and I listened to my parents all the time. Now that I am grown, I don't listen to them as much. That's because our understanding of things is different. There's always a gap between their generation and ours. For instance, in the way we dress: we always disagree about what is in fashion. The older people are always more conservative; they don't like new things. The clothes they pick for me are never colorful, never something that is fashionable in Shanghai. Especially my father, who always says: "What do you want to look so pretty for?"

We have disagreements with them, but I don't think we're rebellious. In China, kids are more filial. We won't oppose our parents sharply. At most, when I really don't want to listen to you, I won't pay attention to you. You say what you want to say, and I'll do it the way I want to do it. We won't contradict them outright.

Other disagreements with your parents?

Our views on international affairs. Most girls are not too concerned with international affairs. Usually it's the boys who pay attention to these things. My father always wanted to have sons, but the fact is, we are girls, and so he wanted us to be like boys, to be interested in the things they are interested in. He tells us: "Look at the boys. They care about what is going on—the real facts. They always read the paper, but you girls have no interest in these things. You should learn from them." And whenever he watches a news program, he always calls me: "Yao Chen-lin, come and look at this! See what is going on."

Our news program is set up like this: first we have national news, and then we have international news. On the international news we learn such things as which foreign leaders are visiting our country. We also learn, for example, that the Russians have pulled their athletes out of the Olympic Games. We know about these things, but because of the way they deliver the news we don't really understand why they happen. I think the boys most of the time don't really understand what is going on either. They have to rely on what the grownups tell them about future political trends and so on. . . .

We are all scared about another political movement like the one in 1966, the Cultural Revolution. Kids of my age are lucky—we didn't have to go through it. I think because we are all scared of [political] movements, we are not really interested in politics. We are all more or less "book learners," and we feel that it's more sensible to study and learn from books, to do well academically. With any political movement, today they say it's good, but tomorrow they say something else. But no matter how unsure we are about political movements, we are always sure about what we learn from books. It is always the same. It is always accurate, always solid and real. And also no matter whether one is in China or in the United States, scholarship is always valid and objective. But with a political issue, let's say a war between two countries, China may have one view and the United States may have another. That's why we don't like to think too much about political issues. It is better to be concerned about our own studies. If academically I make some achievements here, it's measured the same way in the United States.

My parents want me to be more concerned with what's going on in the world and understand what is happening in our country. . . . Actually we still have to give some attention to politics because we have to take exams in political affairs. But I think our parents' generation give more thought to politics than we do. They are older and they have better insights. Sometimes when we children say something that doesn't sound right to them, they tell us not to repeat it again—they are more cautious. Their attitudes are different. They always leave a way out for themselves [*liu-hou-lu*]. They are more prepared in case something happens. They are not like us young people. We don't think about consequences.

Any other changes in your relationship with your parents?

When I was younger, they looked after me in every way. When they noticed small changes, they asked me questions. They worried. Now they think I am more mature, and so with some things, they let me decide for myself. They still ask me about studies and grades. But they don't say too much about other things. They can't watch every step I take. They just make sure I'm well fed and dressed, and that's about it.

What are your parents' hopes for you?

Five years ago I told you that someday I wanted to go to the United States to study. That's still my wish now and also my parents' wish for me. In the United States the technology is more advanced and I could learn a lot.

What about the changes in your environment?

Well, our home is larger. Five years ago, our home was very small. They have extended it by nine square meters. In Shanghai, we can't take down the houses and rebuild them. But we have so many people here, so we make the houses larger by extending the front sections. Every home in our neighborhood was extended by nine square meters. In this way we can temporarily solve some housing problems. They are building new housing in some places, but there's no way that can satisfy everybody, and so we can only do it a little at a time. In America and other countries, it seems that there are a lot of flowers and trees. In movies I've seen children running around on the grass. We can't do that here. In Shanghai there are very few places like that. As it is, living space is already small and crowded, and so it's almost impossible to find even a small plot of grass in our environment. In our school we have playgrounds and soccer fields but no grass or trees. And because we grow up here, we don't have much of a relationship with nature. When we were in grammar school some of the boys, the mischievous ones, liked to catch cicadas—and that was only during the summertime. In the country it's different. I have two cousins who live in the country. They love to go swimming and fish in the lakes and ponds and roll around on the grass.

Also, five years ago when you were here, that was not long after the Gang of Four was crushed. Since then the Party Central Committee has made many policy changes. The first thing they did was to rehabilitate many of the old revolutionaries who had suffered a great deal during the Cultural Revolution. Afterward, they met many times to reorganize the Party and clean out the undesirable elements. Also recently, it is our country's policy to give the peasants a lot of benefits. For instance, they are letting the peasants sell their grain to the government at a higher price, although they've raised food prices only by a small percentage. Anyway, all of a sudden the peasants are becoming richer. Also they are allowed to have a side occupation: they can raise chickens and ducks, grow flowers, or dig a pond and raise their own fish. In the past, our impression was that the peasants had a hard life. But now, it's different—they are rich now.

What is the boy-girl relationship like in your high school?

It depends on the classes. In some classes, the boys and the girls are clearly divided. They don't even talk to each other. In others, the boys and girls get along very well. But there is no such thing as any one boy being close to any one girl. We are all so busy with our schoolwork; there is no time to think about these things.

What kind of music do you like?

Classical music and popular music. Rock music is not allowed and so I don't know what it sounds like. I like music very much. . . . I like to play the piano. I've studied it a little in high school. There is a typing class in school. I know that it will help me with my English. But our school has only a few typewriters, and there are too many students registering for the class, and so they have to choose the best qualified students. When I heard about the class, I decided to take up piano first, to make my fingers more dexterous. I registered for the course in my sophomore year, but I didn't get in until a year later because they take the most qualified first, and the literature and foreign language majors usually have priority. I don't play the piano anymore. I don't have the time. I have my electives, my regular classes, and on top of that, computer science and typing. And we also have extracurricular activities—group activities—at least once a week. In elementary school, there is the Young Pioneers. In middle school, we have the Communist Youth League. The Communist Youth League has a lot of activities—meetings, outings, and study sessions when we discuss newspaper articles.

What do you do during the summer?

I read a lot, but then I can't read books all the time. My eyes would get too tired, and so sometimes I'm a little bored.

What kind of books do you read?

Novels, classics—Chinese and Western. We read the world classics in translation. We have a lot of them at home. At school our teachers introduce us to such world classics as *Anna Karenina, Madame Bovary, Pride and Prejudice* and *Jane Eyre,* and Mark Twain's books. We read them during our free time but there are also selections in our textbooks. We also read a lot of Russian literature. Now, it's easy to buy these translated works. In the past, it was hard to find them. Then, I didn't even know there were so many good books in the world! It was after I entered this middle school that I was introduced to these books. We have a very good library. At first I didn't know what to look for, and so I'd ask the librarians. There are two librarians, a man and a woman. They usually give me suggestions. I like natural science very much, but I also like literature. I like *The Godfather* and Sherlock Holmes, English mysteries and French mysteries . . . the Belgian detective, Poirot, in *Death on the Nile,* and *Sin Under the Sun.* Now I am reading Romain Rolland's *Jean Christophe.*

In class we also have to read classical Chinese . . ., chapters from *Mencius*, for example. Then we have to write essays on ideas like "I will let life go and choose righteousness."*

How do you or most Chinese students feel about Confucius and Mencius?

In the past I know that we were supposed to criticize them, but then I was too young. I didn't understand why we had to criticize them. Now we know that it is wrong to criticize them and also wrong to say they were perfect. Now we feel that everything has two sides, and this is the same with Confucian thinking. It has its progressive side, but then it also served the ruling class in a feudal society—it helped them to exploit the working class. We say that Confucius and Mencius were great educators and literary giants, but their thinking . . . we are more realistic now. We no longer do such things as saying someone is good one minute and bad the next. We don't jump from one extreme to the other anymore. We are more tactful.

There's another kind of situation we have here: what the books tell us and what we say to our friends, classmates, and colleagues at work are sometimes different. When that happens, we always have to bear in mind the political implications. Let's say our teachers make us memorize something in our textbooks, but we students have a different point of view. In our school, among classmates, we love to argue and debate. If we don't agree with what we're taught, we love to put in our two cents' worth. Our teachers let us say what's on our minds, but then at the end, they have the last word. They tell us, It's all right to say these things here, but don't do it when you are out there. Sometimes they're in a very difficult position. They have to tell us the truth about things, but that does not necessarily agree with "the spirit at the top." They let us say things during class. Then they tell us to be more careful when we leave. "Don't talk wildly and don't be reckless," they warn.

What are some of the issues that you debate?

Mostly politics. The way politics is being taught now makes a little bit more sense than before—before, we simply had to memorize everything and we didn't understand what we were taught—and what we learn has more relevance to our lives. We understand better, for instance, what

* This quotation is from *Mencius*, 6A:10.

Marx said. When we discuss economic theories, we always compare our country to the United States. Whenever we talk about capitalist societies, we use the United States or Japan as our examples. It's easier to make comparisons that way. Let's say we are on the topic of how capitalists exploit factory workers. Our teacher first explains what is in our textbook. Then she gives concrete examples. She may also give examples that demonstrate how our socioeconomic theory works. This way she can contrast the two societies. Sometimes it's hard to see any differences, but they can't just say that there is no difference. When our teacher is forced to make such a contrast, we as students usually understand her predicament. Even though we might have our own ideas, we would not pursue the issue to the end and force the teacher to take a clear stand, one way or another. And the teacher also knows that her students will not, as a result, criticize her. There is a tacit understanding between the teachers and the students.

* * *

I had a marvelous interview with Liu Zi-jin in Zhongxin Elementary School in 1979. He was twelve then and he could not stop talking. He spoke pu-tong-hua *fluently, but the Shanghai intonation energized his speech with a regional color that marked his personality. He was a good student (he told me this unabashedly) but not an obedient one. As we talked, he had questions for me, most of which were* statements—*criticisms—about America and capitalism.*

Liu Zi-jin remembered a great deal about living under the Gang of Four and was eager to share his knowledge with me. This was unusual for 1979. He held back nothing, and even when he was judgmental, he revealed how he really felt. He impressed me with his openness and sureness and with the sparkle in his eyes.

Liu Zi-jin came from an unusually large family with older and younger siblings. His mother was a high school chemistry teacher and his father a factory worker, retired early because of a heart condition.

I saw him again in 1984. He wore a wrinkled white shirt buttoned halfway and shorts. His round face had become angular. A soft, youthful beard had grown on his chin. The sparkle in his eyes was less playful. Liu Zi-jin still made statements, but did so more with his presence than with words. And when he did speak, he focused more on himself than on others. He remained self-assured and independent, but now his singularity seemed to close him off. I was astonished by his change and told him so. He acknowledged it with a cool smile.

In both interviews, two other schoolmates are present. Zhao Wen, just seven days older than Liu Zi-jin, is in the same grade. He is shy and quiet. Both his parents are factory workers. He has two brothers, both in their twenties, one a brickmason, the other not yet assigned a job.

Zhao Li-wei is three years younger than both. He is in the second grade, but has a brother who is thirty-two and a sister who is twenty-three. His brother, who is already married and has a child, lives in Anhui Province and comes home once a year.

(The transcript begins with our first conversation.) Liu Zi-jin and Zhao Wen, are you two in the same class?

Liu Zi-jin (LZJ): No. I'm in Class Number One. He's in Class Number Three. There are five classes in fourth grade.

Is there any difference among them?

LZJ: No. In each class the good and bad students are all mixed together. But when we get to fifth grade, it's going to be different. We are fourth-graders now. In a couple of weeks, we are going to take an important exam. The exam will determine which class we will be in next year.

Tell me what your regular school day is like.

LZJ: I get up around five in the morning. I study some English and review some vocabulary. Then after breakfast I start out for school. I get there around seven. At twelve-thirty we have our lunch break. We always go home to have lunch. In the early afternoon we return to school. We finish our classes around four. After school we always have homework to do.

Do you always finish your homework first before you play?

LZJ: Nowadays we don't play at all. We study until eight-thirty or nine and then we go to bed. We help with the chores—washing clothes, sweeping and mopping the floor. Actually my gege and jiejie do most of the chores. My jiejie also does the cooking at home.

Do you sometimes wish that you were outside playing instead of doing your homework or helping out with the chores?

LZJ: I don't go out and play. I stay home and read. Sometimes we play in the hallway or in our apartment. We use the table where we have our meals as a Ping-Pong table. But nobody plays outside.

Why?

LZJ: Because most people are either preparing for their college entrance or for their junior high or senior high entrance.

What about kids your own age?

LZJ: We play inside our apartment buildings. The only thing is that we don't play outside.

You've been studying very hard. What are your hopes for your future?

LZJ: I want to go to college. Because of what the Gang of Four did, our country became very backward. Now we have to catch up to the international standards. We have to catch up and go beyond them. So we all have to study diligently. When we have a college education, we can help to build our country.

Are all students diligent students? Is there any student who has to repeat a grade?

LZJ: In each grade there are about six students who have to repeat. They're the ones who fail the finals. But two or three years ago, even if you failed the exam, they'd let you continue to the next grade.

Why was that?

Zhao Wen (ZW): Then we were still under the Gang of Four. During class we talked to the kids near us, and we didn't listen to what the teacher was saying.

Why weren't you paying attention?

LZJ: That's because the Gang of Four told us things like: good students are weak and meek, like little lambs. They also said that it was useless learning from books and from teachers. Every day we heard this type of propaganda on the radio. So we behaved as they wanted us to behave.

We didn't pay attention to our teachers. I remember some classes were completely out of control. Students would fight, talk back to the teacher and argue with her. Even little kids in the lower grades did this. The teachers could not maintain order in the classrooms. They couldn't discipline the students. If the students wanted to play, they played. If they didn't feel like coming to class, they didn't. They came and went as they pleased.

Did most students behave like that?

LZJ: I would say about half and half. A small portion of the students were very good. Another small portion were somewhere in between. Then the remaining half was very bad. But that was in another school. I was transferred here in the third grade after the Gang of Four was toppled.

What could you do if you wanted to study?

LZJ: I asked my mama to teach me when I got home. My mama is a teacher. At that time she could hardly teach at all, and so she usually came home early and gave me lessons.

In the last two years, what has happened to the students who were troublemakers?

LZJ: Most of them are all right now. They've changed their ways. The schools put all students under strict discipline. There are rules we must follow.

What happens to the students who have violated the rules?

LZJ: If it's a light offense, he gets a warning. If he repeats it, he is kicked out of school. . . . There was this boy from our school who stole money from his parents. The money was in a closet, and he forced open the lock. Our teacher told us about it.

And who told the teacher?

LZJ: You see, he first started stealing in school. He stole other kids' pencils. He stole everything he could lay his hands on. He also stole things from home. He got mixed up with a kid from the middle school.

He learned all sorts of bad things from him, stealing and fighting. His teacher got suspicious. She questioned him. His attitude was pretty good. He confessed everything, even what he did at home. Since he was honest, his punishment was light. He only got a warning. If he continues to behave well, the school will eventually take away the warning. But that won't be for a long time yet. I think that most students who do something terrible are found out at the end. If the school doesn't, his parents will. And when they do, they usually tell the school about it. Why? They want their children to be good. They want their children to do well in school and to go to college someday. They all wish that.

Do you think that the bad will always be exposed at the end?

LZJ: I think so. At least that's what we see on television and what we read in storybooks. But in real life, sometimes it's not true. In class a lot of kids do bad things, and the teacher doesn't know. But if they use reason and correct themselves before the teacher finds out, then that's all right too.

Do you watch a lot of television?

LZJ: We don't have one at home, but my uncle has one, and so sometimes I watch it in his house.

Zhao Li-wei (ZLW): We don't have one either, but two other families in our building have it, and so I go there to watch it.

ZW: Our next-door neighbor has a television set. When there are good programs, I go there and watch. But now it's exam time, and I don't have time for that.

LZJ: I like to watch programs and listen to stories on the radio about the war, stories about capturing enemy agents and about the underground activities against the Japanese.

Who are the enemy agents?

The Japanese, the KMT, and also American agents. This was when we didn't have any relationship with the United States, when Americans were still very close to the KMT. At that time they trained agents of Jiang Jie-shi [Chiang Kai-shek]. Recently there have also been plays about the Cultural Revolution. There is one about Zhang Zhi-xiong, a woman who was not afraid to speak out when an old cadre had been falsely accused by Jiang Qing and her renegades [the Gang of Four]. At the end they seized her and took her to court. They forced her to confess to a crime she had not committed. She refused. Finally she died in front of a firing squad. But before she died, she shouted: "Long live the Chinese Communist Party!" She kept on shouting, and they had to cut her larynx to silence her.

On weekends and holidays, what do you do with your parents?

LZJ: My baba has been home sick for the last two years. He has heart problems. Sometimes when he feels awful, he sleeps for the whole day. He has problems breathing and feels very uncomfortable. When his illness doesn't act up, he's all right. I like to tease him and play tricks on him. My mama is a chemistry teacher. She gets Sundays off, but most of the time she's busy preparing lectures.

Tell me more about your relationship to your mama.

LZJ: She's the one who punishes me when I misbehave. Sometimes when she gets very angry, she spanks me. Once I was home and she asked me to read those old classical novels. I said, "No." Instead I played Ping-Pong. Well, I got a beating that time. I have problems reading classical novels because the words are difficult. But whenever I get stuck, I ask my mama to explain them to me. Sometimes when I don't understand what I'm reading, I ask her to tell me the story to give me a general idea. But when she is in a good mood, I tease her, too.

Tell me something you did that you didn't tell your parents about.

LZJ: Well, once I gave somebody a bloody nose and I didn't tell my parents. This boy was always trying to tease me. One day I was just standing by a tree, and for no reason at all he pushed me up against the tree. I got very angry and hit him. You see, I just wanted to show him that I was not a pushover [excitedly]. I gave him a punch on the nose.

Do you have a best friend?

LZJ: Yes, someone from our neighborhood. He is very nice. He also doesn't like to go out and play. His name is Song Hua. He's not very bright. He has some difficulties with learning, but he works very hard. We are both twelve. We do a lot of reading together. Sometimes I go to his home and we have our own class. Since I am doing well in all my subjects, I help him most of the time.

There is also an empty field near my home. One of my classmates has a soccer ball, and sometimes we play soccer there. We don't do that very often though. When I go shopping for my mother, I have to pass by that place, and I watch other children play.

ZLW: Before I was six, I used to go out and play with my neighbors every day. Now I like to play chess at home. Sometimes we tried to catch birds. We use slingshots or an air gun. My neighbor has one. We also like to find stray cats at night. We try to hit them with pebbles.

ZW: I play with kids in my neighborhood. Sometimes my older brothers take me to the park or to a movie. My father works in Hubei Province. He has been there since the beginning of the Cultural Revolution. He only comes home once a year for about two weeks. When he comes home, he helps with the chores and he rests. I write to him regularly. My mama gets off on Saturdays, and she washes clothes and cooks. She doesn't have time to do things with me.

What dialect do you speak at home?

LZJ: Before we went to school, we spoke the Shanghai dialect at home. But once we are in school we have to speak the *pu-tong-hua*. Now we are more used to speaking the *pu-tong-hua* at home. My parents still talk to me in the Shanghai dialect, though.

Can you describe your home a little?

ZW: We only have one room with two beds. When the weather is hot, we all sleep on the floor. There is a radio, a sewing machine, a big closet, a big table, and a clock. There is a kitchen and toilet shared by three families.

LZJ: We have three rooms—two bedrooms and a living room, which is also the place where we eat our meals. I sleep with my younger brother in one bed. My sisters sleep in another. My older brother sleeps in a separate bed by himself, and we all share the same room. My baba and mama, they have a separate room. We have our own kitchen, but two other families share a toilet with us.

ZLW: Originally we only had one room. Then we added another level on top. I sleep with my baba. My older sister and my mama sleep in another bed. In the wintertime some of us would use the upper level, but most of the time we sleep in the same room. We also have a sewing machine, a radio, and a big closet.

Do you have any questions about America?

LZJ: We learn that Americans live in high buildings. Actually, the rich live in the high buildings, and the poor live in shacks and slums. Why is that?

There are problems in America, many problems. So it's not easy to answer your question. In fact many poor people from the slums live in high apartment buildings, and many middle-class and well-to-do families have single-family houses.

ZW: What do Americans eat for breakfast, lunch, and dinner?

We have dried cereal, very much like your puffed rice, and cold milk for breakfast. Then there are also eggs, toast, oatmeal, and things like that. For lunch we can have a sandwich with cold meat in between two pieces of bread. For dinner it's usually a hot meal with meat, vegetables, and potatoes or rice. What about you?

LZJ: For breakfast we have soupy rice with pickled rice or some other sort of vegetables. For lunch and dinner we have scrambled eggs with tomatoes, or stir-fried vegetables and meat. Sometimes we also have steamed buns. I like steamed buns.

September 1, five years later: we are all assembled in Zhongxin Elementary School. The Yao sisters are also there. Liu Zi-jin and Zhao Wen are now both juniors in Caoyang Middle School, a so-called key school in Shanghai. Zhao Li-wei is finishing junior high this year at a different middle school.

We talk mostly of changes: changes in relationships, personalities, attitudes, interests, and environment. Yet what emerges plainly, though we were unaware of it at the time, is the continuity within the changes: references to the past as a way of making sense of the present.

[*Speaking to Liu Zi-jin*] *How is your father?*

LZJ: He is still very ill. He has not gone back to work since the last time we talked.

Do you remember our conversation five years ago?

LZJ: Yes, I remember it well.

Do you still like to joke around with your father?

LZJ: My father has gained a lot of weight. He is very fat now. We call him all sorts of names, comparing him with all the fat people and creatures we know. He looks like the Maitreya Buddha.*

Does he have Maitreya's temperament?

LZJ: Not at all. He has a bad temper, quick and explosive.

What about your relationship with your parents? Do you see any changes in the past five years?

LZJ: Our differences are greater. Our relationship is not so harmonious as before. We are older now and we want to be independent. We want to have the right to make decisions for ourselves [*zi-zhu-quan*], but our parents still want to mind our business. So there are more conflicts. A simple example would be the way we dress. We want to wear more fashionable clothes, but they think that that sort of clothes will give our teachers a bad impression. We have different points of view. Also, I like to read novels. If my mama catches me reading novels, she tells me that I should be studying. She thinks that reading novels distracts me from doing more serious work.

What about you, Zhao Wen?

* The future Buddha, a Buddha yet to appear. According to Buddhist teachings, his coming will mean the initiation of a new, peaceful, and harmonious age. In Chinese art he is depicted as a big-bellied, jolly, laughing figure.

ZW: In the past when I was little, I didn't understand much. So I was very close to my parents. But now I am grown up, and I can make sense of things myself. So our relationship is not the same as before. For instance, we can never agree on how to organize my life.

Do you enjoy sports?

ZW: I like soccer and basketball.

LZJ: I like to do body-building exercises. I know that's very popular in the West. I have some simple equipment at home like the chest developer and the barbell.

Other things you do during the summer?

LZJ: This summer I was in a work-study program. I worked twenty days, and I got paid for it. The pay was one-and-a-half yuan a day. This was a program sponsored by our school. You could either work in a food processing plant or for an architectural and construction company. The work was very light. We worked an hour each day, and the rest of the time we had lunch and just sat around. But during the hour when we worked, we worked very hard: we cleared fields, removed steel beams from the crane, and carried bags of limestone. We were supposed to work six hours a day, but since we were young, the construction workers didn't want us to overexhaust ourselves. So they gave us a lot of time to rest. Every student can participate in the work-study, but you have to apply.

ZW: But I didn't know anything about it.

LZJ: A student in our class knew about it, and he told us about the program first. This year there were about twenty students from our school in the program. Some students weren't interested in applying because they thought the work would be too tiring for them.

What do you intend to do with your money?

LZJ: I want to buy some clothes and save the rest for pocket money.

Are there many opportunities like this around?

ZW: There are some, but usually circumstances don't allow us to have this kind of experience. We have to study and study. Our parents much prefer we spend more time studying.

LZJ: My parents think my studies always come first. They think we can let everything else slip a bit.

YCL: My parents want me to be more independent, to have more practical experience. But at the same time, they're not quite sure I can handle it all by myself. Last fall my school organized the juniors to go to the country and work in the fields for two weeks. We went to Jiading Prefecture, and we lived among the peasants. We picked cotton, harvested rice, and hauled manure. During the whole time my baba was worried about me. One Sunday he showed up with my meimei. He wanted to make sure that I was all right.

How did you like those two weeks?

YCL: I was tired. We lacked tempering. But since it was just two weeks, I had a good time. I wouldn't have been happy if it had gone on longer. We got along with the peasants pretty well. Some were very kind to us. But in the villages where the peasants were poor, we were not treated so nicely. In the richer villages, it was much better. The peasants there wanted us to tell them all about Shanghai, the streets and the interesting things that went on there. They didn't want us to do any heavy work. But in the poorer places, the peasants asked us to do all sorts of work and usually we had to work the whole day. I had a classmate, and every day her "master-worker" came to fetch her early in the morning. We were all so angry about the way he treated her. We said we weren't there to do physical labor but to learn from the peasants. . . .

Each day the peasants begin work before dawn and then about eight they come home for breakfast. After breakfast they go back to the fields and work until twelve. That's when they have their lunch. After lunch they go back again. They don't come home until it's dark, around six. When we were there, they sent us home early to rest. But this peasant I just told you about, he was terrible. He hardly ever let my classmate have any rest. Last year all the juniors had to go to the countryside for two weeks. It's the same this year.

In the future would you prefer to work in the city?

All: Yes, definitely.

Isn't the city very crowded, especially Shanghai?

ZLW: Nanjing Boulevard is crowded but not here. [Laughs.] The city has more to offer than the country. We grew up in the city, and we are not going to feel comfortable living in the country.

YCL: My great-grandparents live in the countryside. We visit them during holidays and sometimes during vacation. And my mother's family is in the suburbs of Nanjing. The people there are very poor and life is very hard. We don't like to go there.

But you did enjoy staying with your great-grandparents when you were little.

YCL: Yes, everything seemed fresh then. Even watching the peasants working in the fields was fun.

LZJ: Life in the country is too monotonous. My waipo is from the country. Last summer I stayed there for ten days, and it was kind of boring. When we were children, we were playful and mischievous. Everything seemed fun. But now we are older, and we don't catch birds and insects anymore. . . . Of course, we like to be in the midst of nature; we enjoy the scenery in the country. On Sundays, we like to get together with a couple of friends and ride our bikes to the suburbs. We have a good time then. But if we were to work and live in the country, that would be different.

What about your attitude toward the peasants?

ZLW: The responsibility system has made the peasants richer. They are better off than us, and so I don't see why there should be any prejudice against them. Last year some of the kids in our school did a survey for a newspaper. We were in the country for just a day to do this survey. We found that they make about 2,200 yuan a year while those who live in Shanghai make about 800 yuan a year. The peasants do work a lot harder than us. They are in the fields all day long. With the money they earn, they buy appliances and television, and they like to build their own houses. The rest of their income is put into savings. They are beginning to put greater emphasis on educating their children. [The law says that] children cannot join the work force without a junior high education. If you haven't graduated from junior high, even if you work in the fields, you don't get paid for it. But if you are able to go to college, when you come back to the village, you can easily become a cadre. Now there are only a few kids who have made it to college.

YCL: During those two weeks when we worked in the country, our teacher from our politics class asked us to look into the living conditions of the peasants. Afterward we had to write a report. We found that their income is higher than ours, but we all felt that we'd rather live in the city with a lower income. Their life is much harder, and we are not going to go to the country just because we can be richer. . . . There is also this gap: the peasants are vulgar; they lack knowledge and culture. I don't know if we are prejudiced, but I am sure that if a peasant's child attended our school, we wouldn't treat her differently. We'd just see her as a classmate. We wouldn't look down on her because she came from a peasant family. Our school doesn't have any student like that, though. They have their own key schools in their prefectures. They wouldn't come all the way to Shanghai. In the past most peasant children had only an elementary school education, and if they had a junior high education, that was considered pretty good. But now more and more are taking the college entrance exams.

Do you want to stay in Shanghai or go away for college?

ZW: In Shanghai.

LZJ: My parents want me to stay in Shanghai, but I would like to go away. I want to be more independent. I want to get out and see the world.

YZL: Before, I wanted to go to Beijing. Then my father told me that I wouldn't get used to the food there. They eat noodles all the time and things made from flour. He wants me to stay in Shanghai. Now my first choice will be Jiao-tong University in Shanghai. It's closer to home, and I can come home on weekends.

Do you listen to your parents in this regard?

YCL: Yes, I think so. The final decision, I believe, is still mine. Parents usually take into consideration what their children want. So if a child insists on going away to college, I guess there's nothing her parents can do: they have to give in at the end. But most parents want to have their children close to home. If their children are too far away, they can't look after them.

ZW: I usually follow my parents' wishes.

What about questions like what to major in when you are in college?

ZW: I know what I want to study in college. I do better in the sciences, and so I'll probably major in the sciences.

LZJ: According to my grades, I should be studying science in the future. But I like literature better. In language class our grades have a lot to do with our point of view. The teacher very often disagrees with how I understand something. On a test I may feel happy with the way I answered a particular question, but when I get the test back, I quite often find that the teacher sees it very differently; he thinks that my answer deserves a big fat zero. You see, the difference is in understanding. . . . I know how my teacher wants me to write essays, but I still write them the way I want to. What the teacher says in class serves only as a reference. I have to do my own thinking. For instance, in one essay we were asked to write what we liked to do best. Most of the kids wrote that they liked to read and study. I said that I liked to play; I liked to go on outings; I liked sports. I told the truth, but the teacher was not pleased with that, and so he gave me a grade based on "impressions." Usually I get about a seventy on my essays. My classmates get at least seventy-five on theirs.

Liu Zi-Jin seems to have changed. Five years earlier he had told me that he always played at home, that he did not like to go out and his best friend was the same way.

Do you ever have discussions with your teacher about your grades?

LZJ: No, we don't do things like that.

YCL: Usually students don't ever challenge their teachers.

LZJ: I don't question him about my grades, but then the next time when I have to write something, I still express how *I* feel. My parents think I'm too stubborn. I have a classmate who's just as stubborn as me. And I talk about these things with my friends. We all feel our grades in school are not so important. There are more objective standards. How you are evaluated outside the classroom counts more. Even if you have low grades, it's no big deal. What matters is how well you do when you are competing against students outside your school. For example, I was the number one student in my class, but some kids in other classes had better grades than me. On the entrance exam I scored higher than most of them. My friends and I all agree we should not make too much out of our grades at school. What's important is not to go against our inclinations, to say what we mean.

You said that you like literature. Whose works do you read a lot?

LZJ: I like Lu Xun and Hugo. I have read most of Hugo's works, all in translation though. I have also read a lot of Dumas. Dumas' works are different from Hugo's. They are not as deep or complex. Dumas was just a great storyteller. Recently I have also finished *Three Comrades* and *All Quiet on the Western Front,* both by Remarque. I am also beginning to read Henry James. . . . I also like to watch Kung-fu movies from Hong Kong. I watch movies for entertainment, to relax. Usually I don't remember what I have seen. I only have a vague notion what it was about. I never watch films made in China. [Laughs.] Sometimes when there is one on television, after about fifteen minutes, I can pretty much guess what the ending is going to be like. So I turn off the television and go to bed.

ZLW: All the Chinese movies are so "black and white." It's always the same routine over and over again.

YCL: You have the same movie being made several times. It's all right to see it once, but to sit through it a couple of times is boring. . . . I think there are many talented young Chinese writers today. That's because they have gone through so much during the Cultural Revolution.

What about the movies based on their stories?

YCL: They're pretty bad. Once they're made into movies, they become uninteresting. Why? Because there are things you can say in a novel but not in a movie. When the subject touches on reality, then there are many other considerations. But a writer is usually more daring. . . .

ZLW: But when a writer goes too far, he will be criticized. There are radio programs debating the values of various books.

YCL: I think that writers should speak the truth.

LZJ: Their works should not be separated from reality.

YCL: The problem is that if you say too much, you'll be criticized, and if you don't say enough, you'll be blamed. Anyway, I think writers should not lie.

What do you consider as lying?

YCL: If something is obviously bad and you insist that it's good, that's a lie. What's the point of saying something that's not true? We are not children anymore. It's not that easy to fool us.

With such high academic pressures, do you still find it possible to develop your own interests?

LZJ: I am absolutely sure I will always be interested in literature. I am certain because I know my character and I know that literature is close to my grain.

YCL: I think we should develop in other ways—

ZLW: But I don't think it's possible in our society. If you want to develop your interests, you won't have enough time to study. Once you have decided on your area of study, you have to fulfill its requirements.

YCL: I think our education should be reformed. First under the Gang of Four, we were told not to study. Then all of a sudden after the Gang of Four is gone, they say we have to study, and the whole purpose of studying is to get into a college. The college entrance is divided into two areas, sciences and humanities, and we have to concentrate on one. We are instructed to do this one minute and that the next. So much homework, so many books to read! So when do we have time to pursue our interests?

LZJ: I think first of all we should be given a sufficient amount of autonomy and also more time for ourselves. We have about seven to eight hours of class, and then the rest of the time we have to do homework. When do we ever have any time to do the things we like? And when do we have time to understand society?

Do you find the knowledge you have gained in school to be useful?

ZW: The knowledge we have gained in the classroom gives us a foundation.

LZJ: I think only half of it is useful. What I consider to be useful is the basic knowledge, math and grammar, something we can't learn outside of the school.

ZLW: The textbooks we use were written a long time ago. We learn what's in them, but there is little that we can actually apply. Some of the textbooks have been revised, but a lot of them are out of date. They were written right after the Liberation.

YCL: I feel that most of what I have learned in class is useful. Teachers don't know everything, and then there are things they can't say in class, but what we get in school is only one kind of knowledge. Then there are things we learn from reading, from watching movies and television, and from actual experience. What we get from actual experience helps us to gain a foothold in society. School gives us something very different.

In class most of the time we listen to the teacher. We prefer to have more discussion time, though.

Do you ever request discussion time?

LZJ: That's impossible. And even if we asked, it wouldn't do any good.

YCL: We have discussion outside of class. We realize that it's useless to make any suggestions to our teachers. Actually no one has thought of making suggestions to the teachers.

Whom would you consider as a good friend?

ZLW: Let's say a teacher makes a mistake, and you bring it to his attention; just to get back at you, the teacher might try to find a chance to bawl you out; the person who stands up for you and defends you is a true friend.

YCL: We make friends when there is a conflict, a break, when a few students are alienated from the rest of the group. . . . I don't really have any good friend. I feel the competition in our school has an effect on friendship. I think that this is probably more true with the girls, but it's also true with the boys. Maybe it's just our school. We are brought together because of our abilities. Everybody is good, and everybody wants to be better than the other. It's terrible in our school.

LZJ: It's not true in our school, unless we are talking about narrow-minded people. Basically *boys* are not that way.

And girls?

LZJ: I don't know. In our class boys and girls don't even talk to each other.

ZLW: Now that's something sensible passed down to us through tradition. You asked us about [our relationship to] our history and tradition. Well, this is part of it. I guess we have gotten this from our tradition, and it has to be good whether we like it or not.

Earlier, Zhao Li-wei said: "Technology is so advanced now that some of the old stuff has no use anymore. But there are things we still value like 'human relations and worldly wisdom' [ren-qing-shi-gu]. *I think the Chinese have a lot more understanding of human relations than Westerners."*

When do you see the boy-girl relationship begin to change?

LZJ: We are fine in elementary school. . . .

YCT: No, no, only in the first and second grades. Beginning with the third grade, we talk to each other only when we have to.

In junior high?

LZJ: All right.

ZW: Not that much going on.

What about high school?

ZW: Not at all.

LZJ: And our teachers support this. Actually there was a classmate of mine who raised this issue in class. He said that we should communicate if we are going to understand each other. Our teacher didn't like that. During class he criticized this student, saying there was something wrong with his way of thinking. He made a point that boys and girls should not talk to each other, that they should be studying instead. He didn't give any particular reasons. That's the way things are, and you can't change them. . . . But boys do spend a lot of time together. We talk and have a good time, and so it's natural that we become good friends. I have a best friend, and we talk about everything. He is not from my class though. I don't have a good friend in my class. My classmates and I have very different personalities.

If you could, how would you like to change yourself?

ZLW: I've never thought of that. [Pauses.] Actually I like the way I am. I don't want to change. I have a good temper. I get along with people, with my classmates.

LZJ: I wish I could be more introverted. I've already changed a lot since elementary school. My environment has forced me to change. You see, in this environment, most people say very little, so I'm gradually becoming that way too. I don't think it's wise to reveal to others everything about yourself. Most people feel this way, my parents, for instance. They tell me all the time not to say too much.

YCL: We all feel that if you are too extroverted, you will suffer in the end. [Pointing to Liu Zi-jin.] I think he is one of them. [Laughs.] If you are too direct and blunt—not saying things in a roundabout way—you might offend people. Most people choose to keep their opinions to themselves, especially if the opinions are negative. People who are too straightforward and say everything on their mind often give others a bad impression. If you show yourself to be different, others will keep a distance from you. But if you don't reveal yourself, no one will ever know what you are thinking and so the relationship continues. On the surface there's harmony, and you won't hurt anyone's pride.

A more cautious person acts according to the circumstances. He first thinks about the consequences of his words. Even when it's safe to say them, still he'll probably hold back half of what he really wants to say.

I don't think that's right, though. I've always been extroverted. So I know I'll suffer at the end. [Laughs.] Parents are different. They are much more knowledgeable when it comes to "human relations and worldly wisdom." They are much more experienced when it comes to handling things. So when we are faced with a certain situation, they always show us the steps to take. They won't let us go all the way and do what we think is right. From the time we were children we've been very influenced by our parents. . . . Those who are open and direct often have to suffer the consequences of being open and direct. So many have decided to change. I think that he [pointing to Liu Zi-jin] is one of them. [Laughs.]

LZJ: I have decided to change because being open has hurt me. For example, if I felt that a teacher didn't know how to teach, I'd tell my classmates what I thought. Some would agree with me, but some would go to the teacher and repeat what I'd said. Well, that did it! An impression is formed, and it's hard to change that teacher's opinion of me. Several of my classmates are like that. During my third year in junior high, we had to elect a student who was "excellent in three categories" [learning, character, and service]. Many of my classmates thought I was qualified, but one teacher had a strong bias against me, so I was eliminated from the list of candidates. Later, that teacher had a talk with me—she told me I had been disrespectful to my teachers and so on. She repeated some of the things I had told my classmates privately. I knew that someone had been an informant. So I learned my lesson. It's smarter to keep my mouth shut.

If you could change your parents, how would you change them?

LZJ: I think it's hopeless to try to change them. Their thinking is so "antiquated." I wish that they were like us, more open.

YCL: I wish my father were not so mean. He is very strict with us. If we do something wrong, he beats us. [Laughs softly.] Most of the time he's fine. It's only sometimes that he . . . he has a very bad temper. He is very autocratic. He won't listen to us at all. We have a television set at home, and he decides which program to watch. My mother is more democratic. She is more compassionate. She, my sister, and I are always on one side, opposing my father. [Laughs.] I wish my mother had more education. She is not as educated or as cultured as my father. She has already done very well, though. She is a supervisor at the radio and television factory, and she has achieved this all through her own effort. She didn't have much education because she came from a very poor family. . . . When my meimei has a question with her math homework, for instance, she always goes to my father for help. Sometimes at the dinner table, the three of us will be involved in some discussion, and my mama will be left out. She just sits there and listens. She can't really join in the discussion. If my mother was more educated, we'd have more to talk about.

ZLW: I wish that my parents could be like us. I wish that they were more *ling-de-qing*. [Someone explains that this is a Shanghai expression, meaning "understanding" or "clear-minded."] It's hard to turn them around. They worry too much and nag too much.

Which relationship is most important to you?

LZJ: I think friendship, the relationship between very close friends.

ZW: I think the parent-child relationship.

YCL: I think none is important. I don't want to be connected to any person. I want to be by myself.

ZLW: I think the parent-child relationship. Parents exhaust themselves trying to bring up their children. A lot of painstaking care has gone into it. So it's not right for a child to abandon his parents when they get old. He should serve them and care for them. I wish that my parents were more understanding, but even if they are not, it wouldn't affect my relationship with them. We complain, but soon everything is forgotten. Of course sometimes I resent my parents. But resentment is one thing; it doesn't hurt the relationship.

YCL: The feelings, the affections remain the same despite the conflicts. If our parents won't accept our views, and if we cannot accept theirs, we just each do things our own way.

Will you return to their side when you have your own family?

YCL: Yes, most definitely. I'm positive I will return. Parents are the closest to us. I am sure we can all live together. I think most of us will live with our parents when we have our own families.

LZJ: I don't want to live with mine in the future. I definitely will visit them and I will be filial. I will fulfill my duty as a son, but I wouldn't want to live with them. Between the young and the old there is a deep gap. I know many of my classmates who have a lot to talk about when they are at school but when they are home don't say anything. They listen to their parents, obey them, and respect them, but there's no talk between them. They don't share a common language. Basically this is how it is for most kids. I'm the same way. When I go home, I hardly open my mouth. Of course, sometimes I tease my father, but that's just goofing around. When it comes to serious matters, I don't express any opinion. When he tells me how he feels about something, I just nod my head and say, "Yes, yes." But when it comes to actually doing it, I don't have to follow his way.

YCL: I'm the same way. My father is autocratic. He won't accept my views. Sometimes I still listen to him when I think what he says makes sense. Other times, I pretend to listen to him, but I do things my way. When I live with them in the future, it doesn't mean that we will have more to say to each other. It's just that when people get old, they miss their children; they are lonely. In fact I can't say that I will enjoy living with them, but it's an obligation, something that I *ought* to do. Otherwise they'll be lonely. When the whole family is together, there is more life and energy.

What about your relationship with your brothers and sisters?

LZJ: We don't get along. Our personalities are different. There are fundamental differences. My relationship with my younger brother is a little better. There is not much of a relationship with the others. We talk but not much. We joke around, but there is no deep relationship. My gege and my jiejie do their own things, which have nothing to do with me. There is no need for me to communicate with them or to understand them. My gege is very dependent on my parents. He is already a medical student. But at school—his school is in Shanghai—he can't do anything for himself. He can't survive without my parents. But I am different. I am independent, and I want to train myself to be even more independent.

ZW: My two older brothers are much older than me. My relationship with them is like an adult-and-child relationship. I think that brothers should feel at ease with each other. But our age difference is so great that it is almost impossible for me to be at ease with them.

YCL: My younger sister and I fight all the time. [Laughs and looks at her.] But actually we are O.K. We don't talk about anything serious because she is still too young. We are fine at home, but we argue too.

Zhao Li-wei has told me earlier that his brother, who is thirty-eight now, will soon be transferred back to Shanghai. He has been working in Anhui for many years, but now his factory is going to be relocated to Shanghai. He explains the move: "His factory is like an old hen that only eats and lays no eggs. Every part they make costs the government two yuan. In the past they made cannons, but the kind of cannons they made is outdated. The parts have become scrap iron. Now they are manufacturing meters, and that's why the factory will be relocated here. The technology in Shanghai is better. He will be living at home with us."

ZLW: My relationship with my gege and jiejie has always been very good. They are much older than me. My cousins, too. They are all in their twenties. I am the youngest in the family. We get along very well. We talk and laugh, and we always get together during holidays. My parents are pretty open-minded, not like some parents I know. They are not autocratic, and when we are in front of them, we don't have to watch what we are saying.

6

In Glittering, Variegated Changes

Throughout my travels in China, I was guided by Walter Pater, though at the time I did not realize it. In his powerful coda to *The Renaissance,* Pater writes:

> Not to discriminate every moment some passionate attitude in those about us, and in the brilliancy of their gifts some tragic dividing of forces on their ways, is, on this short day of frost and sun, to sleep before evening. With this sense of the splendor of our experience and of its awful brevity, gathering all we are in one desperate effort to see and touch, we shall hardly have time to make theories about the things we see and touch. What we have to do is to be for ever curiously testing new opinions and courting new impressions, never acquiescing in a facile orthodoxy of Comte, or of Hegel, or *of our own.*[1] [My italics.]

Pater speaks of discriminating "every moment some passionate attitude in those about us." My own effort was much more humble. In a short period of time several children and I shared some moments together. We lost ourselves in those moments—in the listening and the telling and the to-and-fro of playing. Each experience was an end, as

Pater might have put it, and perhaps for that reason no two children seemed alike. Each, shaped by her own curve, colored by her own dyes, and enclasping her own "inward world of thought and feeling," was a distinct person. And for a brief interval I gathered all I am "into one desperate effort to see and touch" and listen.

The effort extended a little further: I also tried to catch my impressions and their words without letting all the "volatile essence" get lost in translation and diffusion. But do I stop there for fear of reducing the "volatile essence" to fixed principles? Again it is Pater who reminds us:

> Philosophical theories or ideas, as points of view, instruments of criticism, may help us to gather up what might otherwise pass unregarded by us. . . . The theory or idea or system which requires of us the sacrifice of any part of this experience, in consideration of some interest into which we cannot enter, or some abstract theory we have not identified with ourselves, or what is only conventional, has no real claim upon us.

In my effort here "to gather up," as I try to pick up the pieces, I rely on Pater's good sense. It is my intention not to sacrifice "any part of this experience in consideration of some interest," "some abstract theory," or "what is only conventional."

WHEN THEY WERE VERY YOUNG . . .

Childhood in China is marked by simplicity. The Chinese believe in the restorative power of the morning air, so the young ones rise early, around six; for many the daily learning begins at that hour. They briefly review their lessons and physically get ready for school. They walk to school, and once there, the hours are long and the work rigorous. During the two-hour respite around lunchtime, everyone goes home for a hot meal and a brief nap (which no one likes to take). Usually one of the parents comes back from work to cook the meal and to be with his children for a while. The schooling continues when the children return in the afternoon to finish the remaining classes. Then it is home again: homework, some playtime with neighborhood friends or classmates (but only occasionally), a family meal together, more homework and review, and bed.

Since they all get home earlier than their parents, Chinese children carry their own keys, and in their solitary afternoons they give themselves over to entirely habitual activities. They have the habit of starting homework right away; the habit of washing their own clothes and the vegetables to be eaten that night; the habit of cooking the rice and setting the table. With a few exceptions (notably when there are doting grandparents at home), Chinese children are expected to perform these daily tasks. It is not a source of conflict with their parents, and they gripe only if someone brings up the subject. Besides, they take pride in sharing the responsibilities. For them, washing their clothes every night is proof of their independence, and being allowed to handle the more complex aspects of cooking is an extension of their parents' trust in them.

In China children are expected to take their learning seriously, and they comply because learning is what they desire: expectation and desire coincide, and it is therefore not a matter of having no choice. From the Chinese point of view, adult's and child's alike, why would anyone not want to learn when given the opportunity? Tradition has demonstrated to them the power and potential of an education. An educated person has a better chance to realize his dreams and ideals—this is what they see from their vantage point. Attempts were made during the Cultural Revolution to abandon this position. Pupils left school to partake in a cause they saw as larger and grander than the sum of their hopes, but the ideological struggle of those ten years left them feeling confused and bereft. Now *their* children are saying: "We are all scared of [political] movements. . . . Today they say it's good; tomorrow they say something else. But . . . we are always sure about what we learn from books. It is always the same. It is always accurate, always solid and real." In reverting to this attitude, the Chinese feel more at home; their children are building their lives with materials that are "solid and real." They believe that they are safer and steadier now, that they can anticipate and make adequate provision for the future.

Chinese children love to play. Their lives are filled with dragonflies, sparrows, and stray cats, but they are not sentimental about them. They tie sparrows to trees and dragonflies to bedposts. They stone stray cats and sentence caterpillars to die. They spank cicadas that can't sing and create wars among ant nations. They play with animals and sometimes put them to work. And very few pets survive their captivity. When Yu Sha's yellow bird starved to death, she made a small coffin and buried it. Wang Wei's friends built a small funeral mound for their dead animal. They even burnt incense and clasped their hands. They liked the ritual.

The children also enjoy playing with friends. They like playing "war" best. They love the thrill of running and chasing and sounding battle cries. They are right and wrong, Right and Left in their games, but that's not the point. There are guns and swords, offensive and defensive tactics but no militarism. It is all playing at this age. Boys even play with girls: wars, hide-and-seek, and insect-hunting.

As they grow older, important changes occur. Wang Lian told me: "My feelings and impressions . . . are beginning to lose their colors. They are becoming hazier. Maybe things are changing. . . . I want to be even younger because I remember seeing things even more clearly then, and the world was full of wonder." What has dimmed the colors of Wang Lian's early impressions? Time and the aggregates of knowledge and experience, perhaps. Rilke says that we should not worry about the fading memories: "For memories themselves are not important. Only when they have changed into our very blood, into glance and gesture, and are nameless, no longer to be distinguished from ourselves."[2] But what of the later apperceptions—the apperceptions of an older child? How do we explain the fading brilliance, the gradual disappearance of the magic and delight that were once inseparable from his experience of seeing?

D. H. Lawrence wrote passionately on this subject. For him the sense of wonder is the "natural religious sense," a permanent element inherent in all life. He believed that with the assumption of knowledge, the wonder "decreases," and seeing becomes apprehension, being no longer an experience of the present. The present lacks color and light because the seer is somewhere else. His mind has carried him to the "abstract space" of right and wrong and of principles, thoughts, and issues; he inhabits the world of meaning but not *this* world. For this reason Lawrence was hostile to didacticism and sentimentalism, which he saw as blocking us from having a direct—"sensuous"—contact with the world.[3]

Chinese children live close to the essence of things because their situation allows it. Their two-parent families, together with the extended relationships of grandparents, aunts, uncles, and neighbors, give them immense emotional stability, and their socialist state guarantees them a basic material security. Their life pattern is simple; the fabric is that of cotton—naturally durable. "What is" is unadorned, yet suffused with light and energy. But that will change. The luminosity diminishes as the children grow and develop; the wonder of "actual living," living through instincts and intuitions, lasts only for a while. By the time they are twelve, they sense the change in their temperament and attitude. They feel weightier, and they are a little relieved. For they have the promise, from their parents and teachers, of being taken more seriously. Very few are like Li Dong-wu, who simply refuses to grow up, or Wang Lian, who remembers being very young and realizes the loss.

There are, then, external pressures that underly the change, and the children themselves wish for an internal transformation. Why? Is it possible to attribute their desire and thereby their change to what Lawrence called "the assumption of knowledge"? We know that from the time when they were very small, a great array of knowledge is poured into them. Aside from school studies, there are moral instructions: Confucian rules and decorums learned within the family, and the charges of socialism urged on them from the state. Young Chinese children generally accept these teachings on faith. Even though they may complain that their parents or teachers are too "preachy," they rarely challenge their elders; they are not sufficiently educated to be skeptical, and the obligation to be filial and respectful weighs on them. Their acceptance, in turn, affords them a sense of order, which allows them to be truly carefree and content; they roam the neighborhoods, carrying their wooden guns, and they know every insect and animal in their environment. Their upbringing, though moralistic and strict, does not rob them of their sense of wonder. In fact, with order and clarity, there is freedom—freedom from thoughts and the freedom to be children.

For the Chinese, the first twelve years of life are not a time to raise questions about autonomy, fairness, or the right of choice. They concentrate on learning, playing, and living, and think it strange that anyone should ask them whether they are happy or bored. Life is straightforward and plain. There are simple rules to obey, but compliance does not mean that they are obedient. It is the way things are, and they are only children.

In the West we believe strongly that individuals are separate entities, and we express this belief in our notions about childhood. We give our children space, we respect their "rights," yet we also expect them to be self-regulated. Young children are often confused by this. They relish their freedom to choose but at the same time are exasperated by the decision-making process. Their emotions tell them that they are not ready for this freedom, and their parents are anxious. In China, where children follow the rules of life with minimum resistance, they are at the same time immensely curious, playful, and plucky. The emotional balance and the clear joyance are a wondrous blend, and for a while they take possession of the child; they become the child. Gao Min was a "possessed" child, I was certain, when I listened to his story. It began in the crib when he rocked himself to sleep and to laughter. Gao Min *was* the calmness and the delight, but that would change—I was also certain of that.

On "change" Lawrence wrote: "If the one I love remains unchanged and unchanging, I shall cease to love her. It is only because she changes and startles me into change and defies my inertia, and is staggered in her inertia by my changing that I can continue to love her."[4] But it is easy to be afraid of change when one is among schoolchildren. Very often I found myself looking at the older children with an inexplicable sense of loss. But it was they who reminded me, "We can't play hide-and-seek forever." No, they cannot. Again we can take solace in Rilke's optimism regarding past experiences and memories. Perhaps the temporary can become the permanent when it has "changed into our very blood, into glance and gesture," and is inseparable from our being. Perhaps Gao Min will never change because of those magical moments in the crib.

NOW THEY ARE TWELVE

Adolescence is a stage of life when a person begins to *think* about who he is. The contemplation is the source of an intense conflict: who he is must have a distinctive identity; he, therefore, struggles to separate himself from others. The self-awareness does not imply an awareness solely of the self, even though his thought and behavior at this time may appear to be egocentric. To separate means to sort out one's relation to others, primarily to one's parents. The child is more conscious of the distinction between this and that, himself and others, but he does not actually prepare for a separation. He may be vocal about his parents' deficiencies, and his behavior at times may even seem rebellious, but he has no intention of usurping their positions. There are still dependent yearnings, and the desire for harmony at home is strong.

Psychologists in the West have attributed the adolescents' fondness for venturing criticisms and a different point of view to their cognitive development. According to them adolescents are merely testing their analytical abilities; they love to reason and hypothesize, but they are also easily carried away by impulse. Most parents do not appreciate their children's enthusiasm for their new-found abilities because frequently they find themselves to be the subject of analysis: Knowledge is, after all, associated with power or a loss of power depending on the point of view. Perhaps adolescents want to know too much about their parents, even their reasons for the inconsistencies between their intentions and their actions, between their professed values and actual deeds. And since children are by nature untactful, they can be a little cruel at times, especially to their parents.

The changes in parent-child relationships may vary from culture to culture, but one can still observe similar patterns and shared characteristics. In China when little children were forced to sleep with blankets on hot summer nights or were forbidden to explore on their own on a hiking trip, they didn't like it, but most of them did what they were told. But once they are adolescents, differences become issues. Life is still characterized by order and stability, but more questions are raised. The rules, once simple, now need clarification, and children no longer accept them on faith. They query their viability and insist on more flexible interpretations. Reality begins to appear more amorphous to them, and amidst the ambiguity a paradox is at work: adolescents begin to see rightness as a function of circumstances and moral decisions as a matter of judgment, but at the same time they strongly desire consistency and clarity. They strive for consistencies in their intents and responses in order to achieve a unified self in a differentiated world, some permanence in the transiency. They are building a character they can call their own so that they will not become muddled in the moral vagueness.

Nowadays young people in China like to use the phrase "everything has two sides." For instance, they find it absurd to weigh Confucius' world view on a Marxist scale, to impose socialist standards on him. And as for their judgment of Mao Ze-dong, they make careful distinctions between his deeds before and after the Liberation and then between deed and intent. One apologist, a teenage boy from the city of Yentai, simply said, "We should forgive Chairman Mao." If the Chairman's vision seemed myopic, he explained, it was because he had not been anywhere else outside of China, except for Russia, and "in Russia the idea of personality cult . . . must have had a strong influence on him."

At home Chinese adolescents are less tolerant of moral compromises. When her mother cast a vote against her conscience, Mei Jing did not regard it as a matter of expediency; she wanted to know how her parent really felt and why she had succumbed to political pressure.

To affirm values that were learned in categorical terms of right and wrong, Chinese children at this age may question their parents' actions, but they are not impudent or presumptuous, for they sense that in the real world things are complex, and more importantly, *they* don't want to lose their respect for their parents. They refrain from hurting their parents with words and in their behavior, though the idea of transgressing the boundaries of propriety does occur to them, especially when there is a conflict. Mei Jing mentioned her wish to get away for a while until her anger was quelled—something she "could never carry . . . through." The thought that her parents might be worried would make her feel uneasy, and so instead of spending a night at a friend's house, she'd "just quietly sneak back."

Lao Zi said, "Knowing when to stop, one can be free from danger."[5] The *Doctrine of the Mean* said, "When feelings are aroused and each and all attain due measure and degree, it is called harmony."[6] These teachings have become part of the Chinese conscience. A Chinese adolescent knows intuitively not to go too far when he disagrees with his parents; he realizes that when he steps beyond what is considered "due measure and degree," he disregards his parents' feelings and thereby infringes a fundamental principle in their relationship.

Chinese children at this age, like adolescents everywhere, have a strong desire to be independent. They have their own ideas and their own way of doing things and are reactive toward external authority. They want to get away from their parents' influence but find the process "very slow." Many told me how they protected their autonomy: "If we cannot accept their views, we just do things our own way." They claimed, however, that their differences with their parents did not lead to "real confrontations." They were careful not to wound them, though their anguish was genuine. I believe that in some complicated way these adolescents sense that a serious wound of this kind would fundamentally alter the nature of their relationship to their parents, which to them is sacred. So can we say that the restraint they demonstrate in their behavior expresses a native yearning for harmony? Is this a weakness of the will or of the heart? I find it hard to decide.

In their independence, Chinese adolescents observe decided differences between their relationship to their fathers and to their mothers. The differences were probably there from the start, but they become more aware of them as they grow more discriminating in their own needs and expectations. When they were little and dependent on others, they loved their mothers because they could always find affection and warmth in their mothers' arms. Many at that age feared their fathers because fathers were "serious and rarely smiled." But now, when they are "more capable of independent thinking" and feel that "acquiring knowledge is more important," they believe their fathers give them more than their mothers to develop their intellect and character. I asked them, Do they now feel closer to the better-educated parent? Is education an important factor in their preference? They seemed to say, Yes, but added that ultimately they felt closer to the parent they spent more time with and the one who gave them direction but allowed them "the freedom to think and analyze things" for themselves. And only in a few cases was that parent the mother.

The mothers of all the Chinese children I talked with had jobs, and several were more successful professionally than their husbands. Yet their children found them narrow-minded, unconversant, and at times even petty and dull. A mother may be well versed in technical materials, but, to her child, her vision lacks breadth and imagination. Is this a biased view? Does the child perceive his mother to be the smaller and lesser being at home because his father treats her as such and she, too, is convinced this is true? Are children, like adults, influenced by men's opinion of women and women's opinion of themselves? But many of the children also observed that their fathers prepared dinner every night and waited for the mothers to come home from work. It is difficult to know how this simple routine is worked into the Chinese consciousness, but I believe that Chinese people are revising their notions about the nature of a woman and her function in society: a new identity is emerging though the old one still lingers. The attitudes of the new generation of women express this change: teenage girls have definite ideas about what they can achieve and what sort of mother they want to be in the future, but their perception of their own mothers is shaped by traditional renderings. These girls may seem a little arrogant and self-assured, but they also have high expectations of themselves; they do not want to assume the personae they identify with their mothers.

There are exceptions, of course, to what I have generalized about adolescents' relationship to their parents. Some children did not associate their independence with struggle—Li Dong-wu being one. When she was little, she was hard to handle, but her parents most of the time just "let her be" and "didn't try to impose a lot of rules" on her. When I saw her, she was in her teens. Her childhood energy remained unchecked; it continues to animate her speech and movements. Confident and self-possessed, she was not conscious of her singularity, yet we know she was one of a kind.

Fang Kan's relationship to his parents, especially his mother, was another exception. His own account was full of contradictions and conflicting emotions. He claimed there was no "real communication" between them, yet he considered a child's relationship to his parents as most important, because talking to parents brings "great results." In his view one may share similar ideas with one's siblings and friends, but it is not the same as conversing with one's parents—they can "make suggestions based on their experiences." Fang Kan thought that his parents' experiences during the Cultural Revolution had made them "very sensitive," suspicious of "the most trivial things." He was glad to have grown up under different circumstances and was sure he was more trustful, yet when the subject of friendship came up, he emphasized the importance of "not exposing too much of yourself" before knowing someone well, lest that person turn against you. The inconsistencies in his story raise the question of whether children, despite their passionate rhetoric and relentless efforts to achieve distinctive identities, can really get away from their parents' influence. What happens between parents and children is a strange process. Parents are absorbed and at the same time rejected by their offspring, and then one day, without any warning, they appear in a smile or rationale. Fang Kan said that nothing got through to his parents, but clearly they were in him. Children may not share the same "language" with their parents or the same taste in music and clothing, but they can and often do internalize their parents' moral and social values and, through them, begin to see the logic of the adult world.

The young people I met in China did not like to associate their attitudes and behavior with their parents; instead, they enjoyed telling me about the long hours they spent with classmates, exchanging ideas and debating issues. They prefer to be with their peers because they feel more at ease with them, not having "to observe distinctions" between older and younger. In their conversations they rarely talk about the things they own or hope to acquire because they do not have the economic basis to do so; instead, they chat about school, teachers, other classmates, political issues, and social trends. They value friendship, but I suspect it is something complex. Most have a few trusted friends, but academic competition gets in the way, not to mention the politics of the Communist Youth League. When friends have time, they sit and talk but rarely do things together. At this age, except for a few games on the basketball court or the soccer field or an occasional outing or party organized by the school, playing literally comes to a stop. Even in the summer, Chinese children spend most of their time alone, reviewing schoolwork, studying ahead, or reading novels.

By the time children are in middle school, scholastic work has become more difficult and demanding: physics and chemistry, geometry and trigonometry, and so on. The children are filled up and weighed down by a mass of accumulated knowledge and a burden of expectation. They are expected now to choose between science and humanities, and their choice will be their field of study in college if they manage to get in one. Very often their decision has little to do with a love for the subject, and many do not want to choose at this point—they want to learn everything—but they are forced to see the logic of the adult world and make a pragmatic decision for their future. During this period their minds have little time for thought beyond school, yet the middle school students *do* think. In fact, I believe, it is their thoughtfulness that makes them seem "old." Their growth is now spurred on by thoughts, thoughts have replaced experience, and the magic of being is recalled—felt through the opacity of memory.

Something else happens, too. While their minds are given full play, their spirit is reined in. Their instinct urges them to let go—just to be happy—but ideas of what they should be like have gotten into their heads, and they begin to cut themselves to pattern. They blame external pressure—parents, teachers, and Communist Youth League cadres—for their conformity. And there is also the power of words; having "no sense of propriety" or being "lax in discipline" is a reputation that is difficult to reverse in Chinese society. Adolescents cut themselves to pattern in order to avoid being trapped with an unfavorable image. They fear what others might choose to perceive. But freedom from judgment (which can never be complete in the first place) has its own trap. Chinese youths can (and some actually do) end up distrusting their own instincts and intuitions and become what others expect of them. They say, "Our society approves of thoughtful and sensible persons."

This is what I understood them to tell me, but the reality is more complex. Adolescent children grope for clarity with their whole consciousness, but the incongruity of mind, heart, body, and spirit makes their task difficult. Some are troubled by the difference between intent and action, by how they really feel and what they usually end up doing. They are unsure if this is right, if who they are is who they want to be. There is a strong desire to be true to themselves, but they must weigh the situation, and they must think. The issue is, I believe, not that of the will or of "the courage to be," to borrow Tillich's phrase. How easy it is for adults to become the body or the mind, to personify courage or chastity! We have the *will* to do it. Children are different. They are more complete. There are exceptions, of course—children who are more like us, who resist becoming what their parents and teachers expect and are not afraid to say what they think and to act accordingly. (Liu Zi-jin, a boy from Shanghai, comes to mind.) But I wonder if they, too, are cutting themselves to pattern, though the pattern is of a different sort.

HOW POLITICAL AND HOW MORAL?

When I first met Yao Chen-tao (she was seven then), she drew me a picture of her imaginary brother, Yao Chen-jie, doing morning exercises, and of herself, standing next to him and holding a red-tasseled spear. She looked proud and confident in this self-portrait, and on the bottom was the inscription: "I am a Little Red Soldier." Five years later, Yao Chen-tao has grown softer and more reticent. Occasionally I could catch a glimmer of her mischievous side, but the spirit of the "Little Red Soldier" had vanished. Her sister, who five years earlier had talked enthusiastically about the stripes on her sleeves that indicated her status as a platoon leader, now said, "We are not really interested in politics." She called herself and her classmates "book learners," more concerned about doing well academically.

This process of "de-politicization," already evident in 1979, was closely linked to the changes in the Chinese government's educational policies. In 1978, the examination system had been restored for the first time since the Cultural Revolution, and the classroom disruptions that had been prevalent were swiftly brought to a halt. Yao Chen-lin, at that time, told me: "Chairman Hua encourages us to study diligently," to shun political involvement and to concentrate on schoolwork. Parents and children alike were relieved, but for the younger children the symbol of the "Little Red Soldier" continued to play a central part in their conscious lives and in their dreams and reveries.

In 1984 the younger children told me they quarreled before starting their "war" games about who would play PLA soldier and who KMT agent; nobody wanted to be a KMT agent, of course. But while their games may remain "revolutionary" in content, are they truly "children of revolution"? Do they still *believe* in the points of view expressed in their textbooks and the political slogans taught in their school drills? Are they still moved by stories of class struggle and by the history of Chinese Communism? Are they still possessed by the spirit of the revolution? Are they still in awe of their revolutionary heroes, or have they become banal too?

Both in 1979 and in 1984 all the children I talked with had their mind set on college, that being a springboard to higher goals. In 1979, when he was only ten, Liu Zi-jin told me, "I want to go to college. Because of what the Gang of Four did, our country became very backward. Now we have to catch up to the international standard. We have to catch up and go beyond them. So we all have to study diligently. When we have a college education, we can help to build our country." This declaration was a set of "learned statements" from school drills and radio and newspaper propaganda. He was "indoctrinated," and he was passionately sincere. But in 1984 he made no reference to his earlier declaration. He had changed, but his country, too, had also evolved. He still talked of goals, but now they were immediate, specific, and private, and sometimes they did not coincide with the expectations of his parents, his teachers, or even his country. Earlier, Liu Zi-jin did not know that the path from "studying diligently" to "building our country" was not a straight one, that "studying diligently" might create doubts and cause alienation, that it might alter one's original vision and talent.

Although knowledge and experience taught older children to be more controlled, they were honest about their political indoctrination in the classrooms. As Lin Qing told me, "There are certain things we can't say to our teachers so directly. . . . Teachers and students understand problems differently. Many of us fear that our views may be wrong. But we *have* to express them, and so we tell each other." He mentioned a recent study conducted by the magazine *Chinese Youth:* "Ninety-five percent of the high school students in Beijing do not like politics class. . . . Kids don't like their politics classes because they are mechanical. You have to memorize everything. . . . They feel constrained. They want to express their views in their own words, and they want to be able to question the existing views."

What about the younger children in 1984? How high and how public were their goals? How political? Chen Hai-qiang, an eleven-year-old student from Liu Zi-jin's old elementary school, at one point during our conversation chided a younger boy who preferred playing soccer and cards to doing homework: "We have to do our homework because we have to learn and we have to build the foundation for the four modernizations. We have to establish far-reaching goals." He chanted these slogans mechanically, without pause, without enthusiasm or conviction. Even the younger boy sensed his insincerity, and cut him off abruptly: "Oh, please don't say these things!" Covering his ears, he continued: "I hate these slogans. My father says them all day long: 'We have to lay the foundation for the four modernizations. We have to study every day and make progress. If we don't, we won't have any future.' I am so tired of it!" Such an exchange would have been unthinkable in 1979, though I must add that the younger boy was not a "typical" Chinese boy; most Chinese children would not have gone that far.

Robert Coles, in *The Political Life of Children,* asks how "a nation which calls itself 'revolutionary' " and is committed to Marxism-Leninism, "*and* which takes a strong interest in the education of its children, might go about the task of reaching the minds of those boys and girls and to what effect." Alfredo, an eleven-year-old Nicaraguan boy who lived in a Managua *barrio,* taught him a great deal. The boy's impassioned declarations—"I wouldn't be alive, maybe, if I'd been born before the Revolution. I'd have died. We kept on dying. . . . That was the doings of Somoza"—appeared to be rehearsed, his phrases drilled into him by "ideologically zealous teachers." But Coles, going further, suggested that Alfredo was "imbued with both Christian and Sandinista values." He was also very interested in the material things from "North America," and enjoyed playing with other children. A child "whose mind works independently," he recognized that "the commandantes aren't the only ones with the answers," though he was thoroughly convinced that Nicaragua, at one time "a slave," was now a country, "his country," to which he owed allegiance. "The Revolution Lives" and "Nicaragua cannot die" may be mere slogans to us, but Alfredo and his friends uttered them out of *belief*.[7]

Chinese children are all fluent in Marxist-Leninist ideological language. They can articulate the materialist point of view and chant slogans as well as—perhaps even better than—Alfredo and his friends. But their words lack conviction. They love their country, but they are not fervent believers; there are no reasons for them to be passionate. The revolutionary flame appears to be quelled.

Sixty years ago, following the 1927 mass execution of members of the peasant associations in Changsha and Wuhan, the poet-scholar Wen Yi-duo[8] wrote a "Prayer":

Please tell me who the Chinese are,
Teach me how to cling to memory.
Please tell me the greatness of this people
Tell me gently, ever so gently.

Please tell me: Who are the Chinese?
Whose hearts embody the hearts of Yao and Shun
In whose veins flow the blood of Ching K'o and Nieh Cheng
Who are the true children of the Yellow Emperor?

Tell me that such wisdom came strangely—
Some say it was brought by a horse from the river:
Also tell me that the rhythm of this song
Was taught, originally by the phoenix.

Who will tell me the silence of the Gobi Desert,
The awe inspired by the Five Sacred Mountains,

The patience that drips from the Rocks of Mount T'ai,
And the harmony that flows in the Yellow and Yangtze Rivers?

Please tell me who the Chinese are,
Teach me how to cling to memory.
Please tell me the greatness of this people.
Tell me gently, ever so gently.[9]

Wen Yi-duo lived through the mad, violent period between 1924 and 1949 when the Communist Party and Nationalist Guomindang were involved in an intense struggle to control China. For him and many of his contemporaries, knowledge of "who the Chinese are" was vanishing from the Chinese mind. Hatred and disintegration had muddled their senses. In his "Prayer," Wen Yi-duo was desperately seeking his China; he was trying to cling to the memory of a past that had an identity—the "heart" and "blood" of a particular kind. Most historians would agree that the Chinese Communist revolution gave Wen's question an answer, though the telling was not "gentle." It helped the Chinese to regain their sense of "who the Chinese are," not through "clinging to memory" but through the creation of new images, new symbols, and new heroes.

The Chinese children with whom I talked grew up with these new symbols and heroes. They know that China is "their country" and that "China will not die." But unlike Alfredo and the children of Nicaragua, they have no memory of past "bitterness"; they have not witnessed acts of oppression and deaths and suffering of loved ones. And unlike their parents or aunts and uncles, children of the Cultural Revolution, they have not had the experience of the revolutionary life: no ardent crowds, no huge political rallies, not even regular study-group meetings. Alfredo in Nicaragua saw himself as a "beneficiary of a historical event." The Chinese children are no different, but they have not known it through experience. They were born into stable homes and communities with basic necessities satisfied and with an education awaiting them. Benefits are bestowed upon them from the time of their birth. Thus they are not consciously aware of the act of giving-and-receiving, and in expressing their gratitude to their benefactor, they do not share Alfredo's passion.

This lack of passion allows the Chinese children a certain clarity in vision, especially since they can now gaze horizontally at other socio-political systems. Very often they begin by asking of another nation, "What is wrong with your system?" and end up realizing, "Perhaps China is not always right." They have become less scornful of other people and more critical of their own benefactor. They question the assumptions and theories their political education teaches them. Their concern is not so much with the ideological basis of China's system as with its practical applications. They compare systems and judge them on the basis of their efficiency and how much material and spiritual comfort they yield.

There are other kinds of doubt in these young minds, too—questions related to the dramatic shift in their country's economic policies, for instance. Chinese youths are worried about the effects that this new direction has on their moral life. "People have become more selfish" is what they observe, and they also feel greater friction in social relationships. Most attribute this phenomenon to the influx of material goods and foreign influence in the last decade, but one girl in Xian suggested that perhaps human relationships in China have always been "in a big mess," the recent economic development being a mere catalyst in a reaction of forces that are elemental but very powerful.

Values imbued from the West also seriously challenge the fundamental values of the Chinese Communist state. The comfort that material goods bring can weaken the spirit and test the will of those who are involved in a socialist revolution. Most of the older children told me pointedly that they did not want to go to the country and work with the peasants, who, according to them, were regarded by city-dwellers as "uncultured" and "vulgar." Many of them were skeptical of the "tempering" this experience was supposed to give them. Even Wu Jin-song, the most ardent of all the Young Pioneers I met, liked talking about the vending machines in Nanjing, stored with soft drinks she could not name, and the sweets of Beijing, which she had only seen on television; she relished the thought of tasting these goodies even though only moments earlier she had spoken admiringly of a friend who evoked the spirit of the revolutionary heroes to resist "temptation."

Chinese children would make general observations about material goods and their effect on human behavior, but they themselves rarely spoke of things they desired. When they were asked what they might like to own, they spoke only of modest gifts. As one boy put it, "We all understand the situation [at home] and we try to be frugal. And usually we don't have any big requests." It is not because the revolution demands self-sacrifice or the children's moral upbringing has taught them to refrain from excessive selfishness, that there are no such "big requests"; rather, it is that the children all sense the stringency of their parents' lives and so try not to impose extra burdens on them. This inborn consideration is a natural part of a relationship that most children agree is the most important one of all. Certainly the parent-child bond is more important than their relationship to the state, and their filial piety more than a simple affirmation of the ancient rule which says that children should serve their parents as they grow old. These children, it would appear, truly grasp that their parents have given them much (even the parents' high expectations are a gift—a gift expressed as a belief in them), and this parental devotion is reciprocated with genuine affection and unflinching loyalty.

Chinese children may, to be sure, think their fathers "autocratic" and "mean" and their mothers "meddling" and "tedious," and they may acknowledge differences and tension; but they assure the listener that nothing can ever alter the primordial feelings. In a Chinese child's relationship to his parents, not remembering the source of conflict ends the conflict. But what brings on his forgetfulness? Is this the result of witnessing how hard it has been for his parents to bring him up? Is this his way of accepting a relationship that is considered permanent and sacred in his cultural tradition? I have mentioned a conscience that "knows when to stop." Mencius called it "deference and compliance" and "the beginning of propriety." In the West we call it a weakness of the will, probably from having known only one kind of strength and only the will. Of course, the conscience is not the only element underlying a child's sense of propriety. No matter how earnest he may sound when talking about repaying his parents' kindness, he thinks and behaves in ways that are socially acceptable. The collective conscience is always watching, and he knows that he is judged as he judges himself.

There is yet another kind of mystery when we consider Yao Chen-lin, an intelligent, vivacious, and self-possessed girl who attends one of the best middle schools in the country and who has her mind set on pursuing a career in electrical engineering or physics. She is eighteen, yet occasionally she still gets whipped when she does "something wrong." She is critical of her father and speaks openly and freely of his bad temper and his authoritarian ways. I met her father twice in their home. A willful and impetuous man but at the same time warm and generous, Mr. Yao has made his daughters the central purpose of his life. They are his labor and his love, and to him there is no reason that they should fail him. He would not tolerate it.

Having been told of her fierce relationship to her father, I imagined fear and resentment in the daughter's love. But I could only see understanding and forgiveness in her smile. In her voice, too, I sensed more cheeriness than anger, and a transparent optimism. Yao Chen-lin also revealed to me what she would like to do for her parents when they grow old. She wanted to live near them or even with them. "It doesn't mean that we will have more to say to each other," she assured me. "It's just that when people get old, they miss their children; they are lonely. In fact I can't say that I will enjoy living with them, but it's an obligation, something I *ought* to do."

When Yao Chen-lin thinks of what she intends to do for her parents in the future, she is not making plans to repay their affection and devotion. Serving her parents is not a duty or a moral obligation, though she uses these words herself. It is, as she imagines, an act that will comfort and assuage them when they are old and tired. The essence of this particular parent-child relationship lies in this *image*—an image that evokes moral feelings and inspires a moral commitment. But exactly what is passed between a child and her parents? Why is it that this child "cannot bear" the thought of her parents being alone and lonely? (It was Mencius who said that "all persons have a mind which cannot bear to see the sufferings of others," his proof that all human beings are born good.) What gives rise to a compassion that is still in the imagination? *This* is the enigma.

When we think of Yao Chen-lin, do considerations of her cultural tradition help us to unravel the complexities and ambiguities of her relationship to her father? Or must we think in terms of a context when it is the individual who creates *her* morality from *her* knowledge and experience? In the case of Yao Chen-lin and her peers, the intense concern and the self-denying devotion of their parents are what is real for them. As they grow older, this reality or truth becomes a constant presence in their conscious and unconscious lives. They are annoyed when their privacy is taken away or not enough autonomy is allowed, and they are pressured when academically they have not lived up to their parents' expectations. But at the end it is out of concrete images of that "undeniable reality" that they knead and shape their own sense of what is moral. Yao Chen-lin's plan for her parents, though imagined, incarnates that "vague" sense.

The concern and devotion of Chinese parents are inspired by their belief in the continuity of their biological and moral life through their children and grandchildren. In this way the parents and the children make sense of each other. Limited living space creates a physical closeness in which parents and children are always watching and observing each other. From the children's point of view, parents are both caring and meddling. The "watching"—usually accompanied by constant verbal reminders—is to protect them from illness and injury, and it also extends to behavior and to intellectual and moral development. At home the children feel like "birds in a cage," "flowers in a greenhouse."

Yet while parents are watchful, the children believe they are not observant, not of them and not of the world around them. Wang Lian offered an explanation: "Maybe they have seen too much, and so everything seems commonplace to them. Things just don't seem strange and wonderful to them." To him, the adults' minds lack the responsiveness and sensitivity to be observant. Children, on the other hand, are detailed observers, and when home is only two small rooms, their parents' words and actions are always within close range. Though parental words may sound like no more than chants to the children, actions leave deep imprints on their sensibilities.

As Chinese society evolves, new elements are introduced into the parent-child matrix. At this point it is impossible to calculate its sums and products. We do not yet know, for instance, how the one-child family policy or better living standards alter this relationship, though there is evidence of ongoing change. Parents with one child tell me that they dote on their child, giving him the best to eat and the best to wear, excessive attention and affection, and very few chores; he is treated like a "lord" or "a little emperor" at home as long as he excels in class and scores well on his exams. As for the child, the pressure to succeed is greater than ever, burdened by the knowledge that he is the only one who can fulfill his parents' expectations.

In 1984 I noticed other changes that altered my earlier sense of Chinese children as a whole. The children, as I understand them now, exhibit more independence in mind and spirit. They think that perhaps it is all right to pull away from their parents while they are still at home or later when they go away. They are more aware of and certainly more vocal about the "gaps" in their relationship to their parents. The gaps still include differences in political views (the focus during the Cultural Revolution), but now the conflicts are in general more "ordinary"—about schools and friends, about how to handle certain situations with teachers and classmates and how to organize their time, about clothes and music, movies and television programs.

Chinese children today are largely preoccupied with the everyday. But as each child recounts her daily agenda or recollects a scene from her past, she reveals an attitude about the world around her. Is it possible to summarize the "attitudes" gathered? There are tendencies and common traits shared by these children, obviously, given the same cultural assumptions and historical circumstances. But each child also carries her own idioms, present in the story she tells and in how she tells it. The idioms are essential elements of her being; they occasion a particular life. And they are the loose ends that I am choosing to leave behind.

I will always remember Li Dong-wu describing with vivid transparence the day that she and her brother and their friends "followed the river downstream." "They walked very fast, and I was running most of the time, trying to catch up. This was far from the bridge—the place where we caught all those fish. It was in the spring, and the frogs were laying eggs. The eggs were floating on the river in a huge patch, sticky and slimy. I didn't know what made me trip, but I fell suddenly and touched the eggs." A pulsation, a moment in a child's life, dancing still in the memory as it makes sense of itself.

Notes

INTRODUCTION

[1] *Zhuang Zi,* chapter 4, "Ren-jian-shi." I followed closely Burton Watson's translation in *The Complete Works of Chuang Tzu* (New York: Columbia University Press, 1968), pp. 57–58.

[2] Hans-Georg Gadamer, *Truth and Method,* Garrett Barden and John Cumming, trans. and ed. (New York: Seabury Press, 1975), pp. 269, 271.

1. A BACKDROP FOR . . .

[1] Clifford Geertz, *The Interpretation of Cultures* (New York: Basic Books, 1973), p. 52.

[2] These are terms that Joseph Needham used. See *Science and Civilization in China,* II (Cambridge: Cambridge University Press, 1956), p. 302.

[3] Benjamin Schwartz, *The World of Thought in Ancient China* (Cambridge: The Belknap Press of Harvard University Press, 1985), p. 52.

[4] *Analects,* 12:11.

[5] Augustine, *Confessions* (7:17), R. S. Pine-Coffin, trans. (Penguin Books, 1961), p. 151; (8:9), p. 173.

[6] See *Mencius,* Book 7.

[7] *Analects,* 4:15.

[8] Ibid., 8:2 (see Legge's translation, in *The Chinese Classics,* I (Hong Kong: Hong Kong University Press, 1960), reprinted from the last editions [1893–95] of Cambridge University Press, p. 208), and 3:3 (see W. T. Chan's translation in *A Source Book in Chinese Philosophy* [Princeton: Princeton University Press, 1963], p. 24).

[9] Ibid., 2:7.

[10] Ibid., 14:45.

[11] Ibid., 4:18 (see Legge, pp. 170–1).

[12] Ibid., 7:8.

[13] *Zhuang Zi,* chapter 4, "Ren-jian-shi" (see Burton Watson's translation in *The Complete Works of Chuang Tzu,* p. 62).

[14] Ibid. (see Watson, p. 55).

[15] *Analects,* 12:17–18 (see Legge, p. 258).

[16] *Zhuang Zi,* chapter 4 (see Watson, pp. 55, 62).

[17] Ibid. (see Watson, p. 55).

[18] *Dao-de-jing,* chapter 8; chapter 17 (see D. C. Lau's translation in *Tao Te Ching* [Penguin Books, 1963], p. 73).

[19] *Zhuang Zi,* chapter 17, "Qiu-shui" (see Watson, p. 178).

[20] See Schwartz, *The World of Thought,* p. 412.

[21] *Analects,* 1:1 (see Chan, *A Source Book,* p. 18); 6:18, 5:27.

[22] Ibid., 3:14; 6:25.

[23] Geertz, *The Interpretation of Cultures,* pp. 49, 53.

[24] Schwartz, *The World of Thought,* p. 88. Also *Analects,* 15:5 and 4:15.

[25] Fung Yu-lan maintained that Confucius was "the first man in China to make teaching his profession." See Fung Yu-lan, *A History of Chinese Philosophy,* I, Derk Bodde, trans. (Princeton: Princeton University Press, 1952), p. 48.

[26] This is an exaggerated figure, though accepted by most Chinese. The Han historian Si-ma Qian (145–87? B.C.) was responsible for making the claim. According to works earlier than Si-ma Qian's *Shi-ji (The Records of the Grand Historian),* the number of Confucius's disciples was around seventy. In the *Analects* only twenty-five are mentioned by name.

[27] *Analects,* 7:7 (see Legge, p. 197); 15:38.

[28] Ibid., 6:17 (see Chan, p. 29) and 17:2 (see Chan, p. 45).

[29] *Mencius,* 6A:7 (see Chan, p. 56).

[30] Ibid., 2A:6 (see Lau, p. 82).

[31] Ibid. (see D. C. Lau's translation in *Mencius* (Penguin Books, 1970), p. 83, and 6A:8.

[32] Ibid., 2A:6 (see Lau, p. 82).

[33] Translated in Fung Yu-lan, *A History of Chinese Philosophy,* I, p. 17.

[34] *Analects,* 4:6 (see Lau, p. 73).

[35] Benjamin Elman, *From Philosophy to Philology* (Cambridge: Harvard East Asian Monographs, 1984), p. 3.

[36] Coles, *The Political Life of Children* (Boston: The Atlantic Monthly Press, 1986), pp. 11–12.

[37] Coles, *The Moral Life of Children* (Boston: The Atlantic Monthly Press, 1986), p. 16.

[38] Schwartz, *The World of Thought,* p. 9. Schwartz borrowed the two phrases—"ancient opinions and rules of life" and "untaught feelings"—from Edmund Burke.

[39] Ibid., p. 413.

[40] As translated in Yang Xianyi and Gladys Yang, *The Complete Stories of Lu Xun* (Bloomington: Indiana University Press, 1981), p. 4.

[41] Ibid., p. 12.

[42] Jonathan Spence, *The Gate of Heavenly Peace* (New York: Viking Press, 1982), p. 153.

[43] Lu Xun, "The Diary of a Madman," in *The Complete Stories of Lu Xun,* p. 11.

[44] For an illuminating discussion of "the burden of culture" during the Ming, see W. T. de Bary, *Self and Society in Ming Thought* (New York: Columbia University Press, 1970), pp. 8–12.

[45] *Shu-ching (Book of Documents),* "The Counsel of the Great Yu"; see Legge's translation in *The Chinese Classics,* III, p. 61.

[46] As translated in *A History of Chinese Philosophy,* II, p. 44.

[47] Ying-shih Yü, "Individualism and Neo-Taoist Movement in Wei-Chin China," in Donald Munro, ed., *Individualism and Holism* (Ann Arbor: Center for Chinese Studies, the University of Michigan, 1985).

[48] "Diary of a Madman," pp. 2, 3. See also Coles, *The Moral Life of Children,* p. 8.

[49] "Diary of a Madman," p. 12.

[50] "Among School Children" in the *Collected Poems of W. B. Yeats* (New York: The Macmillan Company, 1940), pp. 213–14.

[51] Cf. Plato's parable as told in the *Symposium,* 189c–193d.

[52] *Sonnets to Orpheus,* 2:5 (see M. D. H. Norton's translation, p. 79).

[53] Coles, *The Moral Life of Children,* p. 10.

[54] Ibid., pp. 9, 8.